Crossing the River at Chamberlain, 1898

SOUTH DAKOTA

Land of Shining Gold

by Francie M. Berg

Old West Region Series

Published by
Flying Diamond Books

dedicated to this dakota land and its people

First Printing

Library of Congress Catalog Card Number 81-67726
ISBN Number: 0-918532-07-8 hardcover; 0-918532-08-6 softcover;
0-918532-09-4 Old West Region Series

FLYING DIAMOND BOOKS
Box D301, Hettinger, ND 58639
Printed in the United States of America

Contents

Lush lemon-yellow flowers of prickly pear cactus bloom on ba
above Missouri. Native wildlife, such as antelope above, blend w
with the golds of native prairie. And golden fall leaves flutter
glorious sunshine of Indian summer.

PART I

Land of
Shining Gold

Skies are radiant gold and crimson at sunset and sunrise in this cle
air.

1. DAKOTA GOLD

In South Dakota—the Sunshine State—the sun shines golden nearly every day, every season. There are sparkling reflections on the snow and colorful sundogs to flank a January sun. The bright, clear freshness of spring. The heat of July. And the melting warmth of golden Indian summers that drift into October and even late November. In any season the sunshine touches the tops of hills and shimmers on the surface of many lakes. Skies are radiant gold and crimson

Meadowlark pours out a golden melody: "Time to plant your sweet potatoes." Soft golds of prairie grasses at right make a carpet for mating dance of sharptail grouse. A rainbow arches high after thunderstorm, and sunshine touches badland buttes.

Corn gives a golden harvest of fresh roasting ears, full silos and fat corncribs.

'There's gold from the grass roots down,
    but there's more from the grass roots up.'

> Like liquid gold the wheat field lies
> A marvel of yellow and green...
>
> The wild hawk swoops
> to his prey in the deeps;
> The sunflower droops
> to the lazy wave; the wind sleeps;
>
> Then, moving in dazzling links and loops
> A marvel of shadow and shine,
> A glory of olive and amber and wine,
> Runs the color in the wheat!
>
> **Hamlin Garland**

at sunrise and sunset. At night a million stars dazzle and the cold green-gold of northern lights flash across an open sky. A golden moon seems to linger a moment on the horizon before lifting off.

Gold is in the native plants and animals of this land. It blooms in a profusion of wild flowers—softly in the heart of the crocus, boldly in a waving sunflower, delicately in the exotic cactus.

Gold shimmers on the feathers of the golden eagle and gleams bright on a dozen species of waterfowl. It vibrates at the throat of the meadowlark as this well-loved bird of the prairies and plains pours forth a golden melody to lift the very soul.

Most pervasive through the state in late summer and fall are the soft golds of prairie grasses. Tall golden grasses wave on east river hillsides, while in the west short grass cures

A golden stubble lights the landscape.

There's Gold in the Land

and in the products of the Land—

golden on the stem. Wildlife blends well into these soft golds: the coyote, the antelope, deer, prairie dog, jackrabbit, rattlesnakes—all true survivors of this land.

Gold dazzled the faces of Sun Dancers in the ancient ceremonial, once known as the Sun-Gazing Dance. Gold was and is in warm and generous hearts of Indian people, ever willing to give what they have in help.

And surely those were golden dreams which led pioneers to settle sturdy towns and quarter-sections on thousands of gravel and gumbo hillsides. Not always was the golden promise borne out, as history here and elsewhere reveals all too clearly. But many golden dreams of homesteaders, cattlemen, miners, sheepmen, brought forth a rich treasure from the land.

Corn has perhaps been the greatest of the golden produce. Introduced into Missouri River bottomlands in the dawn of civilization, this native American crop was vital to survival and growth of numerous Indian cultures. Later it meant as much to pioneers. Today much of eastern South Dakota is true corn land—and corn cribs grow fat in harvest. At Mitchell a fantastic fairy castle has been built to the honor of corn and what it symbolizes to South Dakotans now and in past ages.

There's gold in the wheat, oats and barley fields, and after harvest a golden stubble lights the landscape. There's a wealth of gold in the pastures and range country to feed great herds of cattle, horses, sheep. California Joe, an early horse rancher north of the Black Hills gold camps and Custer's inimitable scout, voiced the rancher's sentiments. "There's gold from the grass roots down," he said, "but there's more from the grass roots up."

Still, the gold that tempted and tantalized, that fed great stampedes of gold fever and panic, that created outbursts of jubilance and mayhem and murder and greed—was the gold found in creeks and diggings of the Black Hills. It was gold nuggets in the pan, gold dust in the riffles of the sluice box, gold sparkling through crushed rock—and the never-ending search for the "Mother Lode," the heart of it all. The gold rush that began with Custer's well-publicized expedition to the Black Hills in 1874 is an exciting chapter in South Dakota's history. In the wild mining camp towns that sprang up overnight were tough miners, rough and ready women, outlaws, shrewd-eyed gamblers—all stung by the fever of gold. There was gold in the streets of Deadwood, Custer and Keystone. Yet it could be that more gold dust settled on those who worked the miners than on those who worked the mines.

Today the largest gold mine in the western hemisphere is Lead's Homestake. In 104 years it has produced nearly two million pounds of gold, worth over a billion dollars. The romance seems nearly gone, though, from this modern industrial giant—until one catches a glimpse of the pure gold bars, the ultimate outcome of all this lifting and crushing of great rocks.

With the price of gold soaring, people are now going back into the rocky creeks and gulches with pan and shovel. Again the breathless search is on for gold flakes, grains and nuggets which might have washed down from the underground gold-bearing rocks. The question teases: Is the Mother Lode still hidden there, somewhere, untouched?

Still another bright shine here is tourist gold. South Dakota's second greatest industry is tourism. (Agriculture is first.) The state offers many things to see and do, but the prime goal of every tourist is to see the great stone monument at Mt. Rushmore. There the faces of four presidents—Washington, Lincoln, Jefferson, Roosevelt—symbolize American democracy to the entire world. More than two million come each year to see. The view and the programs are free, but most visitors find plenty of places to spend money.

Many choose an elegant reminder of their visit—a piece of well-crafted Black Hills gold jewelry. This jewelry, designed in varied colors with grapes, leaves and vines, is a timeless favorite with South Dakotans and has a history as old as the gold mining camps.

Gold bars from Homestake. Black Hills Gold Jewelry at right twines grapes and leaves into timeless favorite.

'Liquid gold' in the wheat field.

Shortgrass cures golden on the stem to feed range cattle year round.

Corn Palace celebrates a golden treasure—the central role of corn here.

Gold nuggets and gold fever continue to lure today's miner.

Gold has been found at several places...
I have upon my table
forty or fifty small particles of pure gold,
in size averaging a small pin-head,
and most of it obtained today from
one panful of earth

Custer's Field Report
Black Hills, August 1874

Pumpkins, like corn, are native and grew for centuries along Missouri River bottoms.

Tourist gold focuses on the inspiring faces of four presidents.

'and surely they were golden dreams—'

The gold-shimmering pheasant—South Dakota's state bird

SOUTH DAKOTA SYMBOLS

The State Seal

In the foreground: to the right a farmer with his plow, at left a smelting furnace and mining. Farther back a range of hills, a herd of cattle and field of corn. Between the two parts, a river bearing a steamboat.

State Flag—The seal surrounded by a flaming sun on a field of blue, encircled with the words 'South Dakota the Sunshine State.'

State Bird—Chinese Ringneck pheasant
State Tree—Black Hills Spruce
State Animal—Coyote
State Flower—Pasqueflower, also known as the Crocus
State Mineral—Rose Quartz
State Gem—Fairburn agate
State Insect—Honey bee
State Motto—Under God the People Rule
State Nicknames—the Coyote State, the Sunshine State
Origin of Name—Dakotah was the name for the Sioux, meaning allies or friends.

Facts in Brief

SIZE: 77,615 square miles, 16th among states; greatest length, 380 miles, width 245 miles.

LOCATION: Geographic center of U.S. at Snake Butte in Butte County.

HIGHEST POINT: Harney Peak, 7,242 feet; lowest, Big Stone Lake, 962 feet.

STATEHOOD: Nov. 2, 1889, the 40th state.

CAPITAL: Pierre.

LARGEST CITY: Sioux Falls (Rapid City, 2nd; Aberdeen, 3rd).

COUNTIES: 67 (3 are unorganized).

POPULATION: 690,178 (1980 census), increase of 3.6% over 1970; 638,955 white; 45,101 Indian; 2,144 black; 1,728 Asian; 2,250 other (self-identified).

SCHOOL ENROLLMENTS: Elementary, with kindergarten, 97,701-88,399 public, 9,302 non-public; High School, 49,414-45,440 public, 3,974 non-public; Vo-Tech, 2,259 at 6 schools; Higher Education, 28,313-21,763 at 7 public, 6,550 at 9 private institutions.

INDIAN RESERVATIONS: CHEYENNE RIVER, 4,584 population, 1,410,346 acres; Teton Sioux—Minneconjou, Sans Arc. Two Kettle. Blackfeet. CROW CREEK, 1,790 pop., 125,000 acres; Yankton Sioux and Teton Sioux—Brule. FLANDREAU, 378 pop., 2,356 acres; Santee Sioux—Sisseton, Wahpeton. LOWER BRULE, 973 pop., 119,944 acres; Teton Sioux—Brule. PINE RIDGE, 13,500 pop., 1,670.753 acres; Teton Sioux—Oglala. ROSEBUD, 9,326 pop., 958,472 acres; Teton Sioux—Brule, SISSETON, 3,990 pop., 107,000 acres; Santee Sioux—Sisseton, Wahpeton. STANDING ROCK, 3,899 pop., (S.D.), 844,525 acres (total); Teton Sioux—Hunkpapa. YANKTON, 2,411 pop., 34,089 acres; Yankton Sioux.

LEADING INDUSTRY: Agriculture (tourism 2nd).

RANKING IN U.S. AGRICULTURE: 6th in nation in total acres in farms and ranches, 45,450 acres. 1st in production of oats, rye; 2nd flaxseed; 3rd in honey and sunflowers; 4th in hay and spring wheat excluding durum; 5th sheep; 9th cattle, (1979). Other important products: barley, corn, hogs, milk, eggs, soybeans.

FARM SIZE AND INCOME: 1184 acres, average size; annual revenue from agric. over $2.5 billion, 73.3% from livestock, 26.7% crops; no. of farms and ranches, 38,000; average gross income per farm, $66,436; average expenditures, $61,292.

MINERALS: Gold—largest gold mine in western hemisphere, Homestake, producing annually 250,280 troy ounces worth $75,084,000 (1979); sand and gravel; stone; oil.

The coyote, state animal

The Coyote

I don't think there is nothin' as bad—good an in between as a coyote...everything has had a hard time to survive but I think the coyote has had the worst. Ever since the first settlers came he has had a price on his head an been bush-whacked with every kind of weapon known to man...With all of this the ol coyote is still with us while other species has lots of help ta keep goin...I think the whole human race could take a lesson from coyotes an jest dig in an look out fer themselves an fight their own battles. How many people can live a day of turrable hardships and then sit on a hill an sing that nite.

Byron Bradfield
WHITE RIVER PETE SEZ

2. VACATION HIGHLIGHTS

Pageantry, a fantastic golden castle, lakes and rivers, western ranches, rodeos, a holy mountain, caves, wildlife, and of course "the faces." These are just a few of the fascinations that South Dakota holds for the visitor.

Pageantry is summertime with many communities celebrating centennials and other events. The smallest town can present a spectacular.

Some, like DeSmet, give dramas every year. More than 100 local people take part in the Laura Ingalls Wilder pageant at this historic little town on the prairie. Most of the Wilder books are based here (though the TV series has erroneously labeled Walnut Grove, Minnesota, where the family lived a few years, as the "little town's" location.) Devotees of the Little House series can tour the Ingalls homestead, the house in DeSmet that Pa built and in which he and Ma lived until their deaths, as well as 16 other sites mentioned in Laura's books.

Summer theater is also held in Wall, in Yankton, at Madison's Prairie Village, and in the Black Hills.

The heart of community heritage is found in its museums and historical landmarks. Almost every South Dakota town has one or more. In Mitchell this has grown into an entire town—Prairie Village—with 40 restored buildings. A steam threshing jamboree is held here. The Prehistoric Indian village at Mitchell goes back much further—700 to 1000 years. Two ancient houses have been excavated and restoration plans are underway.

State Capitol at Pierre

South Dakota is cattle country.

Shrine to Music display of Far Eastern instruments.

Harvey Dunn's paintings of Dakota pioneer life are viewed at Memorial Art Center.

Full size bronze casting of David, by Michaelangelo, stands in Sioux Falls.

Scenic lakes and rivers are typical South Dakota. Boating at sunset above.

Magic, still evenings, surpassing in beauty the most fantastic dreams of childhood!...Out to the westward—so surprisingly near—a blazing countenance sank to rest on a white couch...set it afire...kindled a radiance...a golden flame that flowed in many streams from horizon to horizon; the light played on the hundreds and thousands and millions of diamonds, and turned them into glittering points of yellow and red, green and blue fire...Such evenings were dangerous for all life. To the strong they brought reckless laughter—for who had ever seen such moon-nights?

O. E. Rolvaag
Giants in the Earth

Costumed Sioux watch dancing.

Indian boy performs hoop dance.

More than 60 rodeos each year.

Canoeing a quiet river

Four big dams block Missouri.

Bathers sun selves at full swimming beach.

Old Time Fiddling Contest makes footstomping music at Yankton.
Above, yucca pods frame view of White River from cutbank.

Mitchell is also the site of the famed Corn Palace which attracts half a million visitors annually. It is newly decorated each fall with 2000-3000 bushels of corn for the Corn Harvest Festival. Inside are large corn panels representing both Indian and non-Indian heritage in South Dakota. The Corn Palace, with its turrets and spires, might be viewed as an example of what Charles Kuralt has called "America's screwball architecture." Such buildings, he insists, are in continual danger of being replaced by structures of glass and steel, and should be protected.

Specialty museums include the Shrine to Music in Vermillion. Here in four galleries are displayed one of the world's finest collections of vintage musical instruments. Of more than 2500 items, less than 10% are shown at one time. Included are instruments as expensively crafted as the most respected concert grand pianos and as wistfully tuneful as a homemade banjo.

At Brookings the South Dakota Memorial Art Center displays over sixty Harvey Dunn paintings. Born in Manchester, South Dakota, Dunn became a noted illustrator and war artist-correspondent. But it is his warm strong paintings of pioneer life on the Dakota prairie which won him highest honors. The Art Center also shows other South Dakota artists, and houses the complete 1500 piece Marghab collection of fine embroideried linens.

South Dakota's Indian reservations are interesting places to visit. St. Francis Mission has an especially fine museum on the Rosebud Reservation with collections of Sioux artifacts, dress, music, medicine. Another Sioux museum is in Rapid City. The Sioux cultural center at Eagle Butte depicts legends and displays beadwork and other arts. Monuments to Sacagawea and to Sitting Bull can be seen, not far from the place of their deaths, west of the river near Mobridge. Wounded Knee Massacre site on the Pine Ridge Reservation offers a painful lesson in history.

Rodeos and pow-wows are especially fascinating times to visit South Dakota's Indian reservations. In South Dakota, rodeo is everywhere—more than 60 are held each year in the state. But it is more interestingly experienced in western ranching towns where roping and the challenge to ride an outlaw horse grew up from the grassroots. Rodeo still retains a non-commercial flavor at such towns as McLaughlin, Lemmon, Bison, and Buffalo. A Dakota wagon train may be joined for tours out of Eagle Butte.

Every county holds fairs and celebrations culminating in the State Fair at Huron in early September—where the best of

Range horses come down to drink at reservoir on Standing Rock reservation, at left. Pine Ridge is the land of Red Cloud and of Wounded Knee.

Laura Ingalls Wilder pageant relives Laura's teaching days in one room school. Above, summer fun for the young on Moccasin Creek in Aberdeen.

everything raised in South Dakota can be seen, including young people with their achievements. Ethnic festivals, such as Czech Days in Tabor, meet with enthusiasm and seem certain to increase in number. Hutterite colonies may be visited along the James River, and produce often purchased there.

Lakes and scenic rivers are well distributed in South Dakota, so there's plenty of boating, swimming, fishing, canoeing, camping, water skiing, and pleasure at being near the water. Guided tours are given at the four big dams: Gavins Point, Ft. Randall, Big Bend, and Oahe. Visitors centers are open. South Dakota has 12 state parks, plus a historical park at Ft. Sisseton, 19 state recreation areas and two nature areas. Most of these are along rivers or lakeshores. Farm Island, a state park near Pierre, has a 200 year history of change from native vegetation (Lewis & Clark stopped here to pick up an elk killed by their hunters), to the garden farming of fur traders, to a developed recreation area, to the present time when cars are outlawed and the island is returning to its natural vegetation.

Near Farm Island is the Ft. Sully visitors center. Other old forts to see are Ft. Meade, Ft. Sisseton, and the ruins of Ft. Randall. Missouri River history buffs might want to cross the Missouri by the bend at Running Water on the old style paddlewheel ferry.

Zoos are found at Aberdeen and Sioux Falls. There's an old mill at Milbank, where American Legion baseball got its start in 1925. Lemmon has a 2-block petrified park which includes huge petrified logs and petrified chunks of rock cemented into various formations. Also pyramids of natural cannonballs.

Scattered remains of ghost towns can be found throughout the state. Many of these were short-lived boomtowns, many died when they were by-passed by the railroad. But old-timers recall them with zest, "That was a thriving town. Had a lively dance every Saturday night and a big fight!"

Travelers from other states--but most especially South Dakotans themselves—should not neglect to see the backways, the farms and ranches, the small towns and cemeteries, the creeks and small rivers and lakes, the buttes and badlands and hilltops, of areas of the state they have not seen before. To do this they need to get off the Interstate, drive down the smaller roads and visit with the people they find there.

Thundering Falls along the Sioux at Falls Park.

Eroded castles and pinnacles at Slim Buttes.

Polled Hereford is washed and fitted for show at the State Fair.

Old Army posts such as Ft. Sisseton at right, Ft. Meade, Ft. Sully and Ft. Randall, recall South Dakota's military history.

Cross-country skiing and other winter sports are popular.

Museums reveal the heart of local heritage.

Dancers wear colorful and skillfully beaded costumes at pageants and pow-wows.

Visitors enjoy restored ghost towns, gold mining camps.

The Black Hills and Badlands

The Black Hills and Badlands area offers many varied attractions to the visitor. Here within a relatively small region are two national parks, Wind Cave and the Badlands; a national memorial, Mt Rushmore; a national monument, Jewel Cave; a national landmark, Bear Butte; and two state parks, Custer and Bear Butte.

An extremely well developed commercial tourist business, in addition, provides every sort of diversion on themes from gold mining to dinosaurs, to such seemingly unrelated topics as marine life and wax museums.

The Hills are perhaps unique in the world in the features which coincide here. The internationally known mountain sculpture. A big modern gold mine. A colorful history of gold rush days, outlaws, cattle kingdoms, Indian culture and battles. Intricate caves and caverns which are among the world's largest. Numerous fossil beds with bones of the early horse, camels, dinosaurs and wooly mammoths—30 in one sinkhole which probably contains 60-70 more. Remarkable mountain scenery and a wealth of wildlife.

Paha Sapa is the Sioux name for the Black Hills.

Mt. Rushmore

One of the leading tourist attractions of the nation, the Mt. Rushmore sculpture ranks second only to Golden Gate Bridge as one of the seven man made wonders of the United States.

"I want to create a monument so inspiring that people from all over America will be drawn to come and look and go home better citizens," said sculptor Gutzon Borglum.

His success is evidenced by the visits of over two million people each year. The mountain sculpture is known throughout the world as a symbol of democracy. In the faces of the four presidents can be seen the vision, the ideals and the accomplishments of the American people.

The mountain carving was first conceived by South Dakota's state historian Doane Robinson to depict heroes of the west, such as John Colter and Jim Bridger. On Robinson's invitation Borglum came to the Black Hills to consider the possibilities. After much searching he found a mountain dominated by a crown of even-grained granite which faced most of the day into the sun. He spent the rest of his life near that mountain, carving out—not western heroes—but the faces of four presidents, each face as high as a five-story building.

Borglum chose his subjects for the ideals they represent. George Washington, the struggle to win and found a new nation; Thomas Jefferson, the spirit of democracy, independence and high vision; Abraham Lincoln, a man of the frontier who fought for equality and justice; Theodore Roosevelt; a fair-minded conservationist of just such lands as these.

The monument has not been without critics. An eastern paper once said, "Borglum is about to destroy another mountain. Thank God it is in South Dakota where no one will ever see it."

The mountain itself is named for an early New York tourist, Charles Rushmore, who happened to ask his guide the mountain's name. Jokingly the guide replied, "Mt. Rushmore," and the name stuck.

But the huge project gained momentum, through donations of pennies from school children in its beginning, to full scale federal financing. Of nearly one million dollars spent

An eye 11 feet wide, a nose 20 feet long

One of world's most popular spots for a family photo

on the memorial in the 14 years of construction between 1927 and 1941, $836,000 came from federal funds.

The year Borglum died, in 1941, the work and the funds came to an end. Although the sculpture is unfinished as planned, it is complete in the minds of those who view it.

At the Sculptor's Studio visitors can study Borglum's working models, scaled one inch to one foot on the mountain, and inspect the tools used. "The faces" are best viewed by morning light. Each evening in summer programs are given at the amphitheater, memorably climaxed by dramatic floodlighting.

The Caves

Caves include the national park and national monument at Wind cave and Jewel Cave, plus many others privately owned and perhaps more conveniently located. The Hills contain many caves due to upheaval and water erosion of an underlying bed of limestone 300 to 650 feet thick.

In Jewel Cave, 60 miles of passageways on four levels have been explored and mapped, making it the fourth largest cave in the United States. In Wind Cave 27 miles are explored; total extent unknown. Temperatures are about 47 degrees (8.3 degrees C) in Jewel Cave and 53 degrees in Wind Cave, year around. (A light jacket or sweater is needed.) A variety of guided tours are offered. Visitors may take a short easy walk

'Sylvan Lake...is the most beautiful spot in the Hills and has few equals anywhere else.'

Robert Casey
The Black Hills

Rugged peaks reflect in mountain lake

Stave church, Rapid City's Chapel in the Hills, reflects Norwegian heritage. Old mine shafts and mining camps are still found. Mountain goats, below right, skip across rocky chasms.

Council scene in Crazy Horse Pageant at Hot Springs depicts last stand of the Sioux. At right, one of many attractive campsites.

After cutting through eight miles or more we fell into the most beautiful valley remembered. Narrow, no where spreading to a greater width than half a mile; hidden almost entirely by steep, wooded cliffs, which rose on either side, so that in the middle of the afternoon it was nearly as dark as twilight. The air was cool and fresh, while on the hills we had suffered from a sultry heat, with the thermometer at ninety-three, and was laden with the perfume of millions of flowers. The whole valley was a nosegay, and so rich was the soil that everything grew with the greatest luxuriance. Our eyes were opened then to the beauties of the Black Hills.

Wm. Curtis, reporter with Custer
in the Black Hills, 1874

Spunky prairie dogs entertain visitors at Black Hills prairie dog towns. Below are towering spires of the Needles. Above right, Terry Peak and Deer Mountain offer breathtaking ski runs.

through improved portions, or the longer more strenuous tours through primitive unlighted sections carrying their own candle lanterns. Special spelunking tours give the adventurous a real taste of cave exploring, partly on hands and knees and wriggling through passageways on the stomach.

Deposits in the caves vary and include: boxwork veins and formations, needlelike frostwork crystals, popcorn nodules, delicate gypsum flowerlike crystals, stalactites, stalagmites, columns, bubbles, and helictites in huge bushes and twists, spirals and curves.

Custer State Park

A specialty of Custer State Park are the wildlife and scenery. The Needles Highway is here, plus hiking trails, camping, fishing, horseback riding. Here is the famous herd of more than 1000 buffalo begun in 1914. A buffalo auction is held in the park each fall selling some 400 head of calves and surplus buffalo. In spring the buffalo are corralled and worked in a three-day roundup. Lots of excitement from the high-spirited buffalo especially during these times.

Other wildlife to see are bighorn sheep, mountain goats, elk, deer, prairie dogs and friendly burros, first brought in during the 1920's to carry visitors to the top of Harney Peak.

Within this park is the Game Lodge, summer White House for two presidents: Coolidge in 1927 and Eisenhower in 1953. The Black Hills Playhouse provides summer theater six nights a week.

Bear Butte

Bear Butte is called Mato Paha, Bear Mountain, in Sioux because of bear legends and its resemblance to a sleeping bear, which can be distinguished for many miles. Prehistoric man had camps here more than 4000 years ago.

For centuries Bear Butte has been a place of pilgrimage for Sioux and Cheyenne, who regard it as the birthplace of their religions. The Sun Dance is said to have originated here with the Cheyenne. It was the site of a great council of the Sioux nation in 1857. Indian people come to this mountain from all over the United States to meditate, pray, seek visions, present offerings, undergo personal sacrifice.

Hiking trails lead up this historic holy mountain. Even the most casual visitor on the trail has the sense of this being a special hallowed place with pine trees hung with prayer cloths and the Indian campground and sweat bath below.

The Badlands

The Badlands National Park, also called the White River Badlands, is a vast area of strange and desolate shapes almost

Prayer cloths flutter from pine tree on Bear Butte.

devoid of vegetation. The most amazing feature here is the great Wall that extends for 80 miles along the White River. The Wall is actually one-sided—a steep and deeply eroded drop-off from grassy plateaus above to bottomlands below.

Traditionally there were only four places to come down the Wall. One of these, near Interior, is called Big Foot Pass for Chief Big Foot who brought his people down this pass shortly before they were massacred at Wounded Knee in 1890. There's no need for range fences, either above or below the Wall. But in one blizzard, 10,000 unlocated Texas cattle went over the Wall, pushing ahead of the storm. Bands of sheep have also been lost over the Wall in snowstorms.

Settlers who lived on the plateau above got their supplies only with great difficulty from railroad towns below. In some places they unhitched their wagons at the brink of the Wall and rode or led their horses down. After purchasing groceries and supplies, they loaded the horses and climbed back up the Wall. While in town they watched anxiously for signs of rain and, if a thunderstorm developed, hastened to outrun it. Otherwise they were stuck below the Wall for days waiting for the slippery clays to dry out.

The Badlands are sculpted by wind and water erosion of the softer soils, exposing and isolating harder layers of soil and rock. Nowhere, it is said, can the influence of erosion be better studied or more easily understood than here. Variegated colors—influenced by minerals mixed with sand and soil—are exposed in layers. There are the soft purples of oxidized

Jewel Cave at left, is fourth largest in world. The flat grassy plateau above the Wall, where antelope graze, drops off into scene of desolation. Erosion continues to cut into plateau.

Camels troop across stage of outdoor amphitheatre in Passion Play.

'Let us place there, carved as high, as close to Heaven as we can, the words of our leaders, their faces, to show posterity what manner of men they were.'

Gutzon Borglum

manganese, the orange and rusts of iron oxide, the white layers of volcanic ash, the grays and tans of silt and clay mixed with soil and ash. The Wall is continually changing, says one man who has lived all his life beneath it. "Every fifteen minutes the shadowing and the colors are different," he says.

Extensive fossil beds have been excavated in the White River Badlands. Remains can be viewed on the fossil trail.

Other Attractions

In addition to national and state supported attractions, the Hills and Badlands abound with things for the visitor to see and do.

Somewhat north of the Wall, on the plateau above, is the town of Wall. Here is Wall Drug—said to be the most famous drug store in the world. Wall Drug came to fame during the hot dry '30's by advertising free ice water. Today it's a full-fledged tourist center with dozens of specialty shops and attractions drawing some 10,000 people a day in season, but still advertising free ice water and selling 5¢ cups of coffee.

Because settlement patterns in the Black Hills national forest included mining claims and forest homesteads, many islands of land within the forest are privately owned. Therefore commercial enterprises directed toward tourism are not only clustered around national forest perimeters, but are sprinkled throughout.

There are restored ghost towns, fascinating museums, drama and melodrama. The Passion Play at Spearfish attracts large crowds. At Deadwood, many watch the "Trial of Jack McCall" and walk up Boot Hill to see the graves of Calamity Jane and Wild Bill Hickok. There are Auto Museums, Wax Museums, pioneer, western and Indian museums, 1880's train rides, Thunderhead Falls, the Cosmos, Bear Country, trout fishing lakes, gold mines, covered wagon trips, Story Book Island, petrified forests, Reptile Gardens, Flintstone City, and many more.

At Lead, tours are given through the big Homestake gold mine. The Museum of Geology at South Dakota's School of Mines has excellent displays on dinosaurs, fossils and minerals. Deadwood's "Days of '76" includes a parade, rodeo and the finale of a wagon train. Custer offers "Gold Discovery Days." Stavekirke, the Norwegian chapel, can be seen near Rapid City as can horse racing and greyhound racing. Keystone and Rockerville are both restored gold mining camps with souvenir and specialty shops of all kinds. At Thunderhead Mountain near Custer, sculptor Korczak Ziolkowski is carving a monument to Crazy Horse, the great Sioux leader.

To get the most from a trip into the Black Hills, as anywhere, it's not enough to "see and buy"; one also needs to "do." In the Hills and Badlands there's plenty of space for walking, hiking, backpacking, boating, water skiing, camping, lake and stream fishing, rock hunting, panning for gold, spelunking (exploring caves) and trail riding, with horse camps for those who bring their own horses.

In fall there's hunting of big game and wild turkeys. In winter, skiing is excellent at Terry Peak and Deer Mountain. Many come to the Black Hills in groups for snomobiling and cross-country skiing.

Old buildings and restored ghost towns attract visitors from many countries.

Deeply eroded badlands Wall extends 80 miles along the White River. At left, life-size dinosaurs on Rapid City skyline depict the many prehistoric reptiles found. Road winds below the wall; every 15 minutes a change in shading.

Sculptor Korczak Ziolkowski carves Crazy Horse Memorial on Thunderhead Mountain.

Black Hills are a haven for wildlife

The Badlands—

Then see the pass by moonlight. No clear-cut edges, but shadowy shapes and figures now. A city dead; untenanted. A thousand monuments; their faces blank, their feet in shadow. And over all a deathless stillness reigns, save when some later car roars through the pass, leaving a stillness deeper than before. This whole frozen sea is waiting, has been waiting almost since the beginning of time, is still—waiting.
Archer Gilfillan
*A Goat's Eye View
of the Black Hills*

No fresh green things in the Bad Lands bide;
It is all stark red and gray,
And strewn with bones that had lived and died
Ere the first man saw the day...

The place is as dry as a crater cup,
Yet you hear, as the stars shine free,
From the barren gulches sounding up,
The lap of a spawning sea.
A breeze that cries where the great ferns rise
From the pools on a new-made shore,
With the whip and whir of batlike wings,
And the snarl of slimy, fighting things
And the tread of the dinosaur.
Badger Clark
Grass Grown Trails

Buffalo herd in Custer State Parks numbers about 1000; 400 are auctioned each year.

Panning gold in the Hills is a new attraction as well as an old one.

Springtime—chokecherry and wild plum trees are in full bloom. New colts cavort on the range.

3. CHANGING SEASONS

Spring, summer, fall, winter.

Nearly every day in every season the Dakota sun is shining. The air is light and clear. Weather is usually pleasant, but unpredictable here at the center of the nation.

Every season heralds a striking change in nature, and in the activities of those who live here and work the land. Every season has its magic moments.

There is the swift freshness of springtime. Creeks suddenly running bankful with melting snow and ice. Hills are tinged green one morning, then deepen into emerald day by day. Crocuses push through the pasture grasses to bloom in beds of purple softness. Lambs and calves leap along the hillsides, bucking, flipping tails, glistening clean and impudent in their newness. As fields dry farm work begins, turning up black loam, planting seeds. Spring fever hits the young and they think of playing in the mud, trackmeets, proms, graduation and the day school's out. The meadowlark greets the spring morning with a song of melodic joy.

Summer brings fast-paced activity. It's time for growing and building. A time for outdoor recreation, for vacations, camping, lake cabins, barbeques, picnics, rodeo. It's swimming lessons and going to camp. It's company coming. In summertime there's work to do. South Dakotans know the deep satisfaction of work well done: stacks of hay, rows of apple jelly, colorful petunia beds, a new patio built, a young tree started, calves growing fast on good pasture, ripening grain, clean cultivated corn, neat gardens, and a blue ribbon won at the county fair. Days can be hot, but nights are cool and the air light. Summer storms come suddenly. Hail is foreshadowed briefly by swift chilling of the air on a hot afternoon. But a summer thunderstorm is pure joy for all its fearsome flashing and crashings. In its wake comes the exhilaration of fresh clean air, hills glistening green, rainbows arching across a far ridge.

Average Date of Last Spring Frost

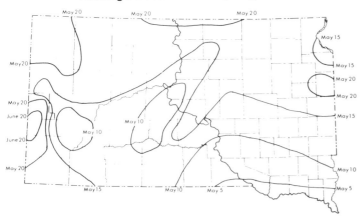

Average Date of First Fall Frost

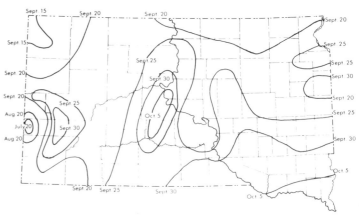

U. S. Weather Service

Fall is the glorious season of Indian summer that follows a quick September frost and perhaps a week of drizzling rain. The melting warmth of the Indian summer breaks through with many weeks of crisp sunny mornings and golden afternoons. Harvests are complete, corn cribs burst with golden nuggets, calves go into the feedlot. And even the farmer and rancher who dried out, hailed out, or sold his calves on a losing market, views his glorious land and can't help being swept by a familiar western optimism: Next year will be better. Labor Day and first frost spell the end of summer. In many ways, too, they mean a new beginning. School starts, from kindergarten through college. It's the season of football and hunting. The full harvest moon hangs low in the sky. High above, southbound geese cleave the evening air, calling to each other, unhurried but never wavering from their dangerous journey.

Winter sun dazzles snow crystals and cuts a clean shadow from fenceposts. Snowfalls can be soft and fleecy or, wind-driven, sculpted into delicate drifts against the merest stem of grass. Winter is a time of grandeur and great beauty. Winter air is crisp and bracing, generally pleasant with bright sunshine. Blizzards will strike—perhaps once or twice during the winter but seldom lasting more than a day, and South Dakotans are well prepared. Insulated clothing and new equipment mean winter sports are widely enjoyed. There's skiing, snowmobiling, ice fishing, hockey, skating, sledding, tobogganing and a quiet walk through the snow.

Bright, clear sky over a plain so wide that the rim of the heavens cut down on it around the entire horizon...Bright, clear sky, to-day, to-morrow, and for all time to come. And sun! And still more sun! It set the heavens afire every morning; it grew with the day to quivering golden light—then softened into all the shades of red and purple as evening fell...Pure colour everywhere. A gust of wind, sweeping across the plain, threw into life waves of yellow and blue and green...

O. E. Rolvaag
Giants in the Earth

Spring

Summer

Fall

Winter

The pasqueflower, or crocus, brings
swift news of spring.

Honk of geese overhead, in spring and fall, fills the air
and lifts the soul

Early summer is branding time in
range country.

In woods, the deep cool greens of
summer

Fall-brilliant trees and mellow sunshine make a glorious season for the hunter.

Golden fall turns into the grandeur of winter

Ice fishing houses cluster on a winter lake.

Coyote hunts through winter stillness.

Average Annual Precipitation

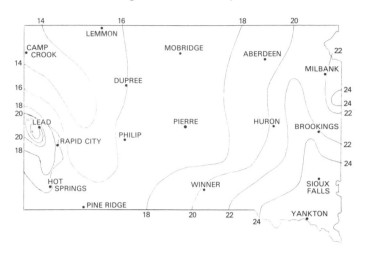

Precipitation Variance at 5 Recording Stations

	1977	1973	1936	1934	Average
Camp Crook	14.07	14.74	4.73	6.60	13.7
Lemmon	23.42	18.02	5.54	8.67	15
Mobridge	24.57	17.18	7.21	6.15	17
Hot Springs	20.12	19.08	10.12		20
Vermillion	25.93	28.66	17.93	21.86	25.25

1977 was one of the highest rainfall years on record; 1973 also high
1936 produced record lows; 1934 also extremely low

U. S. Weather Service

CLIMATE OF SOUTH DAKOTA

South Dakota is known as the Sunshine State, with sunshine about 62% of the time between sunrise and sunset year around. The air is clear with excellent visibility.

Rainfall is the most crucial factor for agriculture, South Dakota's most important industry. Great variation exists from year to year and from one area of the state to another. The northwest corner is the driest, averaging only 13 inches precipitation. Moisture increases almost on the diagonal through the state, with the southeastern corner receiving about 25 inches. Most rainfall comes from the Gulf of Mexico. This moist air reaches eastern South Dakota most easily as it moves north from the gulf and turns eastward. Air flow from the Pacific Ocean brings little moisture over the Rockies; air from the southwest brings none.

Hills and valleys also affect weather patterns. This is most noticable in the Black Hills. There, abrupt elevation of 5500 to 7242 feet increases rain and snow. This is because moisture in the weather front condenses when it meets the rising flow of air at the eastern or southeastern edge of the Hills. As can be seen on the precipitation map above, the Black Hills receive much more moisture than surrounding lands.

Snowfall is 25 to 45 inches for most of the state, with over 100 inches in the Black Hills. Again there is great variation from year to year. For instance, Sioux Falls had only 5.4 inches of snow the winter of 1930-31, but received 94.7 inches in 1968-69. Most years snow does not remain on level ground more than a few weeks at a time without thawing.

Growing season averages 120 days in the northwest to 150 days in the southeast.

Hail can be expected two or three times a year in most of the state, with the highest frequency in and near the Black Hills. Tornadoes may occur—with an average of 29 funnels a year being sighted. A severe tornado hit Rapid City June 18, 1967, causing $2,000,000 damage.

Flooding is a danger with heavy snow and rapid spring melting. Severe flooding occured along the Big Sioux, Vermillion and James Rivers in April 1969. Missouri River flooding has been controlled for the 90 miles of natural river remaining in South Dakota. Flash floods can rise rapidly in steep Black Hills canyons. Extensive building in the flood plain in recent times has increased danger to life and property. In the tragic Rapid City/Black Hills flood of June 9, 1972, torrents of rain fell—up to 10 and 14 inches—in a short time. Walls of water surged down narrow mountain creeks sweeping away houses, cars, campers and trees and smashing them into buildings below. The toll rose to 232 persons confirmed dead with 5 missing; over $100,000,000 in property was destroyed. A subsequent study showed flooding has occurred in Rapid City about every nine years; the 1907 flood probably had even higher water than in 1972.

Sudden weather changes are typical of the entire northern plains. The Guiness Book of Records lists the world's most freakish temperature rise as hitting Spearfish January 22, 1943. This was a rise of 49 degrees in two minutes: from four below at 7:30 in the morning to 45 degrees at 7:32. Water ran in the streets, but by 9:27 that same morning Spearfish had set another record, dropping from a 54 degree high at nine o'clock back to four below.

The Hammond Almanac of 1979 lists five abrupt U.S. temperature drops. Of these, three were in South Dakota, two in Montana. Besides the Spearfish drop, two were in Rapid City, both in 1911. On January 10 temperatures there dropped 47 degrees in 15 minutes—from 55 degrees at seven in the morning to eight degrees at 7:15. Two days later on January 12, a two hour drop changed temperatures 62 degrees in Rapid City from 49 degrees at six in the morning to 13 degrees below by eight.

Freakish temperature differences often exist between Lead and Deadwood—three miles apart. One day in Lead just before noon it was -12 degrees, then rose in 15 minutes to 30 degrees. As temperatures soared to 52 degrees in Lead, it remained a frigid -16 degrees in Deadwood. Not until late afternoon did the chinook hit Deadwood, warming it to 44 degrees by 7 p.m.

South Dakota weather statistics are given below. The year to remember was surely 1936. Or, more accurately perhaps, for those who lived through it, that was a year they could never forget. South Dakota records were set in 1936 for hottest, driest, coldest. Temperatures dropped to 58 degrees below zero in February, rose to 120 degrees in July, and a low precipitation record was set in Ludlow with 2.89 inches. (That same year Sioux Falls had 25.28 inches.) Another dry year, 1980, measured 8.30 inches in Ralph, 8.04 in Camp Crook, 10.27 in Lemmon, and 23.30 inches in Castlewood.

SOUTH DAKOTA WEATHER STATISTICS

Lowest temperature	-58 degrees F at McIntosh Feb. 17, 1936
Highest temperature	120 degrees F at Gann Valley July 3, 1936
Precipitation	13" northwest to 25" southeast, average
Snowfall	25-45" at lower elevations over 100" in Black Hills
Growing Season	Average 120 days (northwest) to 150 days (southeast) except at higher elevations in Black Hills

Towering old cottonwoods shade river's sandy beaches.

4. THE RIVER

Mighty Missouri.

Great surging river of history. River of fur traders, explorers, gold miners, pioneers, Arikara Indians who farmed and fiercely fortified its banks. Longest river in North America with 3000 circuitous miles of navigation. And some claimed the Missouri reached even farther—all the way to New Orleans—that it completely dominates the mild Mississippi from the point they run together.

Dakotans call it simply "the river."

The river. These words evoke subtle memories of mystery, dread and fascination. Traditionally the Missouri was where the west began. Across was a vast land—rugged, semi-arid, with harsher climate. Across was a difference in the people as well; independence, individualism, optimism and tolerance were valued highly.

These distinctions persist today. The Missouri cuts the state of South Dakota quite neatly in half—effectively separating east from west. In defining the vast differences they feel, Dakotans have coined the terms "east river" and "west river," applying them to both land and people. East river contains the institutions and the ways of the east. It is well developed with generally good farm land, higher rainfall, and a long-rooted population with strong nationality patterns. West river is the essense of the west. There a greater mix of people occurred as waves of immigration in good times fell back in drouth, to be renewed by fresh waves as rain increased.

Pioneers saw the Missouri as a barrier and viewed it with fear and unease. Part of this tradition stemmed from the difficulty of crossing. Swimming stock and floating wagons was risky, with strong undercurrents, and deep soft mud along the banks. Ferries operated in places, carrying wagons, passengers and livestock. In low water during summer and fall, pontoon bridges were strung across at Chamberlain and Evarts. Thousands of wild longhorn cattle were trailed across these narrow bridges at shipping time.

Pioneer lore is rich with stories of crossing the wide Missouri. Accidents, and loss of life, goods or livestock were all too common. Those who settled along the river knew well the stories of the river's toll. In winter these people crossed on the ice. Certain individuals always took pride locally in being first to cross in the fall, last across before the ice broke up in spring. Some of these—and others less daring—were caught on the wrong side of the river as break-up signals increased, attempted one more crossing—and failed.

The Missouri is a hungry river that washes at cliffs and soft banks, undermining them and tumbling them down in a roar and muddy splash, shifting sandbars, surging in strong undercurrents beneath deceptively smooth surfaces. At flood stage it tears out living trees and plunges them downstream to lodge as driftwood on a thousand sandbars. Rivermen called her the "Big Muddy" and "the Misery," and navigated with great difficulty. The artist George Catlin riding up on the first steamboat was amazed at the color of the water; he experimented and found it totally opaque at one-eighth inch.

The Missouri was South Dakota's first tourist route. Famous visitors rode those early steamboats: Catlin, the naturalist writer Prince Maximilian and his Swiss artist Karl Bodmer, John James Audubon and big game hunters of every stripe. For half a century and more the Missouri was the main highway of fur trade with a string of trading posts far upriver. Arikara lived on the river and Sioux made winter camp in the shelter of thick cottonwoods.

Favorite craft on the Missouri were steamboats, keelboats, canoes, bullboats and mackinaws. The Arikara used the bullboat, building it like a tub of a single bull buffalo hide stretched over a willow frame. Bullboats were too awkward to paddle upstream; they were used for crossing and downriver trips. The gold miners' mackinaws were also for downstream travel. They were little more than boxed-in rafts; many were floated down from Ft. Benton in Montana to Yankton and sold there.

Brushy banks provide good wildlife habitat.

Dakotans call it simply 'the river.'

Oh Shenandoah, I love your daughter
Far away, you restless river.
She lives across the stormy water.

  Away, away, I'm bound away
  Across the wide Missouri.

Oh Shenandoah, I long to hear you
Away, you rolling river.
Oh Shenandoah, I can't get near you.

  Away, away, I'm bound away
  Across the wide Missouri.

Migrating mallards and other waterfowl land on the big open waters.

'The Missouri is a hungry river, washing at cliffs, tearing out living trees.'

River Sunset...
A Time to Reflect

When the sun ceases to exert its brilliance and changes to its more tranquil mood of yellows, reds and golds, it is a special time to be on a river. There is something mystic about a river, especially at sunset. All is still except for the constant croaking of frogs, the whistle of the bobwhite quail and the movement of water...

South Dakota Conservation Digest

Forest of highline towers replace cottonwoods near Ft. Thompson. At left, 'Last Stand of Cheyenne River Sioux' drawn by G. W. LaPlant.

Ice break-up was a dramatic event for all who lived on the river.

"The river's breaking up—I think she'll go tonight," an anxious settler would say, listening to the cracking, snapping and popping of the ice-locked river. Warily he would move his cattle to higher ground and lay awake listening, wondering if the ice would jam. Most times by morning he saw the river breaking free in a wide channel and his children ran to climb great slabs of ice flung high on the banks in a wonderland of ice castles, caves, tunnels. But there were unforgettable times of flood when families watched helplessly while muddy waters surged higher about their buildings; ice cakes swirled against corral posts and nudged at the front door; cattle and horses were caught in low-lying pastures.

The Missouri could go on the rampage twice a year. Early in spring when the ice broke up and snow melted, again with the June raise of heavy spring rains. Ice usually went out in March. At Pierre in the 90 years between 1845 and 1935, records show the ice went out three times in February—in 1930, 1931, 1934; 20 times in April with the latest being April 20; and the 67 remaining years in March.

The big flood came in Pierre on March 27, 1881, after a winter of deep snow that put two feet on the level and cold temperatures that froze the ice 42 inches thick on the river. Other floods through the years were also memorable.

Then came the Pick-Sloan plan for development of the Missouri River basin and the Flood Control Act of 1944. The sudden flooding is ended now. The Missouri lies shackled and chained by big dams, four in South Dakota. These are: Gavins

Point Dam at Yankton backing up Lewis and Clark Lake; Fort Randall Dam at Pickstown with its Lake Francis Case; Big Bend Dam at Fort Thompson forming Lake Sharpe; and largest of all, Oahe Dam and Oahe Lake above Pierre, backing water into every low spot and tributary throughout the northern half of South Dakota.

These lakes—500 miles long and covering 700 square miles—are called "America's newest water playground," "The blue-water Great Lakes of South Dakota," "America's largest chain of inland lakes."

Big powerhouses at each dam generate great amounts of electricity for South Dakotans and others. Towns which feared to expand into the flood plain, now build with little regard for it. The billion tons of stored water give great promise of irrigation to a drouth-prone land. The lakes provide good fishing: northern pike up to 15 or 20 pounds or more, walleyes

'River development' kills trees and floods bottomlands above Pierre, right, and far up the Grand River in photo at lower left.

averaging 3-6 pounds, crappies, white bass, catfish and the prehistoric paddlefish which are snagged in tailwaters below the dams. Recreation includes also boating, camping, water skiing, swimming, ice fishing and ice boating. At dam sites the Army Corp of Engineers has built effective visitors centers which justify and explain what has been done and depict the history, geology and paleontology of the mighty Missouri. Each year the Corps computes the benefits in dollars.

But there are those who lament the losses and regret values sacrificed to flood control downriver. So little of the original river is left—in South Dakota perhaps 90 miles, most of it well settled. Gone are the quiet bottoms with clear springs and brushy coulees that were havens for deer and other wildlife. Gone is the habitat of thousands of songbirds. Gone are the forests of big cottonwoods, thickly fringing the river's meandering course in bright living green. Gone are thousands of acres of the best cropland and pasture. Gone are rich archaeological sites of ancient civilizations. Gone are the ancestral homes of many, both white and Indian.

Attractive shoreline can be found, but many who knew the green valleys and picturesque river cliffs find stark lack of beauty in the four big lakes with their barren gravel-hill coastlines, with everywhere the dead standing cottonwoods raising silver skeleton arms and lying in bleached stacks along the banks. (A local joke asks the question: "How long will it take for the dead trees to disappear?" The answer: "About as long as it takes for the dams to silt in.")

The question still remains whether it was necessary to flood out so much land and so many people in order to save other people and towns from flooding. Could the same ends have been accomplished less destructively, perhaps with smaller dams, or in other ways? Has the Corps been somewhat overzealous in moving dirt and mapping out new projects for itself?

Many ironies can be found here. Indian people see a bitter humor in this typically "white men solution": Flood land to prevent flooding. Land underwater never floods. Permanent flooding of more than 80% of South Dakota's Missouri bottomlands seems a brutal way of preventing the floods.

Undoubtedly Indian people have suffered most. The forested river bottoms were an important part of their heritage, as well as providing an economic base. There they raised gardens and a great deal of produce; they hunted in timbered draws; they cut fence posts for sale to neighboring ranchers.

Cheyenne River and Standing Rock Indians bitterly opposed Oahe Dam. The word Oahe means a dependable and secure place to stand in Sioux. It seems particularly apt to the Army Engineers—theirs is a dam well built, a good job. But

"If the Corps had its way the entire world would be water and concrete.'

Ellen Ducheneaux
Cheyenne River Sioux

Oahe takes its name from the mission settlement of Oahe, once a firm foundation, washed away by rising waters. Ultimately tribal efforts to block the dam failed. Many whites, too, lost homes and land, however there's much truth to Indian statements that "all the big dams flood Indian land."

The Missouri has always confronted humans with dilemmas and opportunities. The dilemmas and opportunities still exist.

Most pressing is the "Use it or Lose it" dilemma. The water in the great lakes is stored in South Dakota, barely used except for power generation. Coal companies, industry and states downriver covet the great impoundments of water. Increasingly they seek legal rights to water which would be stored here and taken out when they require it. Efforts are underway in South Dakota to attach some prior rights—but to do this, water must actually be used. Various plans for using it include irrigation, domestic water for towns and rural areas, and industrial projects for which the state could grant water rights on a limited-time basis.

Irrigation presents its own dilemmas. The promise of irrigation has been unfullfilled in 50 years since the building of the first of these dams at Ft. Peck. At Garrison Dam the diversion plan has stalled on local resistance to building more dams, taking more land, and digging huge canals paralleling in many places the existing rivers.

The possibility of using the lakes for barge traffic is another opportunity.

All these projects are extremely expensive. But if the water is not used, others might establish prior rights. Use it or Lose it.

The river.

The mighty Missouri of history—now tamed. A tourist brochure goes further and puts in the past tense: *"Once the Missouri River,* four huge earthern dams have created the blue-water Great Lakes of South Dakota." Yet such a judgement may be premature in the scope of the ages.

Meanwhile the old Missouri rolls on ceaselessly, chained, but filling her lakes to full flood in season, pausing only to seek her way past man's obstructions.

Ft. Randall Dam at Pickstown backs up lake Francis Case.

Bowhunt an early season; outwit a wily coyote, left, or mule deer, right.

Chow down in hunting camp.

5. RECREATION

Hunt and Fish
in South Dakota

Angle below Ft. Randall Dam.

Fly fish in fast water; feel the thrill of a first catch; flush out a pair of pheasants; or string up a nice catch of walleye.

Ride horses, whether it's a gentle kid's horse, or a wild horse race at Belle Fourche, center—or on the Bad River Suicide Ride in rough country above Ft. Pierre as seen in photo at right.

Enjoy Horses and Rodeo

Rodeo queens in action with their cutting horses, or on parade.

Try Panning for Gold

Use the skillet—or buy a real gold pan.

HOW TO TELL IF IT'S GOLD: Gold is shiny, wet or dry, and a bright yellow. It's heavy—not the sparkles of mica which might be floating on top. A flake is soft and can be dented with a fingernail. If it shatters or crumbles, it's not gold. Gold may be in the form of flakes, fish, dust, granules, pea gold or nuggets. But gold panners soon learn to think small—lifting the merest speck of treasure out with tweezers or the head of a wooden match and storing it in water in a test tube.

EQUIPMENT NEEDED: Pan, shovel, tweezers, a corked test tube to use as the "poke" for storing gold. You may buy a gold pan at hardware stores and souvenir shops (the 15" size is best.) Or like old-time miners in a pinch, substitute the cast iron skillet. Some use pie pans, wash basins and even hubcaps. Surfaces should not be oily, so local experts recommend you first clean any pan with sand, scouring it out with your foot and rinsing in the creek.

WHERE TO PAN: Panning gold is allowed anywhere in the Hills on public lands except where mining claims exist (usually a notice is posted) and on lands owned by the Department of Game, Fish and Parks. File a claim though, if you want to set up a sluice box. Some suggest panning the same localities that yielded gold to miners in the past—Rapid Creek, Annie Creek, Boulder Creek, to name just a few. Others say, stay west of Highway 385. The pro's head for the backcountry keeping their digging secret. The trick is to find the most ideal spot close to water for digging out your pay dirt. Yours can come from riffles and crevices in the stream or nearby banks. Better yet, look for signs of old creekbeds where gold dust and nuggets may have been washed down and caught in riffles, then hid under layers of earth. A recently crumbled bank might expose the kind of stones that indicate an old creek—black, oval-shaped flat stones which look as if they've been washed.

IS THERE REAL HOPE OF FINDING GOLD? Definitely. There's still gold in the Hills. But panning is hard work, as most tourists soon discover. It may take most of a year for the weekend prospector to accumulate an ounce of gold. But there's always the lure of the big strike. Remember that Potato Creek Johnney found a nugget the size of a candy bar—7¾ ounces, the biggest ever found in the Hills and spent his life looking for another one. The erosion process that exposes old creekbeds and washes gold down from gold-bearing rocks is continuous. You might find "color" in your first pan and be stung by gold fever forever after. Even if you don't, you'll enjoy the experience of prospecting deep in the Hills with the ghosts of miners panning up and down the same creek.

HOW TO PAN: Shovel your gold pan full of the dirt-gravel mixture you've selected. Set it in the creekbed and stir to wash out excess mud. Then face upstream. Tilt pan about one inch below water level and shake back and forth. The heavy sediment—including gold, you hope—will begin shifting to the bottom while lighter gravels slough off into the creek. Occasionally hold pan flat and shake hard. It may take 15 to 20 minutes to work down to fine material. Experts do it in 10. When there seems to be only fine black sand in the bottom, swirl most of the water out of the pan. Trail the black sand out—it's actually iron grains—looking closely at the tailing. If there's gold you should see it here.

Iceboat on Lake Oahe—at speeds of 40 miles per hour.

Get active in sports, organized or impromptu. Spring wrestling meet in Buffalo, below, matches 400 young wrestlers from age four up.

Motorcycles—parked four deep in the streets of Sturgis

The Black Hills Motor Classic

More than 20,000 motorcyclists from across the country come to Sturgis each year for the Black Hills Motor Classic. They ride here alone, as couples, with groups of friends and as clubs to watch the races, to meet other cycle enthusiasts, and to tour the Black Hills by motorcycle.

South Dakota welcomes them, but with caution and concern. Motorcycle injuries and fatalities grew enormously after the helmet law (for over age 18) was repealed in time for the 1977 classic. During the next three years the week-long rally racked up nine deaths—and perhaps the real horror—140 injuries with a high incidence of severed spines, permanent brain damage, amputation and broken necks and backs. Emergency rooms of nearby hospitals have been jammed throughout the event.

Unfamiliar mountain roads prove hazardous for the most experienced and cautious drivers. A particular danger is the stretch of road called Boulder Canyon, between Sturgis and Deadwood. There tourist traffic of autos, campers and cycles is heavy; the road is steep, narrow and winding; slow-moving logging trucks might be encountered at a sudden turn. Of 12 recent motorcycle fatalities, eight occured on this highway.

Besides tricky road conditions, drivers who don't pay enough attention to motorcycles, and heavy traffic, safety authorities blame speeding by cyclists, excessive drinking and lack of helmets for injuries and deaths.

A determined effort by the highway patrol in 1980 (and admitted good luck) succeeded in cutting the toll back to just 19 injured—without any deaths. Extra manpower on the roads was effective, and the patrol say they intend to continue strict enforcement of traffic and liquor laws to maintain increased safety for all.

They caution motorcycle drivers to:
- wear helmets even when not required
- drive a safe speed
- obey the laws on alcohol and drugs
- drive defensively, with headlight on, expecting a hazardous situation around the next bend

They aim a media campaign at local drivers to watch out for motorcycles.

Attending the classic and touring the Black Hills by motorcycle can be a delightful and exciting experience; both cyclists and motorists are urged to avoid tragedy by using extra care and courtesy during the Black Hills Motor Classic.

Motorcycle Accidents During Classic

	Accidents	Killed	Injured	Speed-Related	Alcohol-Related	Helmets Worn
1979	42	2	35	13	13	6
1978	55	5	46	22	14	11
1977	52	2	59	18	12	20
$976	30	0	32	17	4	26
1975	22	2	26	11	4	18

Note: S.D. repealed helmet usage law one month before 1977 classic

Ski the high slopes.

Swim in the river near Platte.

Bike through town and country roads.

Explore—but don't go into old mine shafts.

Wade in Split Rock Creek at the Palisades—or just relax.

Backpack along the Missouri.

37

6. WILDLIFE

Mountain goats skip over rocky terrain.

Rocky Mountain bighorns, above, replace larger Audubon sheep, now extinct. Below, South Dakota's herds of buffalo are among world's largest.

South Dakota's wildlife is a valued resource. It has been from earliest times. Then wildlife was of great economic importance to Indians, fur traders and settlers. Today—although there are financial benefits to hunting and fishing tourism, to trapping, and to maintaining a balance of nature—the chief value of wildlife is in the pure enjoyment of wild animals, birds, fish and reptiles.

The wildlife we enjoy today are survivors of many destructive forces and tremendous environmental change. They've had to be hardy and adaptable in the past 150 years. Some have changed their range—deserting old haunts for new ones. Many were able to adapt centuries-old habits and instincts to cope better with civilization. Some could not change and, being particularly vulnerable—like the buffalo and antelope—were nearly wiped out. Today careful management tries to keep a healthy balance.

Wholesale destruction of big herds, especially buffalo, occured with commercial hunting after 1850. Buffalo were killed by the thousands for hides and meat—sometimes only for their tongues, at 25¢ each. Before 1899, when it was outlawed, deer were also sold in the butcher shops of South Dakota. A Deadwood butcher named Rodgers gave this scornful reply to a Black Hills Times reporter in October 1880:

> What is venison, did you ask? Why venison ain't nothing. There is a saddle of it you can have for 5¢ a pound, and there's a whole row of carcasses. If you will take them all, you can have them for 4¢ a pound. Every day the market hunters send in 50 - 100 carcasses of venison. We have to give it away to keep it from spoiling.

Big game hunters contributed to the overkill. Wealthy sportsmen came to Dakota close on the heels of the first traders. One who earned a bloodthirsty reputation was "that butcher Sir George Gore" of Ireland. Gore brought a great entourage of servants, equipment and wagons. He killed thousands of deer, elk and buffalo, leaving much of the meat to rot. He even had, to the amusement of a local fur trader, "a man to bathe and scrub his highness daily."

Teddy Roosevelt hunted this area without fanfare like any other rancher, while living in Dakota's badlands. But in later years he came by special train to hunt near Aberdeen at Sand Lake where one pioneer says the sky was almost black with ducks, geese and cranes. A sidetrack was built especially for President Roosevelt, so the train could be stationed nearby while he hunted.

Finally when the big herds were almost gone, homesteaders claimed their quarter sections and settled in to subdue the land. They killed what they could for food—deer, antelope, ducks, geese, grouse. And, like the ranchers, they

relentlessly hunted down the destructive species—wolves, coyotes, bobcats, jackrabbits, rattlesnakes.

The last Audubon bighorn sheep, long a favorite with sportsmen here, is now extinct—killed soon after the turn of the century. Grizzly bears and their smaller cousins the black bears, range no more along South Dakota's western rivers and hills. The last bear in the Black Hills area was killed within a few years after rancher Hank Mason was fatally mauled in the 1890's by a bear threatening his livestock.

Buffalo were nearly exterminated in the 1880's. South Dakota Indian people had an important role in saving them.

The last big buffalo hunts were in the Grand River and Slim Buttes areas and along the South Dakota/North Dakota border. Ed Lemmon says in 1881 he saw the tableland known as Delaney Flats in Perkins County swarming with buffalo. Later that fall James McLaughlin, Indian agent at Standing Rock, accompanied the Sioux of that reservation on a last hunt during which they killed 5000 buffalo. The missionary Thomas Riggs also went, as the only white man, with Cheyenne River Sioux to the Slim Buttes on a winter hunt in 1880-1881 that netted some 500 robes. Riggs wrote that the Du Pris (Dupree) boys took a wagon; it could have been during this hunt that Pete Du Pris roped some of the buffalo calves he raised which became the foundation stock for an important number of the buffalo alive today.

A year or so later, probably the summer of 1882, Du Pris—realizing the buffalo would soon be gone—went with friends to the Yellowstone and spent several months in capturing buffalo calves. They succeeded in catching five—another report says nine (perhaps some of them died). Du Pris branded them, turned them loose with his cattle, and kept the increase until he had a large herd. When he died, they were sold to Scotty Philip, a Bad River rancher. Scotty Philip and his wife Sarah—who was a sister of Crazy Horse's wife—are given much credit for helping save the buffalo from extinction. The Philips had at one time 1000 head of buffalo. Sarah Philips said, "My people might someday need them again for food."

The buffalo herds were gone by 1883, with only stragglers remaining. Barely 500 buffalo were alive in 1889. But today South Dakota has large herds of buffalo on preserves and private ranches.

Antelope were close to extinction, too, by the 1920's, and were saved by strict hunting laws. The last wolves disappeared from South Dakota's northwest badlands country about 1920. Older wolves were noted for great endurance and cunning; the pioneers told fascinating tales of famous wolves

Whitetail deer, below, range throughout state, run with white tails raised, waving like flags. Mule deer, above in badlands, carry their black tipped tails low.

Doe hides close with her dappled twin fawns. Antelope, right, and mule deer favor open country.

Sociable prairie dogs watch for danger, ready to spread the alarm. Three night animals common to entire state are striped skunk, raccoon, porcupine.

(such as Three-Toes), their wanton and wide-ranging kills, and the men who tried to bring them down.

Coyotes, however, have proven uniquely adaptable to changing times. As "White River Pete" reminds us, they have always had a price on their heads. Early bounties paid were $1.50 for coyotes, $5 for wolves (1893). Additional was sometimes paid by local ranchers. State control efforts became too efficient for coyotes, finally, during the 1940's, and they became scarce. After 20 years most westerners—except for sheepmen—were pleased to see a coyote or two again. One day a longtime sheepman-trapper-hunter drew a bead on a coyote—an easy shot—then put his rifle aside without firing; he was glad to see a coyote once more run out of a sagebrush draw. But coyotes are again destructive predators of sheep. Ranchers say they have changed old instincts: they howl less, and no longer run out in the open at the swoop of an airplane, but lie low in the brush. There's little question in the minds of sheepmen but that the adaptable coyote will survive. As one South Dakota sheepman puts it: "When the last man dies on earth, there'll be a coyote waiting to pick his bones."

Jackrabbits are frequent food for coyotes—but food well earned. Jackrabbits rely on keen sense of hearing and great speed. An early historian noted, "All they ask of a coyote is a fair start and an open field." In early Dakota settlement days, jackrabbits were so thick that they are described as lying on scoria buttes like droves of sheep, in winter with their white coats. They destroyed crops, shrubs, gardens and trees. Pioneers countered with rabbit drives. During the Hyde Coun-

ty rabbit drive the men chose sides with the north group challenging the south. Losers treated the winners to oyster stew, with the women bringing sandwiches and cake.

In early days there were big prairie dog towns, too, stretching for miles. These interesting and sociable animals have a complex communication system that includes yelps, calls, warning barks, defense barks, fighting snarls, fear screams, teeth chattering and yipping. Their eyes are placed high and to the side to better to keep watch for the predators—coyotes, hawks and eagles. When a person or animal approaches, warning yelps sweep through the town. Those prairie dogs nearest the intruder dash for their holes and watch there silently, or with under-the-breath chattering, while the alarm continues through other parts of the town. Prairie dogs caused serious economic problems by denuding great sections of rangeland with their sprawling towns—and many a cowhorse broke its leg in a prairie dog hole. Prairie dog towns were brought under strict control during the 1940's.

There are also newcomers to South Dakota. The ringnecked pheasant swept the state after being introduced in the 1890's from Asia. Mountain goats and species of bighorn sheep, smaller than the extinct Audubon, have been brought into the Black Hills from the Rocky Mountains and thrive well there. Immigrant wild turkeys now look on the Black Hills and the Slim Buttes as home, and European Hungarian partridges have spread throughout central and eastern South Dakota. The greater prairie chicken, or pinnated grouse, walked into South Dakota of its own accord, following the settlers; it is now

Jackrabbits once were thick as droves of sheep.

Mother coyote brings jackrabbit to her pups.

Canadian geese winter in steamy waters on Capitol grounds in Pierre. Above left, a trio of owls blink sleepily from branch. Left, a ferruginous hawk nests on ground near Leola.

abundant in the southcentral mix of grassland and farming.

Many native animals were particularly well adapted to living on the open plains and prairies. They have keen eyesight, were noted for speed, cunning and vitality. Many get along well without much water—the prairie dog needs none at all. The antelope has, besides keen eyesight, a danger signal that can be seen farther than the animal itself. The white rump signals danger by flashing in the sun "like a tin pan." The antelope has great endurance at speeds of 40 miles per hour. The jackrabbit runs nearly as fast—30-40 miles per hour, clearing up to 17 feet at a jump with powerful back legs. The mule deer uses open spaces as protection, too. When startled, it bounds up an open slope, then stops to see where the danger lies. The buffalo needed little protection except hardiness and its tremendous size, and it made good use of the vast open pastures here.

These traits of living in the open proved excellent defense against natural predators. But they made the antelope, buffalo and mule deer easy targets for the high-powered rifle.

Many plains animals have social instincts: there were the huge herds of buffalo; prairie dog towns with divisions within the town and colonies on the outskirts; large herds of elk; wolves hunting in family packs of 12 to 15; and antelope migrating in winter herds of several hundred.

Walter Prescott Webb, in *The Great Plains*, makes the point that many of these plains animals were misnamed. The buffalo is more properly a bison; the antelope not really an antelope but a pronghorn; the prairie dog is of the squirrel family; and the jackrabbit is no true rabbit, but a hare. Webb blames this confusion on a typical lack of understanding of the west by easterners who came here. But he cites Hornaday as an authority that it is useless to try changing, as the animals are now called these names by millions. Furthermore, it seems without much purpose. Scientists use more technical terms anyway, and the people will speak as they will. Perhaps a third term is superfluous, and adding the word *American* to buffalo and antelope would make the distinction clear.

South Dakota is a border state for birds—between eastern and western species—so a wide variety nest here and migrate through. At least 377 species of birds have been identified in the state. Big Canadian geese are again nesting in South Dakota, as are rare trumpeter swans. Wild turkeys respond to mating calls in springtime, and hunters thrill to the challenge

Robin builds her nest in fence corner.

Sharptails dance in full frenzy—drumming, vibrating, circling, charging—at first hint of light, above. Rare trumpeter swans nest in La Creek refuge.

South Dakota's pheasant population reached peaks of 20 million birds; they wintered thick in shelterbelts and marshy cover like this. Declining cover sparked pheasant decline. Restoration program includes improving nesting cover, predator control, restocking with young birds.

Pheasant chick, newly hatched.

Tom turkeys display full fans of whirring tail feathers.

by initating the enticing yelps and clucks of hens—and the tom turkey's strident gobble; but they are not easy targets. The old ritual of the sharptail grouse's mating dance is still enacted every spring from late March through mid May on favorite mounds and hilltops.

Today the major problem for wildlife is one of sufficient habitat. Civilization continues to close in, with more concrete on the ground, more buildings, more intensive farming. Most natural habitat and cover throughout the wooded Missouri River valley has been destroyed by flooding.

But the state has established many refuges and parks. South Dakotans are concerned about preserving wildlife, not just in these refuges, but everywhere. Hunters and landowners work closely with the department of game, fish and parks in conservation practices. Surplus animals and birds are made available for hunting, thus making a healthier environment for a wider variety of others. With this balanced management, the future looks bright for South Dakota wildlife.

RATTLESNAKES

Many westerners regard the rattlesnake with a bit of the same ambivalence they do the coyote. They are determined to kill every rattlesnake they see and know a rage and horror often born of all-too-real experience. Yet there's respect and even a dry kind of affection for a creature who so rightly belongs in butte and range country and who—like the coyote—is a survivor of man's best efforts to destroy it.

The deadliness of the rattler has been much exaggerated. Few adults die from rattlesnake bite. A number of South Dakota children have died, however; Jones County alone records several deaths in early days—all of them children. The greatest danger is when the snake is unseen, or come upon suddenly before it has time to warn the intruding person or animal. In recent years a boy from northwestern South Dakota was bucked off his horse into some weeds, jumped back on and rode home without realizing he'd been bit. He lay sick in the hospital several days before doctors discovered the cause of his illness. Snake serum was administered, but too late.

When coiled, hissing, rattling, and lashing out with forked black tongue, the rattlesnake may look invulnerable and vicious. But he usually stays put or tries only to escape, and is easy to kill. South Dakota's literary sheepherder Archer Gilfillan claims to have killed one once with a copy of

On warm fall days rattlers sun outside dens.

Jackley, South Dakota's 'snake man,' caught the big rattlesnakes, kept them here in basement for shipment.

Shakespeare, but he says his Shakespeare was never the same again. (Boots and shoes should never be thrown at a rattler, as poison fangs can become imbedded and scratch later on.)

While rattlers may travel some distance from their dens through the summer, they return to den up in the fall, often with bullsnakes. On warm fall days they come out to sun themselves. Prairie dog towns were favorite places to den. One fall a rancher near Murdo went to put out poison in his prairie dog town. As he leaned over to cross the fence, he suddenly heard sharp buzzing from several directions. Frozen astride the fence, he looked around and saw he was surrounded by 12 coiled rattlesnakes. He eased slowly off the fence and toward the largest opening. Finally he reached his team and wagon, knotted the end of the rope and killed nine of the snakes. Still shaken, he took them home hanging from the back of the wagon.

The missionary Thomas Riggs tells of a similar experience while attempting to cross a prairie dog town between Oahe mission and Yankton on a warm October day. His saddle horse became extremely uneasy as he approached the dog town. He saw a rattlesnake, got down and killed it—then saw another and killed it, too. A few feet farther on was another, and another. By this time his horse was dripping wet from terror. Looking ahead, Riggs saw hundreds of snakes, obviously on their way to den up for the winter. He backed out slowly and circled wide around the town.

South Dakota's most famous rattlesnake man was A.M. Jackley, a state control officer, sometimes called "the St. Patrick of South Dakota." He was an expert on the life and habits of the prairie rattler. It was the thought of Jackley, some said, that caused a snake's blood to run cold. He hunted snakes on rocky points, spring and fall, close to known dens and searching out new ones. He knew the favorite haunts of rattlesnakes and the "snake passes" they chose to cross highways. The larger-sized snakes he popped into a sugar sack with a snare and took home alive. He kept them in his basement for shipping out later. Today a few trappers still catch rattlesnakes alive and ship them to serum centers.

People who live in rattlesnake country learn to listen and watch as they walk. The buzzing sound of a rattlesnake is distinctive. As westerners say, "any of a dozen sounds could be a rattler—but when you hear one, you *know* that's what it is." Gilfillan mentions several good imitations: "a weed in this region whose dry pods, when carelessly kicked in walking, give off a sound almost like a snake on the warpath, enough like it anyway to induce a gentle perspiration in a man who has

recently killed a rattler...the sudden buzzing of insects and even a lamb whose rasping blat many a time caused me to jump."

Gilfillan, a herder who killed rattlers and knew their potential for violence, nevertheless called them gentlemen. From his book *Sheep* comes this classic tribute to the rattlesnake:

He is never the aggressor. All he asks is to be allowed to attend to his own business. Furthermore, if he is disturbed, he will even stretch a point and will peaceably withdraw if allowed to do so. He never strikes without warning, if he has time to warn. He will begin rattling at the approach of a disturber, and he will keep on rattling as long as that person is in the vicinity. If he is cornered and believes himself in danger, he will strike with the best weapon he has, and you or I would do the same. His rattle is at first only a warning. If angered, he will no longer try to crawl away, but will remain coiled until the issue is decided. When the stones begin to drop on him, he will try to protect his head with some of his coils, but he will rattle defiance to the last; a fair fighter and a brave one.

'A fair fighter and a brave one.'

7. GEOLOGY

Salty inland seas once flooded into this region from the Gulf of Mexico. Rivers brought down sands and clays, silting in the seas and building up the land.

Eons passed. Seas receded, leaving vast swamps and floodplains. A warm tropical climate prevailed. Thick forests grew in the rich soil—mighty redwoods, dense ferns and leafy brush. Century by century lush vegetation fell into the swamps, building up thick layers.

Then the shallow waters of the inland sea returned. The process was repeated again and again through eons of time. Great trees crashed into primeval swamps as strange reptiles raised their heads to listen. Clay sediments deposited on the sea floor formed the Pierre shale which covers much of west-central South Dakota and is known locally as gumbo.

When vegetation decayed, energy was liberated. But when thick layers of organic material became trapped underwater, silted down and packed through pressure, the energy did not escape. Instead it changed to the coal and oil found in north-western South Dakota today.

At times great upheavals broke and tilted the earth's crust. In this way the Rocky Mountains rose, and underlying rocks pushed the Black Hills into a dome. Hundreds of exploding volcanoes sent great clouds of ash into the sky. Descending, the ash added its white layers to the soil.

Fossils formed, too, when conditions were right. The best preserved fossils pertrified, by staying in a water-soaked condition until the minerals in the water replaced the original cells. An accurate pattern of cells and tree rings was left. Oxides of iron and manganese produced bright streaks of red, yellow, purple and black. Petrified trees and chunks of petrified wood are common through western South Dakota.

Animals left their remains, too. Many dinosaur fossils are found in the Hell Creek Formation of northwest South Dakota. Rich fossil beds of early mammals are found in the badlands of the White River and in the town of Hot Springs. Scientists from the world's foremost museums have come here to collect fossils.

Then after millions of years of tropical climate, there came a great change on this land. It was chilled by great ice ages. At least four or five times glaciers swept down from the north. They covered the land for thousands of years with thick ice sheets, and then retreated for more thousands. The final

The early French explorers named it well—Coteau des Prairies, the "Hills of the prairies." The Coteau is green and innocent land of tree-fringed lakes and ponds, meandering streams, soaring hills and rocky dells, splashy waterfowl marshes, and small farm-centered cities. Sisseton, Sioux Falls and Enemy Swim; Punished Woman's Lake; Devil's Gulch; Waubay, that's Indian for where-wild-fowl-build-their-nests. Today's names still whisper the old legends of the Coteau.

Roberts County History

glacier lasted some 95,000 years and began its retreat a mere 25,000 years ago.

South Dakota's eastern landscape shows clearly the action of these glaciers. The land has been leveled as if with bulldozers. Debris is pushed into piles and ridges. A rich topsoil of glacial drift (rock and soil mixed) covers the eastern part of the state to an average depth of 40 feet, and as deep as 700 feet in places.

The course of rivers was changed. South Dakota's western rivers run due east, and scientists believe other rivers also flowed east before the glaciers. But as the last glacier moved south and west, it pushed ahead great ridges of debris, forcing the eastern rivers and the Missouri in a new course to the south. Glacial lakes formed, and melting waters carved out new river valleys.

Erosion began anew in this part of the state. But less time has elapsed; it is a younger topography, with rounded hills, scoured-out sloughs and lakes; drainage systems are incomplete.

In the west, erosion continued to cut deep into gullies and canyons. Loose soil washed from rocky ridges and buttes, exposing the harder layers.

Walls dropped off cliffs to reveal the earlier story: ribboned layers of dark soil from ocean bottom, coal, white layers of volcanic ash, scoria clay baked red by burning coal. The story is plain and easily understood in the White River badlands, and students from all over the world have come to study the layering.

The face of South Dakota is now a generally sloping plateau from northwest to southeast, as if tipped on the diagonal. (Notable exceptions are the jutting Black Hills and the small region of lower elevation in the northeast corner draining north to Hudson Bay.) This diagonal pattern influences most weather conditions: rainfall, temperature, growing season.

But while much of the state is level or gently sloping, at comparatively few points is the view unbroken by hills or rolling ridges. South Dakota is typified by hills and bluff-bordered rivers, both east and west. Rivers run between great boulders and cliffs, not only in Spearfish Canyon or near Chamberlain, but at the Pallisades, the Dells, and many other places. The mountainous outcropping of Black Hills is echoed to the north by pine clad Cave Hills and Slim Buttes. (Once these areas of high elevation were larger and more numerous, but erosion has worn them down.) East of the Hills are badlands and the 80 mile Wall bordering the White River, which is echoed by eroded walls along the Bad River, the Cheyenne, the Moreau, and the Grand. Near the eastern edge of the state are the rough hills called the Coteau des Prairies which drop off steeply into the Minnesota valley.

Erosion and glacial action have shaped these regions.

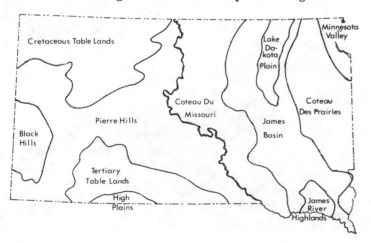

Apatosaurus

Pteranodon

Triceratops

Age of Dinosaurs
200,000,000 to 65,000,000 years ago

Dinosaurs ruled the world for 140 million years. The name means "terrible lizard"—and terrible they must have been, the most enormous and powerful animals ever to stalk this earth.

When South Dakota was tropical swampland, dinosuars lived here, feeding on jungle plants and on each other. The meat eaters walked about on powerful back legs, their gigantic mouths filled with sharp teeth. Some could leap at their prey; others were too massive for this. Many had small useless-appearing arms, but sharp claws for seizing and tearing at their victims. Plant eaters had their defenses. Many were armed with horns, hard plates and spines, had bony frills about their faces and thick hide. Others wore heavy coats of armor. Some spent much time in water, for protection and because of their great bulk. Others were small and fast.

A great variety of both kinds—including the largest known—ranged northwestern South Dakota and are found in the Hell Creek formation. Bones of the following have been found here.

APATOSAURUS—"Thunder Lizard"

Apatosaurus (Brontosaurus) was the largest of the huge dinosaurs. It weighed 30 tons and measured 70 feet from head to tail, about a quarter of the length of a football field. Because of its great bulk it probably spent much time in water to support its weight, and fed off water plants.

TYRANNOSAURUS—"King of the Tyrant Lizards"

This meat eating dinosuar was the most powerful animal ever to walk to earth. It was 50 feet long, weighed 8 tons, and was 18 feet tall when standing up on its powerful hind legs. Tyrannosaurus had an enormous head lined thickly with dagger-like teeth. Each tooth was three to six inches long. Fierce as it was, scientists speculate that because of the size Tyrannosaurus must have been slow moving. Likely it could catch only the large slow dinosaurs, probably battling the well armed Triceratops and the more vulnerable Apatosaurus when it came to shore. Tyrannosaurus was one of the last of the dinosaurs.

Tyrannosaurus

OTHER MEAT EATERS

Both Allosaurus and Gorgosaurus were huge predators similar to Tyrannosaurus in many ways. They were 30-35 feet long with mouths filled with sharp teeth and arms small and seemingly ineffective, but sharply clawed. Allosaurus lived at a much earlier age, however, and was the most dangerous predator then.

TRICERATOPS—"Three Horned Face"

Triceratops was a plant eater, but a solid fighter. About 30 feet long, it weighed 7 tons. The skull was huge and protected with a bony frill or shield that curved up over the shoulders. Deadly weapons included two long sharp horns above the eyes and a shorter horn over the snout. Triceratops probably charged at his enemies; his bones show scars of many battles. This was probably one of the last dinosaurs to become extinct. A Triceratops head 6½ feet long has recently been dug in Harding County for the Museum of Geology in Rapid City.

"Ostrich" AND "Duck Billed" DINOSAURS

The ostrich dinosaur, Ornithomimus, had a small head on a long neck and carried itself like an ostrich, 8 feet tall with its long front legs dangling. The mouth had a flat hard beak and it probably ate small reptiles as well as insects and plants. The 18 foot high Anatosaurus was duck billed and web footed. It probably spent much time in the water scooping up plants that grew along the bottom. It had about 2000 teeth with new ones ready to replace any lost.

ARMORED DINOSAURS

The Hypsilophodon was an extremely ancient animal wearing only two rows of armored plates. It may have been the ancestor of the fully armored dinosaurs which came later. Long fingers and toes show it may have climbed trees. It was only five feet long and carried its head low. The Nodosaurus was much larger, about 17 feet, with bony plates covering the entire body. Hoplitosaurus was well defended with a variety of strong plates—flat, round, triangular, spiked.

OTHERS

Some dinosaurs found here were quite small. The Saurornithoides had a skull less than 7 inches long. Thescelosaurus, a slender and speedy plant eater, was 8 feet long. Camptosaurus grew from 4 to 15 feet long and walked either upright on his large hind legs, or bent over. He had a horny beak for nipping off plants Barosaurus, the "bonehead dinosaur," had a bumpy skull of solid bone 9 inches thick which protected the small brain. Paronychodon and Dromaeosaurus were two other dinosaurs of this region.

OTHER REPTILES, FISH, AND BIRDS

Living at the time of the dinosaurs were great flying reptiles, such as the Pteranodon with a wing span of 15 to 20 feet. Hesperornis was a bird that swam but did not fly. Alzadasaurus was a 36 foot long marine reptile which had left the land and become fully adapted to life in the sea. The monster "Bulldog Fish," longest known bony fish, inhabited the waters, and turtles 11 feet across crawled near the shore.

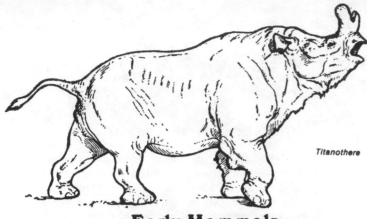

Titanothere

Early Mammals

65,000,000 to 10,000 years ago

Mammals appeared about 65 million years ago and became the dominant land animals. Their fossils were found early in South Dakota. During the 1850's the badlands of the White River were already among the best known fossil beds in the world. Nearly every great museum sent expeditions here to gather bones. The badlands erosion had laid bare the special layers of earth which contained early mammals. (Dinosaur bones would be in much deeper layers.)

These early mammals developed and changed greatly through eons of time. Some lines died out and others thrived. They had hair and warm bodies heated by energy from the food they ate—thus they coped well with the Ice Ages. Their young were born alive and fed from the mothers' milk.

Then after the last glacier when climate warmed, a strange thing happened. Many of the well developed mammals in North America became extinct. Among those which disappeared entirely were the ground sloths, mammoths, sabertooth tigers, oreodonts, titanotheres, and several lines of horses and rhinoceroses. Others, such as the horse and camel, had spread to other continents before they died out here, and thus survived. All these animals had lived millions of years in South Dakota. Why they disappeared is one of the great mysteries of science.

Was it climatic changes, disease, powerful predators such as man? If so, why did certain mammals survive while others died?

TITANOTHERE—"Thunder Beasts"

Indian legends told of great thunder beasts which raged through the sky during storms and sometimes plunged to earth with the sound of thunder, drumming their hooves along the ground. Their bones were strewn on the open plain after a hard gully-washing rain.

The first museum specimen ever taken from the badlands was the jaw of a titanothere, described in the Journal of Science in 1846. A well known skeleton in the American Museum of Natural History, taken from Corral Canyon, measures nearly 8 feet tall and 14 feet long. It is almost 4 feet through the pelvis. The Titanothere was a massive hulking beast with an interesting and grotesque head. Above its snout was a thick blunt horn shaped like the letter "Y", probably used in fighting, giving the head a saddle shape.

It was here in 1886, digging titanothere fossils, that Hatcher discovered differences in the bones taken from different soil levels. He began recording the exact level from which each skeleton was taken and found, in the more recent fossils, a gradual increase in size. Also skulls became longer, teeth changed, the horn grew larger and more grotesque. This was a stunning discovery. Before this time, bones were dug and studied without regard to where they had been originally placed.

CAMELS

Early camels were light and graceful, like a gazelle, about 24 inches high. Eyes were set far back and the foot had two toes with small pointed hooves rather than the present day pads. Several species developed. The giraffe camel, which became extinct, held his head nearly 18 feet high. (An earlier camel found in Wyoming had four toes and was little larger than a jackrabbit.)

Before camel and llama fossil discoveries here and elsewhere in North America, biologists had puzzled at the close similarities between the two which were so distantly separated geographicaly. This was explained by fossil records showing both originated in North America. It seems only camels migrated north across the land bridge into Asia, while only llamas traveled down into South America. It is interesting that camels—apparently better adapted to traveling the cold regions—later developed into heat-loving desert animals, while the llamas made their way through tropical heat in Central America to develop in cold mountainous regions of the Andes.

RHINOCEROSES

Fossils of the true rhinoceros were found in the badlands in 1850, a startling discovery for scientists of the day since rhinoceroses were known only in Africa and southern Asia. All three major kinds of rhinoceroses were found here: the upland, the aquatic, the lowland. Both upland and aquatic are now extinct.

The upland rhinos were small, light chested and swift footed, hooved, without horns and resembling horses. The aquatic rhinos were more like present day hippopotamuses—heavy, short, with four toes and spreading padded feet, eyes and nostrils high as if for swimming, with tusk teeth and an upper lip that tended toward an elephant-like trunk. The true, or lowland, rhino began as a light limbed animal, between the other two types. It did not have horns initially, but began growing them in the Miocene times. These horns were crosswise of the face, in contrast to present day two-horned rhinos which have horns lengthwise of the face. Early rhinos ranged in size from 28 inches high to larger than those of today.

SABERTOOTH TIGER

The sabertooth tiger pounced on his prey, stabbing his head downward and slashing with his sharp fangs six inches long that curved down from his upper jaw. As he slashed and ripped, his lower jaw dropped back nearly flat against his throat. Sabertooth tigers found here were about the size of a leopard, but more powerful; others grew large as the African lion. Earliest discoveries of this terrible beast of prey were in the White River badlands. Food supply was likely the oreodonts and rhinoceroses. Several other kinds of cats, less powerful, preyed on smaller animals here. The sabertooth tiger died out, but many other cats survived.

HORSES

Horses have a long and interesting history in South Dakota.

The earliest "dawn horse," eohippus, which appeared 60 million years ago has not been found in the state. But many fossils were discovered in northern Wyoming, so likely it was here also.

Mesohippus, the second stage horse, was numerous in South Dakota along with its descendeants and offshoots through many millions of years. Of these descendants, only one line survived as forerunner to the modern horse. This was Equus, which later developed into all six species which exist today: the modern horse with its close wild relatives; the ass; the onager or "wild ass" of Asia; and three species of zebra, unlike except for their distinct stripes.

About 20 well developed lines of horses died out much earlier. The little forest horse is gone. Gone, too, are the Miocene pygmies of remarkable grace and beauty, the short footed mountain horses of South America, and the delicate deer-like Neohipparion. The American Museum, which found a near perfect skeleton of the Neohipparion on the Little White River in 1902 described its running mechanism as "surpassing the most highly bred modern racehorse, with a frame fashioned to outstrip any type of modern hunting horse, if not thoroughbred."

The lineage of the horse is well known. Its fossils are widespread through the world and it has probably been studied more than any other animal. Yet the fossils tell a strange story of complex development and dead ends.

In its beginnings the little eohippus lived in both the new and old world. Then it died out everywhere except in North America where nearly all of its subsequent development took place. Less than 25,000 years ago it became extinct in North and South America.

Luckily herds of Equus had crossed the land bridge into Asia by this time. Otherwise there may never have been horses for Sioux warriors, broncs for South Dakota cowboys, Thoroughbreds on the track, or pleasure horses in towns and on Dakota farms and ranches today.

The smallest species of eohippus was about the size of a cat; others grew large as a coyote. They ran on flexible dog-like legs with padded toes, four in front and three in back. At the end of every toe was a little hoof. The head was very different from that of the modern horse, with a short snout, eyes set down toward the middle of the skull, and small brain. The teeth were far less hardy than those of the modern horse, with low enamel-covered crowns, good for eating succulent leaves but not grasses.

The earliest Mesohippus, found in the badlands, had three toes. Most were about 24 inches high, with slender head and eye still very far forward. The back was arched and flexible; the legs long and slender. Teeth were about the same. Mesohippus, like the eohippus, was no grass-eater. These dainty little horses must have looked somewhat like a greyhound or whippet hunting dog.

Millions of years passed and the horses's jaws grew longer. Legs lengthened and became more rigid, giving horses their stiff-legged, but very fast gait. Horses increased in size. As grass increased, horses turned from browse to grass for food. Since grass is harsh and abrasive, this caused a great change in teeth. The old low crowned teeth with their outer shell of enamel, similar to ours, would have worn down quickly. In the new high-crowned teeth, enamel turned on edge and folded into projecting rims through the teeth with a hard cement between. These teeth could be worn down without damage, and they grew exceptionally long to allow this. Horses began to stand more and more on tiptoe, with the side toes rising off the ground. The hoof on the center toe enlarged. The straight line of descent became one-hoofed, though other lines retained three toes and various hoof-pad combinations.

The earliest one-toed horse, a 10 month colt, was found on the Little White River in 1916. The nearly modern Equus survived the Ice Age in America, spread to every continent except Australia, and was still here when the first people came.

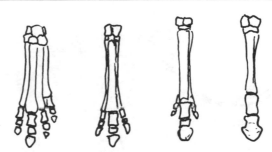

Changes in foot and leg from 4-toed, pad-footed at left; to 3-toed Mesohippus, second left; to dominance of center toe as foot tends to rise on tiptoe; to modern hoof of Equus. Not drawn to comparable size.

In his book "Horses", George Simpson, professor of Vertebrate Paleontology at Harvard, explores the theories that try to explain the mystery of why the great horse herds died out. He finds none of them really satisfactory.

It was not the glaciers, because horses were abundant after the last glacial age. It is doubtful food shortage caused it, because buffalo and other grazing animals were thriving. Competition from other grazers, such as the big herds of buffalo, is ruled out because horses also died out at the same time in South America where there were no buffalo. A sudden climatic or environmental change, likewise, could have hardly affected such a large area as the two continents. Deadly predators, another possibilty, seems unlikely as none appeared at that time, except man (who undoubtedly did kill horses for food, but also killed other animals which survived); certain deadly predators died out along with horses, such as the sabertooth tiger and dire-wolves. Disease cannot be ruled out, says Simpson, but most diseases would have affected other animals.

The answer remains a mystery, a piece of the larger mystery which doomed so many other mammals in the new world.

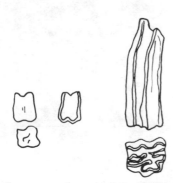

Teeth of early horse at left were similar to ours. Right, teeth of the modern grass-eating horse.

WOLVES, COYOTES

Ancestors of wolves and dogs were abundant in the badlands. More than 20 species have been found which resemble wolves, coyotes, and foxes. The credonta was probably the most primitive carnivore and was about the size and build of a wolf.

OTHER MAMMALS

Oreodonts are among the most common fossils found in the badlands, and were found only in North America. Now extinct, they were not closely related to any living animal, though they resembled pigs somewhat. A female oreodont at the Museum of Geology has unborn twins fossilized inside. The giant pig was apparently only indirectly an ancestor of present day pigs. Size varied up to as large as the modern rhinoceros;

long slender heads of the giant pigs were up to three feet long. Tapirs were also abundant in the badlands fossil beds. They were related to titanotheres, horses, and rhinoceroses. Although tapirs were of ancient ancestry, they did not advance much. They developed in North America, then traveled to South America and Asia before dying out here. Ancestors of deer, smaller mammals and rodents were also present in abundance including ancestral badgers, mink, martens, weasels, ermine, skunks, otters, squirrels, rabbits, beavers, rats and gophers.

NON-MAMMALS

A great many fossil turtles are found in the badlands as well as lizards, crocodiles, fossilized bird eggs, turtle eggs and sea shells. Crocodiles were about 6 feet long.

A Deadly Sinkhole

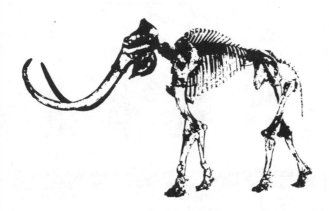

One day in June 1974, contractors bulldozing a sandy knoll at the south edge of Hot Springs for a housing project bladed up a huge bone. Later more bones and big teeth turned up. When informed, owner Phil Anderson halted the work, despite deadlines and schedules.

"Let's stop—and see what we have here," he said.

What they had, turned out to be the most remarkable concentration of mammoth skeletons ever found in North America. The sandy knoll was once a deadly sinkhole where mammoths came to drink about 26,000 years ago, and then could not escape.

A warm artesian spring fed this sinkhole, similar to the warm springs in the region today, as can be seen by the hot-water-leached bones. Perhaps at times of low water the mammoths had to climb down the steep banks to drink and could not get back out. They starved there, or were killed by predators. Later the sinkhole filled with heavy clays and silt which did not erode as did surrounding land, so that in modern times the sinkhole was exposed as a ridge.

Excavations between 1976 and 1979 turned up 59 mammoth tusks and 21 skulls—bones from at least 30 mammoths. The largest measures 14 feet tall at the shoulder, about three feet more than present-day elephants. The biggest tusks are great curves of ivory 14 feet long and 7 inches through at the base.

Less than 10% of the site is excavated; an estimated 100 mammoth fossils may be there. Other scattered bones have been found—bear, camel, coyote, pig, fish, large carnivorous bird. Scientists from Chadron State College, Nebraska, National Geographic Society, Earthwatch and others have been involved in the excavations. Much volunteer help was also needed.

Mammoths and their cousins the mastodons probably came across the Bering Strait during one of the glacial periods. They became extinct more than 10,000 years ago. They were hunted here in the northern Great Plains, but evidence of humans at the mamoth site is uncertain.

The struggle of local people to ensure that this heritage remains here and can be studied and enjoyed at its original site is a story in itself. Too often in the past have South Dakota fossil beds been literally looted by far-off museums. It seems unlikely to happen here.

Cooperation from fossil experts has been excellent. Bones sent for study to Southern Methodist University in Texas have been returned. Chadron State College, which offered the initial expertese retains the skull of "Manfred," one of the first to be studied. Phil Anderson volunteered to haul the 1½ ton encased skull to Chadron, blowing out both rear tires on the way. It is now too fragile to be moved. Ivory fragments of one tusk, broken by bulldozers, is being fashioned into jewelry and sold by the local organization. All other fossils are to be retained within the state.

The local non-profit Mammoth Site corporation purchased the original two acres from Anderson, and is adding adjacent land at the cost of $46,000. Community leaders are seeking funds to finance the kind of visitors' center they envision—an attractive building to cover and protect the site, reconstructed mammoth skeletons overlooking the deep pit of exposed bones, a viewing walkway, with perhaps from time to time a chance to study bonediggers at their work. Cost could be up to two million dollars. The small temporary structure used at this time has tourists crowded shoulder to shoulder in summer.

Earthwatch team digs at Hot Springs.

Part II

South
Dakota
Today

690,178 People

It never is verboten for any South Dakotan
To laugh and talk as freely as he votes,
And if they haven't riches to carry in their britches,
They always carry laughter in their throats.
Badger Clark

1. A SOUTH DAKOTA LIFESTYLE

Growing up close to the land.

South Dakota character is shaped by the land, it is said, and by a pioneer spirit of working the land.

It is strength, integrity, neighborliness; it is filled with optimism. A visitor to Sioux Falls in 1814 wrote on his return: "Essentially the spirit of the west is one of faith. There is nothing there of decadence, as the French call it...The malady of pessimism does not thrive on the sunlit prairies of Dakota." Most would agree the statement holds true today.

Living with the land has meant living with clean fresh air, open sky, space, and all the forces of nature. At times this has brought loneliness and despair; it has demanded fortitude and courage. In presenting his Bluestem Woman sculpture in Rapid City, Dale Lamphere stated, "Only those who could draw strength and purpose from the land, could see its beauty and withstand its bitter disappointments—only those survived and sank deep roots. It is to that spirit of moving with and accepting nature that I offer this work."

John Milton, editor of South Dakota Review, has also seen the force of the land reflected in people here. "South Dakota's landscape is immense, dominating and continual," he says. "It is the major element in the establishment of the South Dakota character, psyche or soul"

Others have pointed to traits which are basic ideals here: friendliness, openness, sincerity, quiet dignity, self-respect and respect for others. Hospitality for stranger, neighbor and friend is the normal way of life. In range country, perhaps more than in close-knit ethnic communities, there is a tolerant spirit of "live and let live".

In the increasing sophistication which movement to the cities, fast transportation and instant media coverage has meant, these sound character values have endured. South Dakotans who once felt isolated and remote from entertainment centers now have the best of both worlds. They can visit big cities, palm strewn beaches, busy centers of world trade—then return home for the pleasures of a lifestyle which is quieter, safer, less congested, with fewer regulations and where the air is clean.

No longer can Dakotans be called provincial. Their world knowledge and extent of travel exceeds that of the majority who live in metropolitan areas. Surprisingly, city people have awakened to this fact. So have our youth, which brings them a new assurance and a sense of the need to preserve the good life.

A high standard of living is generally enjoyed, even though incomes may be low by national standards. A higher quality of life just costs less in South Dakota. High moral character is reflected in a low crime rate, one of the lowest in the nation. South Dakotans generally enjoy good health and longer lives.

According to the 1980 census the state population is 690,178, an increase of 3.6% over 1970. Of these 638,955 identified themselves as white, 45,101 Indian, 2,144 black, 1,728 Asian, and 2,250 other. The last designation is mostly Spanish or Mexican origin. South Dakota averages 9 people per square mile; only four states are more sparsely settled with the U.S. average being 61. Birth rate is 17.1 per 1000, a decrease, but somewhat above the U.S. average of 15.3. Nearly 13% of South Dakota's population is over age 65, compared to a national average of 11%.

South Dakotans have a strong sense of their ethnic roots. By 1890 one third of the white population was foreign born. Many of the immigrants settled together in tight-knit communities. They spoke the language of the old country, kept

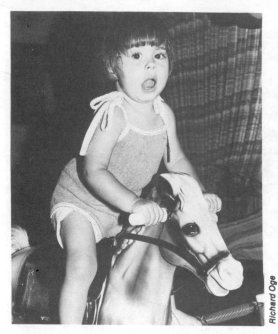

Richard Oge

For youth, new assurance and a sense of the good life.

alive its customs and built their own church. As late as the 1930's many children from these ethnic communities did not know English when they started school. The greatest numbers who came were Norwegians, Germans and German Russians, followed closely by big immigrations from Sweden, Denmark and the Netherlands.

This rich cultural heritage is appreciated today more than ever with the resurgence of ethnic pride. Specialty foods are especially enjoyed: Norwegian lutefisk, lefse and fatigmand; German fleischkuchele, kuchen and homemade sausages; fruit-filled kolaches of the Czechs; fry bread of the Sioux Indians. A Schmeckfest put on by Mennonites features recipes from each of three dialect groups: the Hutter, the Low Germans, and the Schweitzers. Czech Days are celebrated at Tabor with a lively Bohemian band.

Community ties are strong. Neighbors may be 15 miles away—or 30—but if they live in the community, they are regarded as neighbors.

High quality life costs less in South Dakota.

R. Oge

An interesting example is the Lodgepole community which includes most of northern Perkins County, stretching about 25 miles each direction. At the center is the Lodgepole store which is a combination grocery, hardware store, gas station, post office, drug store and laundromat. The country storekeepers have on hand a good stock of livestock supplies, hats, pitchforks, nails, apples, baby food, hair spray, wedding gifts, as well as the latest model dishwasher and refrigerator with all the parts needed to repair those sold in past years. (Plus they do the fixing in no time.) Scattered through the community are six country schools and four churches: Methodist, Lutheran, Christian Reformed (originally Dutch.) Each school and church is a secondary community center, but everyone joins together at the big community hall. Something is usually going on there: a potluck dinner, roller skating, school music program or graduation, a political rally, a meeting such as the Coyote Association or PCA, a health clinic, sewing class, rummage sale, anniversary open house, family or school reunion, dinner for a funeral gathering, or a dance. Community card parties are a winter tradition at the Lodgepole Hall; once a month they include potluck supper. Out front is a blackboard, which can be read from the highway announcing upcoming events, wishing someone a happy birthday or predicting a good morning.

Close community ties have meant learning a sense of responsibility. Young people grow up skilled in human relations, knowlegeable and in touch with reality. Volunteer work is a way of life in most South Dakota communities and towns. This is how needs are met. This is the way things get done. It's the way to keep the hospital going, the ambulance ready, the fire department running. It's how a new swimming pool comes about, or a senior citizens' center. Each person is important and needed in these efforts. Each has countless opportunities for leadership and for service, and learns to accept the challenges.

As everywhere, personality is unique and diverse. Every community, large and small, has its outstanding individuals who enrich the lives of those around them in a variety of special ways.

a time to work

and time to dream

R. Oge.

Close community ties—
neighbors need each other

Right, 8th grade graduation for six schools at Lodgepole Hall; below; a branding in range country.

Today's reservations are places of youth and change.

2. ON THE RESERVATION

Today's Indian reservations are warm accepting places, though often disrupted by conflict and uncertainty. They lure back those who have gone. Ties to the reservation lands and to the tribe remain strong.

South Dakota has an Indian population of over 45,000. Perhaps half live most of the time on the reservations. All are Sioux, but they come from three or four main branches with many historically diverse bands, speaking different dialects.

In Indian country there is a rise of what has been called a new nationalism. For many this has meant a turning back to tradition, a searching for roots long forgotten—or never learned. The Native American Church has many followers, as does the way of the Holy Pipe. Activist groups such as AIM—the American Indian Movement—have set in motion many of these changes—changes which have increased violence and tension. But activists are also polishing and bringing forth into the light a long-hid jewel: the pride of being Indian.

It is time for change, they insist.

One hundred years ago Indian people were forced onto these reservations, stripped of their language, their customs, their religion. For generations government policy allowed no self-determination and tried to destroy every trace of Indian identity and culture. Children were taken to boarding schools, sometimes not allowed to see their families for a year or more. There they were forced to disavow their heritage and become as "white" as possible. It was supposed by both Indian and non-Indian that the tribes would eventually disappear and Indian people would blend into the so-called melting pot. Sioux lands continued to disappear.

The result was a serious identity crisis for people who were not allowed to be Indian and could not become white. The identity crisis manifests itself yet today in many self-defeating ways such as through alcoholism, drugs, suicide, high accident rate, petty jealousies, resentment against non-Indian, and aggression against family and friends.

The Indian, it is said, is an alien in his own land.

"We do not see peace of mind in this generation," says a young Standing Rock teacher. "We hope it for our children."

On every South Dakota reservation there are troubling problems. The beauty of the reservation lands and dark-eyed children contrasts sadly with sprawling junked-car towns and "derelict warriors" on the streets.

Many of the problems center on poverty. There is almost no industry and few jobs except with the Bureau of Indian Affairs and tribal government. Over half the work force is unemployed, although on any reservation there is a trained and talented pool of technicians: mechanics, TV repairmen, computer operators, carpenters, electricians.

Spring Creek is a typical reservation town at the end of the road. About 175 mostly fullblood Brule Sioux live there; many speak their native language better than they do English. Nearly half do not have access to a car; there is no public transportation. There is no gas station or grocery store, few telephones.

Isolation is a real factor in many reservation towns. It is difficult to obtain goods and services; transportation is limited and expensive; cost of living comes high; health services are out of reach in an emergency. Groceries and other stores frequently charge much higher prices than in non-reservation towns. Severe winter weather and bad roads are life and death matters.

South Dakota's reservations have hospitals and clinics in the larger towns offering preventative health programs as well as emergency care, but many seem heavy with regulations and not always flexible to the needs of people who have traveled far and with much dificulty to get there. Don Doll explains some of the problems in *Crying for a Vision:*

Leo Makes Room for Them holds Rocky whose jaw was swollen for two days. It was hard for Victor and Sherry to take him to the Rosebud Service Unit Hospital 20 miles away because they had no car. They couldn't call for help either; only 10 percent of Indian homes have phones. At the hospital out-patients wait three to four hours for treatment from a staff rated at half strength. Less than one-fifth of Indian three-year-olds get complete immunization. Indian children die at three times the national average.

The Indian health service has a poor reputation on many reservations. It has been a training ground for medical students, and many professionals who stayed on have been of less competence.

At the center of some of the reservation's worst problems is alcoholism. Alcoholism is at once a symptom and a cause: a symptom of all that is wrong and impossible to deal with in reservation life; the cause of much tragedy, suffering and crime. Many corrections officials see drinking as the cause of much Indian crime—unlike white crime. "With an Indian," says one, "I don't see the crime being committed unless he has been drinking." Drug abuse is a related problem, and reaches down to small children sniffing glue.

Studies indicate about one in three Indian adults drink excessively. Father Noah Broken Leg, Episcopal priest for Spring Creek explains the cycle: "On the reservation there is little to do; but there is so much to forget. Because of the drinking, almost everyone has experienced tragedy, often at a very young age. To forget, one drinks. But when one drinks, one is liable to do something else that he will regret when he sobers up. He can live with that for awhile feeling miserable about himself—until he can take it no longer, and drinks again to forget. And so the circle so not end."

Many people live on the edge of a crisis.

"Daily life on a reservation is crisis oriented," says Beverley Badhorse in her study *Press Coverage of Native American Affairs.* "You move from one crisis to another—yours or someone else's. Most homes are already taxed beyond sensibility by lack of money, personal problems, transportation, overcrowding and maintenance problems. And yet the householder may suddenly find a mother and four children at the door...at 20 below zero. It may be a genuine emergency—electricity turned off, no food, a drunken father on the rampage. Five more mouths to feed. Five more people using improperly installed plumbing."

On the reservation nearly everyone experiences the death of several close friends and relatives each year. Murder, suicide and accidental death rates are high; so are the reported "accidents" which are probable suicides and murders. Freezing to death is not rare. Sadly, it's a common tale in any small town bordering the reservation to find, on a bitterly cold morning, a frozen body behind the bar or a few miles out of town somewhere between home and a car stuck in the ditch. Life expectancy of the Oglala on Pine Ridge is 46 years.

In the midst of each crisis, inevitably, are the children. In one-parent families, many live with the mother or other relatives. Family problems may be overwhelming. In many cases the sound values of the past have been lost in child rearing. In *Photographs and Poems by Sioux Children* Arthur Amiotte explains:

One is apt to find much permissiveness on one hand and even harsh, physical, inconsistent discipline on the other; little verbal communication or discussion with children; as well as limited freedom in the child's exploration partly imposed by crowded and dangerous aspects of the home environment. The child is confronted with alternating encouragement and restriction of aggression, primarily related to the consequences of aggression by parents. Parents are often oriented toward fatalism, impulsiveness, immediate gratification, distrust of new experience, rigidity, narcissistic behavior, and a sense of impotence in handling children's behavior. Misbehavior is often regarded as that which annoys parents at a given moment.

Government bureaucracy is at its worst on a reservation. For over a hundred years BIA, and its forerunner the Indian Service, has been in charge of reservation policy and services. With one hand it has put forth made-in-Washington solutions, with the other withdrawn them or prevented their success. Much BIA activity in the past, it has been charged, was done to obscure error, protect bureaucratic jobs and gain personal power. Incompetency and fraud cloud many reservation projects, for example housing units built with inferior materials and dishonest inspections.

At best, government has been the all-pervasive force—throwing out lifelines of help, simultaneously with siphons to drain off freedom and initiative. BIA's method has been to direct programs from the top down on every tribe alike, choking off local leadership. Just as programs became workable through local efforts, they were dropped and replaced with others, equally unresponsive. This has meant great job insecurity; jobs were swiftly terminated when money and programs ran out.

There has been much criticism of BIA through the years. Today it is about 75% Indian staffed at all levels and claims to be more responsive and sensitive to Indian needs. BIA protests its role as scapegoat, saying it is Congress which makes the unworkable laws, and the bureau which has had to put them into effect.

Reservations have been the target of many additional programs from government, church and volunteer agencies.

Industry is much needed; projects have been crafts, leatherwork, pottery making, Wanblee Archery, Sans Arc Saddlery. Below, a neat row of fenced homes in Ft. Thompson.

Silent-scars

the post office opens on schedule
a derelict warrior
            decked out in borrowed rags
collects his government pay
(vietnam   we are not proud)
tomorrow the money will be gone
the memories drowned
                        only for awhile....
yes   he's the heartache
of our nation's grandmothers
and the devil's pride
who blinded his soul with the taste
of wine
these useless battles
are wearing our reservations
                            thin....

Rick Traversie
Cheyenne River Sioux

"For bringing us the horse we could almost forgive you for bringing us whiskey. Horses make a landscape look more beautiful." John Fire Lame Deer.

BEHIND GLASS

A man with stone eyes
Banished for a century
Is walking with feet
Heavier than sand
In a barren land
With cactus trees.

Behind glass.

Cliffs of red, orange, and gold
Lie in the shade of a hand

And a humming woman
Under the green cottonwoods
Is sewing a star quilt
Of sky blue and white clouds
with nimble fingers

While a meadowlark sings.

Tony Long Wolf

PRISON ROSES

the scent of love is your black satin hair
on the pillow
in the light of the shadowed moon
reflected from daydreams I collected

sitting here
longing for those nights spent in heaven
the clicking of top-lock brings me back
to a caged world without you

and
the
scent
fades....

Rick Traversie

from An Anthology of Poetry by the Inmates of S.D. State Penitentiary: "Mama said there'd be days like this, but she never said there'd be years of it."

So many people come to help Indians through the years that the ratio has often approached one to one—with frustation levels near saturation. Most stay only a short time before being replaced by others with new enthusiasm and new ideas, but little understanding or experience. Generations of this have increased Indian cynicism and disillusionment. It has become a protection device not to care, not to hope too much, to accept what comes, take what is given.

Three groups of people make up most tribes: Bureau, traditional and urban Indians. The Bureau Indians are the stable working class of mixed bloods, who tend to have the government jobs and understand benefits due them. The traditional full bloods, or "grassroots" Indians, have usually been pushed aside and are the poorest of the poor; they have not been able to fit into the system and not benefitted much from the very programs designed to help them. Urban Indians come and go—to the city for jobs and excitement, back to the reservation for services or money due them, to vote or influence tribal politics; in the past many have been among the most willing to sell off lands and rights. Today many young activists come from this group and align themselves frequently with the traditional full bloods, who look on them uneasily as outsiders who may betray secrets or flaunt what is meant to be intensely personal.

These factions struggle for control of the tribe, which means control over jobs, opportunities for benefits such as new houses, the police and the courts. The ways of using power on a reservation are legion; vindictiveness and favoritism are rampant, says Badhorse. Politics is inbred, a cross between small-town politics and the old clan system, it has been said. Those in power have all the rights; others may have none. Giving the few available jobs to relatives is considered a normal part of reservation government. The enormous power of BIA has strengthened those in tribal control and increased the helplessness of those out of favor. As with any community settled by the same families for generations, the reservation has its share also of petty jealousies, cherishing of old injuries, its various factions working below the surface to gain their own ends.

Tribal membership itself is often in dispute. BIA is rigid in maintaining heirship for all whose ancestors claimed Indian land, a century or more ago. Some have little Indian blood. (In some cases, none—it is said that white men sometimes got on membership rolls dishonestly to obtain land allottments and lease rights.) In other cases, offspring of intermarriage between tribes may have lost membership in both. BIA requires ¼ degree of Indian blood to participate in some programs, 1/8 degree in others. Every tribe has its own rules for membership, and BIA and tribal rolls may not be the same. Vine Deloria Jr. says, "Indian tribal membership today is a fiction created by the federal government, not a creation of the Indian people themselves." With all the legal entanglements, it is impossible for tribes to reform on the natural basis of active community membership.

Law causes other conflicts. Indian people on the reservation are subject to four sets of laws which frequently conflict: tribal, state, federal, and special federal laws for Indians. On the reservation tribal law is supreme—but it is often challenged by state authorities and others. "It's a mess, let me tell you," said one justice official.

Border town law enforcement is probably prejudiced against the Indian offender, as reservation people believe. But under tribal law, Indians have often had it even worse. "Reservation justice," says Philip B. Taft Jr. in *Corrections Magazine*, "is often swift, silent and brutal; many untimely deaths go uninvestigated."

It can depend on who is in power.

Until 1968 when the Indian Civil Rights act was passed, many Indian people did not have civil rights protection. This meant unreasonable search of homes, persons and property could be conducted without warning or warrant. Persons could be held in jail indefinitely without due process. Excessive bail, fine, cruel or unusual punishment was not forbidden. Speedy and public trials were not required. Reservation people did not have absolute right to freedom of religion, speech, assembly, trial by jury, or to petition for redress of grievances. Since 1968 tribal courts have been limited to sentences under six months or $500 fine or both for one offense.

But people denied civil rights sometimes have little recourse. Tribes such as the Rosebud Sioux have dismissed civil rights claims by invoking sovereign immunity which means they are an independent government which cannot be sued without its own consent. The book *Reservation Street Law*, published by Sinte Gleska college, explores the difficulty. The claim is to be filed in tribal court, "but when you do this the cause of action is dismissed on grounds of sovereign immunity. Your civil rights have been violated but there is no forum in which to enforce these rights. For the individual, this situation appears truly intolerable and unfair."

Tribal law is not taught in schools, so there is much confusion over legal rights and responsibilities. Few understand the technicalities. Indian police and tribal judges have frequently been poorly trained. Punishment meted out has been sometimes arbitrary and even cruel. Freedom could be bought in some Indian courts.

If arrested on a reservation for one of 14 crimes covered by federal law, an Indian must be tried in federal court. This seldom happens. What has been called a "tribal protectiveness" takes over—a desire to insulate tribal members from white justice. Guilty and presumed guilty are thrown into reservation jails on other pretexts. These are notoriously the worst of rundown jails. "In Eagle Butte the jail is cramped and battered," says Taft. "Inmates often sleep without mattresses; windows are broken and lighting is poor or nonexistent."

At the state penitentiary in Sioux Falls, Indians make up 25-30 percent of the prisoners, although they are only 6½ percent of the state population. This high rate also holds true for boys and girls at state training schools.

Native American activists say it is a clear case of racism which puts so many Indians in prison. Others point to typical reservation living conditions such as poverty, unemployment, poor health, poor housing, high alcoholism and drug dependency, high suicide and murder rates, broken homes—the highest number of single parent families in America. Most crimes are alcohol related.

Going to jail or prison is so common that virtually every family is affected. In small towns bordering reservations, activists charge that white drunks are sent home while Indians in the same condition are thrown in jail. At prison, Indians serve longer sentences for the same crimes; they also serve longer before being considered for parole. A four year study at the South Dakota penitentiary showed Indian rates of parole were about half that of whites.

South Dakota Indian people feel they meet a great deal of radical prejudice throughout the state.

Vine Deloria Jr., son and grandson of distinguished South Dakota Sioux ministers in the Episcopal church, says Americans in general refuse to accept them as contemporary people. "There exists in the minds of non-Indian Americans a vision of what they would like Indians to be," he writes in *God is Red*. "They stubbornly refuse to allow Indians to be or to become anything else. They insist on remaining in the last cen-

The tribe is like a team or company, some say—cooperative spirit counts more than personal competition.

RESERVATIONS AND EMPLOYMENT

CHEYENNE RIVER - 1,410,346 acres; Teton Sioux— Minneconju, Sans Arc, Two Kettle, Blackfeet; pop. 4584; labor force 1944, 50.2% employed.

CROW CREEK - 125,000 acres; Yanktonnai Sioux and Teton Sioux - Brule; pop. 1790; labor force 658, 49.1% employed.

FLANDREAU - 2,356 acres; Santee Sioux - Mdewakanton, Wahpekuta; pop. 378; labor force 138, 92% employed.

LOWER BRULE - 119,944 acres; Teton Sioux - Brule; pop. 973; labor force 365, 58.9% employed.

PINE RIDGE - 1,670,753 acres; Teton Sioux - Oglala; pop. 13,500; labor force 5356, 43.7% employed.

ROSEBUD - 958,472 acres; Teton Sioux - Brule; pop. 9,326; labor force 4687, 47.4% employed.

SISSETON - 107,000 acres; Santee Sioux - Sisseton, Wahpeton; pop. 3990; labor force 1269, 47.1% employed.

STANDING ROCK - 844,525 acres (N.D. and S.D.); Yanktonnai Sioux and Teton Sioux - Hunkpapa; pop. 3,899 (S.D.); labor force 1761, 18.5% employed.

YANKTON - 34,089 acres; Yankton Sioux; pop. 2,411; labor force 1096, 19.4% employed.

BIA employment figures for May 1980

Note: The employment situation is probably not as bright as shown here. BIA officials agree unofficially that their figures "have been used to justify programs." Also much of the labor is seasonal, not year around. Tribal figures for unemployment are often much higher than those given by BIA.

tury with old Chief Red Fox, whoever he may really be, reciting a past that is basically mythological, thrilling and comforting."

Newspapers in border towns seldom use good news or helpful information from the reservation, such as tribal business and legal affairs, two sides of controversial issues, or even wedding and engagement photos, says Beverley Badhorse. Her study finds instead that Indian news is usually devoted to crime, unnatural death and accident. On the other hand, she says Indians are justly critical of eastern reporters who come to blitz a story, sit an hour in a teepee, and return to write the definitive story and perpetuate "the noble redman syndrome."

Pine Ridge residents say violence by whites towards Indians is common in nearby towns. They cite a murder in Gordon, Nebraska as touching off the fuse for the 1973 Wounded Knee conflict. From the book *Voices from Wounded Knee* comes this description: "In February 1972, Raymond Yellow Thunder, from the reservation community of Porcupine, was beaten in Gordon, Nebraska, by two white men, thrown naked into an American Legion dance, beaten again, and locked in an auto trunk. His bruised body was found two days later. His attackers were released without paying bail, and charged with second degree manslaughter." Relatives were refused a look at the body or autopsy report, according to this source. They went to the BIA for help, to the tribal government, to a private lawyer—all without success. Then they went to AIM.

It would be helpful if news reporters in these towns wrote better Indian news, says Badhorse, but there are many reasons why they don't. Few know where to start. They are ignorant of legal, political, economic and cultural structures on the reservation; obstacles are geographic isolation, language and hostility. They fear the Indian and cannot easily break through Indian distrust of whites. Journalists need to spend a long time with Indian people before they write about them and they must not rely simply on information fed to them by the BIA, she writes. Neither should they take as the whole truth the views of white people living near the reservation, nor those of Indian activists—who tend to be urban, articulate, and wise in the use of public relations. However, she insists it is vital reporters do begin covering reservation news so Indian people, like others, can benefit from freedom of the press. "Bungling in Indian affairs has been covered up for more than 100 years," she says. "This failure on the part of the media has resulted in gross inaccuracies, miscarriage of justice, misuse of funds, official misconduct—all tolerated and perpetuated by U.S. agencies charged with Indian affairs."

Indian newspapers have not been able to do the job, since they tend to be unstable, short-term, operating on a financial shoestring. Some are also tribal, with the political slant of the tribal council; others are run by activists and slanted toward that particular view. Indian people have learned to distrust what they read in newspapers.

But despite the social and economic upheaval of the past 100 years, much Sioux culture and traditional values have been retained. The expected disintegration of the tribes has not come about. In fact many tribes are united as never before in this century by similar causes, powwows and traditional ceremonies. The belief that the tribe will survive long after white civilization disappears is not unusual on reservations today. Indians today are deeply concerned with development of the tribe and preserving their reservation lands.

Traditional culture has become more accepted by both Indian and non-Indian.

In South Dakota's penitentiary, educational, social and rehabilitative programs are now designed especially for Indians, and often administered by them. Indian inmates gather in culture groups such as the Native American Council of Tribes; some build sweat lodges and practice traditional religions.

"It's really helped me with my attitude," says one inmate. "Before, it was to hell with everybody. I was gonna do my own time. But after I went to the pipe ceremony and the sweat lodge, I became concerned for the next person. Now, if there is some way that I can help somebody, I'm going to do it."

The biggest concern for an Indian inmate, says the head counselor, is what he will do when he gets out. "There are no jobs, no recreation facilities. The only thing he can do is drink."

The Swift Bird project on the Cheyenne River reservation, established in 1979 as a minimum security prison for first offenders and possible half-way house, tried to provide an answer. At Swift Bird, inmates went on work release, received therapy and could immerse themselves in Indian culture. It was an exciting and encouraging innovation. But all too soon disagreement arose between the all-Indian activists who ran the camp and the conservative tribal advisory board, over how to solve management problems. A bitter fight for control ensued and the bright hope of Swift Bird fluttered to an end after only two years of operation.

Vine Deloria Jr. likens a tribe to the modern corporation in which all employees work together for the good of the company—in contrast to the personal ambition of competitive society. Being inside the tribe is so comfortable and

'Heartache for a nation's grand-mothers.'

'Beauty of dark-eyed children.'

R. Oge

Powwow-reaffirming traditions.

reasonable that it can act like a narcotic, he says. Those who are away feel lonely and alienated and long to return.

Sharing is believed essential if the tribe is to survive. The giveaway feast, long discouraged by whites, is an example of this sharing. Lame Deer explains, "What they are trying to tell us is that poor people can't afford to be generous. But we hold our otuhan, our give-aways, because they help us to remain Indians. All the big events in our lives—birth and death, joy and sadness—can be occasions for a give-away. We don't believe in a family getting wealthy through inheritance."

Traditional Indian people stand ready to help each other even when it might cause them serious problems. Most families who live by Indian values expect to take in one or several "Stay Away Joe" types from time to time. (Because of its realistic portrayals, the book *Stay Away, Joe* is a favorite among many Indian people.) Usually it's a relative whom they love, scold, become exasperated by, put up with, and protect. Stay Away Joe is accepted no matter what crisis brings him or her to the door—whether to sleep off a drunk, escape the law, hide out from a murderous acquaintance or enraged spouse, or eat until the next check comes in. The same Stay Away Joe will probably be accepted again in the future regardless of what new crisis he or she might precipitate before moving on—even if it is wrecking the family car, bringing in drunken and destructive friends, stealing money or household items, having illicit relations with a daughter or son, committing murder or violence against a family member.

A general frustration with Indian conditions on the reservation helped trigger the rise of AIM and Indian activism and militancy during the early 1970's. AIM has led several South Dakota protests such as the sit in at Mt. Rushmore, the 71-day takeover of Wounded Knee, various Black Hills encampments and demands for return of the Black Hills.

Activists criticize the Mt. Rushmore sculpture, calling it an enormous paperweight. In his book *Lame Deer, Seeker of Visions,* John Fire Lame Deer, an elderly traditionalist, points out Mt. Rushmore as an example of white man's disease for confusing bigness with greatness. Lame Deer is also no admirer of the Crazy Horse sculpture now underway. There are at least two things wrong with it, he says. First: the time has passed when any white man can decide what is an appropriate monument for Indians, especially in the sacred hills. Second: "The ghost of Crazy Horse doesn't want a tourist monument built of him; our dead people don't want it; the trees and the animals don't want it...The whole idea of making a beautiful wild mountain into a statue of him is a pollution of the landscape. It is against the spirit of Crazy Horse." Lame Deer predicts the enormous statue will never be finished.

On South Dakota's reservations, changes are definitely in the wind, partly because of the new activism, partly because of a national willingness to give tribal governments more control. Block grants should mean more flexibility to use federal money for needed local purposes. There are, however, well-grounded fears that block grants could mean less money on the reservation; also that less federal control will mean state controls, fewer jobs, and more tribal politics. Another concept under consideration is that Indian tribes be dealt with as a 51st state with the benefits, independence and responsibilities of other states.

Some tribes are trying to clear up land entanglements. Land ownership in and near reservations is unbelievably complicated. Individual land holdings are fractionated by a hundred years of inheritance during which the government required passing down of undivided shares. Ownership of a small piece of land by 50 or more heirs, in various percentages, is common. No heir may sell, lease or use the land without ap-

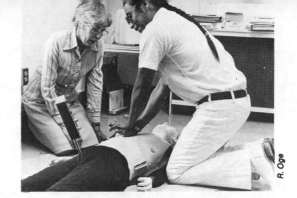
Indian health service gives training.

proval from all. BIA as administrator has kept track of all the paper work and portioned out lease money—which in some cases is very small. Tribes such as the Rosebud Sioux are now trying to buy these fractionated allotments for tribal use; unfortunately funds are limited. Other lands are owned by the tribe, by the federal government, and by whites—purchased during periods when government urged termination of reservations.

Frank Pommersheim and Anita Remerowski say, in *Reservation Street Law,* there is a great need for state and tribe to work out their disagreements over the right to govern reservation lands and Indian people. There have been many expensive legal battles. The authors say both tribal and state authorities need to approach the problems in a spirit of good will and cooperation instead of with lawsuits. "For without this, it is difficult to imagine lasting and fruitful solutions to these problems for the coming generation." In addition claims and threats of claims against both federal and state have kept Indian people uncertain and need to be settled for good, says BIA's area director, with a deadline after which no more claims will be paid.

Churches must face the rise of native religions, perhaps finding new ways to work together in an Indian frame of reference. Schools are now coming under Indian control, with all-Indian school boards and Indian teachers. This should result in better self-images for young people; for example, they will study another view of the role of Indians in American History.

Needless to say, some of the changes are making whites near the reservations jittery as incidents increase against their children in formerly peaceful schools, and as they see tragic results of Indian militancy first hand.

Community colleges are established close to home in Pine Ridge, Rosebud and Standing Rock. As a marvelous omen for the future, Eleanore Robertson, area director of Indian Health, cites the 60 mature men and women who worked hard and earned their GED degrees at Oglala Community College last spring, as well as the many young Indian people returning to the reservations to work for their people.

There is certain to be a rise in women's leadership roles with many career-minded young women today, she says.

There is much that is positive on the Sioux reservations today. This is well expressed in the deep love of Indian people for their lands and tribe, and old values they hold strong such as brotherhood, cooperation, acceptance, wisdom, and living in harmony with nature.

Native Americans hope that—somewhere between the rancher's disillusioned view and the do-gooder's noble red man—South Dakotans as a whole will learn to know Indian people as individuals, neighbors and friends. They are encouraged by a resistance at last from non-Indians toward civilization's obsession to "cut it down, dig it up, tear it out, dam it over, and move on," and believe that this nation may yet enrich itself with an understanding of the great Indian traditions and cultural values.

A long way from the sod house school: new brick buildings, library facilities, school bus service.

3. FOCUS ON LEARNING

Education has come a long way from the sod house school with the pile of assorted books on the table. Modern methods and equipment combine with solid teaching in the basics to insure South Dakota students an opportunity for high quality education from kindergarten through college.

Student-teacher ratio is 16.4, compared with a national average of nearly 20. Of every $1000 in per capita personal income in the state, $47.21 is spent on education. High school dropout rate is low; nearly 85% of entering high school students graduate. (This figure was 91% in 1970.) More than half of these graduates take post high school training.

Nearly 100,000 youngsters are enrolled in South Dakota elementary schools. Nearly 50,000 are in high school. Well over 30,000 attend colleges, vo-tech and commercial schools in the state. Of these 91% attend public schools. (See figures on page 10.)

Teachers, on the average, are 11-year veterans; 20% have a masters degree or more. Salaries of these teachers rate well below the national average, but have more than doubled in the past ten years.

Country schools have been a way of life in the state for nearly a century, but have been rapidly closing their doors in the past 25 years with consolidation and bussing. As late as the decade 1970-1980, nearly ⅔ of one-teacher schools closed, dropping the total from 378. There are now 132 one-teacher schools and 59 two-teacher schools in the state, making a total of less than 200 rural schools remaining.

Many of these are in western South Dakota where isolation and distance have always been facts of ranch life. Parents have traditionally undergone much hardship to get their children to school. In many places buses cannot run efficiently, so parents drive twice a day to school over roads which can be nearly impassible in mud, high water or drifting snow. Youngsters often drive these same roads before they are ready; they drive back roads and try for early driving permits. High school parents are faced with harder decisions: Letting their children drive even longer distances, renting them an apartment in town, or having the mother move in with them during the week. Consolidation has usually improved

educational facilities, but has not answered this problem of distance.

Two boys' ranches in the state offer education and help for boys with special problems. McCrossan Boys Ranch at Sioux Falls, established by Melinda McCrossan in honor of her husband, serves about 60 boys. The ranch features big gentle Belgians and finds that troubled kids and horses go well together. Sky Ranch for Boys is built along the Little Missouri River south of Camp Crook and houses 50 boys. Airplanes are a specialty there. Said the "flying padre," Father Murray, "When a boy first arrives, he generally has a chip on his shoulder. We make a deal; I'll give him flying lessons if he'll pitch in and work on the ranch."

South Dakota provides a variety of vocational education classes for small high schools in two innovative ways. The first method is with multi-district vocational schools which are centrally located; students are bussed in from outlying schools for vocational classes they select. The second method, for more isolated schools, is to take the classes directly to students via mobile classrooms. Each classroom is a specially furnished trailer house, complete with teacher and all necessary materials and equipment for the class. These classrooms are moved to each participating school in rotation so that a student may take a semester of auto mechanics in the fall, for example, then a semester of food preparation and service in the spring.

South Dakota has 14 accredited colleges and universities. Two relatively new community colleges have also been established on the Pine Ridge and Rosebud reservations, Oglala Sioux Community College and Sinte Gleska Community College; another serves Standing Rock at Ft. Yates, North Dakota. Six state supported vocational-technical schools are located at Mitchell, Watertown, Rapid City-Sturgis, Sioux Falls, Springfield and Pierre. In addition, there are private commercial schools at Huron, Aberdeen, Rapid City, Sioux Falls, Yankton and Watertown.

Cheerleading the school spirit, left; innovative vocational classes.

Nearly 100,000 in elementary schools.

At country school: a trackmeet, above; below, one room for nine children of all ages, near Bison.

The stress of registration in USD DakotaDome, left, and relaxing at Northern, above.

At SDSU, below, the Carillon and a free-wheeling bed race.

Campus scenes, winter and summertime, sun and stately buildings.

SOUTH DAKOTA'S ACCREDITED COLLEGES AND UNIVERSITIES
Fall 1980 Enrollment

PUBLIC

South Dakota State University, Brookings	6,848
University of South Dakota, Vermillion	5,968
Northern State College, Aberdeen	2,603
SD School of Mines & Technology, Rapid City	2,393
Black Hills State College, Spearfish	2,099
Dakota State College, Madison	1,000
University South Dakota at Springfield	852

PRIVATE

Augustana College, Sioux Falls	2,115
Sioux Falls College, Sioux Falls	849
Mount Marty College, Yankton	568
Dakota Wesleyan University, Mitchell	543
Huron College, Huron	321
Presentation College, Aberdeen	300
Yankton College, Yankton	272

Colleges with candidacy status are: National College of Business, Rapid City; Oglala Sioux Community College, Pine Ridge; Sinte Gleska Community College, Rosebud. Another without candidacy status is Freeman Junior College, Freeman.

4. SPORTS OF EVERY KIND

For the sports enthusiast there's always another sport, another game, another tournament, another match, another challenge—no matter what the season. What's new is the tremendous upsurge in girl's sports. In high school, college and community, girl's athletics strikes a chord of response that was long dormant.

Spectators are part of the fun.

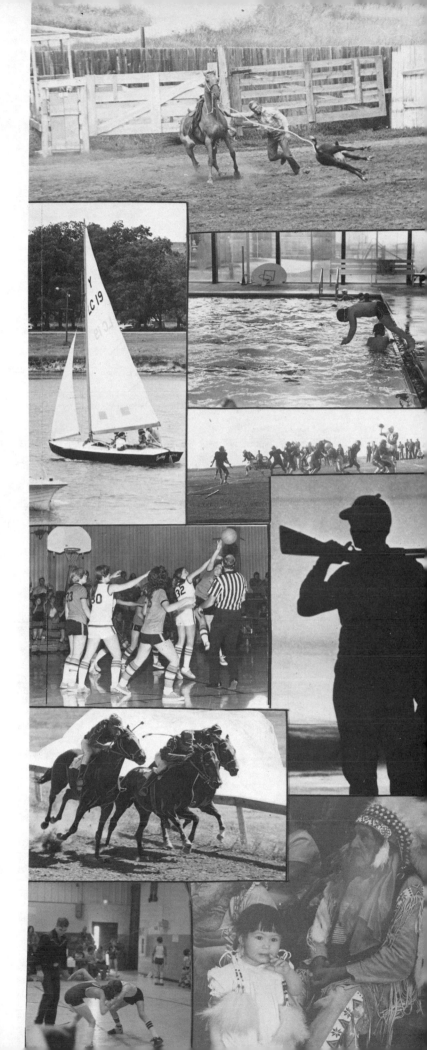

At left, beaded Sioux medallions. SDSU actors stage musical Brigadoon. A fairyland of sidewalk art in Vermillion.

5. THE ARTS

The arts are alive and lively in South Dakota. They are the Memorial Art Center, the Shrine to Music, ritzy events at urban centers and colleges, community musicals and melodramas, books and writings published throughout the state, and an old Indian woman stitching a Star quilt for a grandchild.

South Dakota has a heritage of many fine artists such as Harvey Dunn, and noted writers including Ole Rolvaag, Hamlin Garland, Laura Ingalls Wilder, and Badger Clark.

Increased leisure today has meant a growing interest in the arts. Musical training begins early and high school students give near-professional performances. Student groups tour this nation and other countries. The arts today are part of everyday living across the state. Artists, poets, potters, sculptors, writers, and workers in a variety of mediums all find inspiration where they live.

Music is alive and lively in college auditoriums and community centers.

"Dakota Scout" in acrylics by Herman Red Elk. Below, former bullrider Jim Sayre paints rodeo action in his Black Hills studio.

6. THE CHURCHES

South Dakota's churches have been strongly influenced by ethnic groups. About half the churches, it is estimated, were started by imigrants who settled together and established the same church they had in the old country. The state also has a heritage of many early missionaries—particularly Episcopal—who settled on reservations, establishing churches and schools, and sometimes baptising, marrying, or holding services for pioneers.

Since Scandinavians, Germans, and German-Russians predominated among immigrants, it is not surprising that Lutheran and Catholic faiths became dominant churches in the state. (Most Germans and German-Russians came from provinces strictly divided as to Catholic or Lutheran.) Before 1900, churches had established a number of private colleges in the state. In 1936, with 42% of the state population listed as church members, the ten leading churches were, in this order: Lutheran, Roman Catholic, Methodist, Congregational, Presbyterian, Protestant Espicopal, Baptist, Dutch Reformed, Evangelical and Reformed, Mennonite.

Among Indian people today there has been considerable movement toward traditional religions.

Country churches once dotted the countryside. Almost everywhere the long spires could be seen rising above the prairie. But with decreasing farm and ranch populations, many of these small churches closed. Yet a surprising number do remain open, supported by vigorous membership. Many ministers of small towns still serve one or two rural parishes. Other communities which have closed their country church still maintain a neatly kept cemetery—and occasionally add a grave for another pioneer.

Bells play a morning sunlight pattern on church in Pierre. Below, a country church thrives in active community.

Many country churches are closed as in photo at left, but keep up a lonely cemetery.

Old courthouse in Sioux Falls, now a museum, has stood as a landmark of urban progress since 1890

7. CITY AND TOWN

Typical of small towns, Platte has wide main street with angle parking.

Cities sparkle with the promise of excitement and opportunity and small towns glow with the warmth of an Indian summer morning when everyone you meet says, "Hello."

But cities grow bigger and towns grow smaller. The national dilemma of growing cities and shrinking towns has not escaped this rural state. More than one-third of the population now lives in the ten largest cities, and many more live in surrounding suburbs.

The smallest of small towns are most vulnerable. No doubt there were far too many to begin with, planted by railroads and promoters in the old boomtown days six and eight miles apart, a reasonable journey by team and wagon. In these towns now the weathered false front businesses close one by one, suggesting nostalgic memories rather than an optismistic future.

However, many small towns in the state are not only holding their own, but experiencing growth and vigor. They are usually trade centers for a large area, without close competition from other towns. They are towns with aggressive business leaders who have the courage to build and remodel, to stock their shelves and advertise. They are communities with strong volunteer leaders who build nursing homes and low-rent housing, a hospital, a library. School bond issues pass when needed and students come there to school from a wide area. Somehow these towns have turned the trick to attract and keep good doctors, teachers, ministers, and other professionals. Some have consolidated health services to cooperate with other towns.

Cities, meanwhile, continue to draw off both the talented and the desperate. South Dakota cities are growing and spawning bright suburbs.

SOUTH DAKOTA'S LARGEST CITIES		
	1970	1980
SIOUX FALLS	72,488	80,908
RAPID CITY	43,836	46,340
ABERDEEN	26,476	25,937
WATERTOWN	13,388	15,632
BROOKINGS	13,717	14,915
MITCHELL	13,425	13,917
HURON	14,299	13,000
YANKTON	11,919	11,992
PIERRE	9,699	11,966
VERMILLION	9,128	10,140

Smallest towns are most vulnerable: a branch line closes and the elevator fades.

Agriculture is South Dakota's largest industry, and livestock provide most of the income.

8. AGRICULTURE—SOUTH DAKOTA'S LIFEBLOOD

Agriculture is the state's most important industry. Cash receipts from farm products were nearly two and a half billion dollars in 1980—a low production year. Farm and ranch real estate is valued at $13,950,000,000.

The importance of agriculture to the state is well understood. And not just on farms and ranches. It generates other industry so that agriculture directly or indirectly influences every business in the state. Commercial enterprises based on farming are a big and fast growing industry: meat packing, flour and feed mills, dairy products, other food processing, implement manufacture, handling and shipping of farm products. Many federal and state employees serve agriculture in South Dakota. Retail businesses of all kinds are involved in supplying the farm producer with equipment, feeds, supplies and financing.

No matter what the business, one usually need not scratch deep to find the farming or ranching connection. In South Dakota, agriculture affects everyone. The price of wheat and cattle can determine how many new cars are sold in Sioux Falls. When crops are good and markets high, there's an air of prosperity everywhere—not just on small town main street, or in an implement dealer's showroom, but on every sidewalk in the state. When drouth hangs on, money tightens and workers get laid off; everyone looks anxiously toward the sky. Similarly, when the bottom drops out of the market farm and ranch families curb their spending—and everyone feels it.

There are 38,000 farms and ranches in South Dakota according to the 1980 census. Average size is 1184 acres. Within the state as a whole, 53 percent of the land is range, including native hay; 35 percent is cropland; 5 percent is pasture and hayland (tame); 3 percent is forest; and the remaining 4 percent is in towns, cities, highways and lakes.

Size of farms and ranches and the type of agriculture varies greatly throughout the state. Smaller, intensely productive farms are in the southeast, with larger cattle and sheep ranches in the west.

In Lincoln County, for instance, farms average 275 acres; in Clay County they average 345 acres. In Lincoln, 79 percent of land is cropland, in Clay, 86 percent. Such intensive cropping is reflected in the price of land being the highest in the state at a 1981 average of $673 per acre.

Ranching units on the Pine Ridge reservation in Shannon County, however, average 11,024 acres; in Ziebach County they average 5,500 acres. Shannon has 6 percent cropland, 85 percent rangeland. In Ziebach 11 percent is cropland, 86 percent rangeland. Land prices are lowest in the northwest at an average $171 per acre. Futhermore, some ranch units here include government pasture and forest leases which drives up the selling price of such ranches.

West of the Missouri, most counties are 60 percent or more rangeland (except for Tripp with more crops and Lawrence which is mainly forest.) East of the Missouri the opposite is true. Most counties are half to 86 percent cropland. (Exceptions are Buffalo, Hyde and Jerauld counties with a higher ratio of grazing land.)

Livestock are extremely important to South Dakota farmers and ranchers, with all this grazing land. About three-fourths of all agricultural income is from livestock, one-fourth from crops. Eighty percent of all South Dakota farms have cattle operations of some kind, a total of 29,000 farms and ranches. Range cattle graze over most of the state, especially in the western section. Cattle feedlots are mostly east of the Missouri where feed supplies are heavy; most dairies are also in the eastern section. Over 6000 farms have cattle feedlots. Nearly 7000 have dairy operations.

Sheep are raised on 6000 farms and ranches, a number which has dropped sharply in the past twenty years. These include big sheep ranches in the west, farm flocks and feedlots in the east.

The main cash crop raised in the state is wheat, followed closely by corn. Much of the grain raised here, however, is fed within the state.

On the export market, South Dakota's most important world shipments are wheat and wheat products, followed by feed grains. Considerably behind are soybeans, then hides and skins, meat, lard and tallow, sunflower seeds.

In a typical year South Dakota's ranking among states in production is listed below. (Unusual situations, such as the 1980 South Dakota drouth, or bumper crops or disasters elsewhere, can change the ranking.)

RANK	
1	Oats
1	Rye
1	Geese
1-2	Flaxseed
3	Honey
3	Sunflowers
3-4	All hay; alfalfa hay, alfalfa seed
4-5	Durum; other spring wheat
4-5	Sheep; sheep and lambs on feed
6	Sorghum
6-7	Barley
7-9	Cattle; beef cows; cattle and calves on feed
8-10	Hogs; commercial hog slaughter
9	Corn for grain

South Dakota is sixth in amount of land which is in farms and ranches, with a total of 45,000,000 productive acres.

Crew shears inside custom made shearing trailer. Sheep shear heavier and raise more lambs.

Ranges and feedlots are filled with crossbreds.

A Success Story

South Dakota farming is a far cry from the efforts of the homesteader chopping seed potatoes into sod with an ax; ranching is a much different way of life than when the Turkey Track let their 60,000 cattle drift with winter storms to be gathered in a big spring roundup. Today both farming and ranching are carefully controlled businesses with enormous financial investments.

Four major changes have taken place: first, mechanization; second, genetic improvements; third, chemical developments; and fourth, socioeconomic change which meant all the other changes could be, and must be, implemented. Today a single operator not only farms more land, but gets vastly more production per acre.

MECHANIZATION

New machinery has taken the hand labor out of nearly every farming operation. Sixty years ago mechanization broke the "oat barrier" of feeding work horses...and since then agriculture has never looked back. Wheat harvesting, for instance, was a big undertaking 60 years ago, involving cutting, binding, shocking, hauling—perhaps drying and storing—and threshing. Today it is quickly completed, mostly by straight combining. Haying is another major job for which many different kinds of machinery have been developed—for loose stacking, bailing, and silage. New methods not only preserve the hay in good condition, but provide a mechanized operation from cutting to feeding. The pitchfork is not quite obsolete, but it's on the way out.

Tractors have been improved every year since they replaced the horse, with more power, more versatility, easier control. Today's tractors not only offer mechanized control at a fingertip but comfort, too, with air conditioned cabs and stereo music.

GENETIC IMPROVEMENTS

The second change is genetic. Research and scientific experiment have improved varieties and tremendously increased the yields of all crops, as well as adding pounds to every breed of livestock.

Wheat yields have doubled from 14 to 28 bushels per acre nationally in the past 40 years. Improved varieties have meant not only heavier yield, but better quality wheat, resistance to disease, to shelling out, to unfavorable weather conditions. Control of rusts through introducing resistant strains has, of

Hybrid corn grows more kernels on the cob, more cobs on the stalk.

Tractors offer air conditioned, sound-controlled comfort.

itself, brought great stability to the wheat belt. Recent success with wheat hybrids brings promise of even greater yields.

Hybrid corn has been a great success for many years, increasing tremendously both size and number of cobs per stalk. Similar advancements in genetic breeding have improved all other crops.

Genetic improvement in livestock is a similar story. At one time longhorn steers grazed South Dakota ranges for four to seven years in reaching maturity. Today most steers are slaughtered at about 20 months—a great saving in pasture use and feed. In the past 30 years, sire evaluation and performance testing has improved the quality of every breed of cattle. Then crossbreeding proved again the value of hybrid vigor, unlocking ability for faster growth and better calf survival rate. Twenty years ago few people were crossbreeding. Today ranges and feedlots are filled with crossbred cattle.

New cattle breeds, moreover, are mixing with the uniform Hereford and Angus herds which once claimed the cattle ranges. The exotics, or large all-purpose European breeds, seem here to stay.

Artificial insemination has speeded up quality improvement, making its first impact on dairy cattle. It has been used in registered beef herds to multiply the benefits of a high quality sire. But commercial cattlemen with 200 or more head of range cows were reluctant to start until the possibilities of introducing exotic breeds into their herds nudged them into it. Now many have modified their management practices so they can get better use from highest quality bulls of whatever breed.

Hogs and sheep have made similar advances. The hog silhouette has changed dramatically from the chunky homesteader pig with layers of lard, to the long sleek hog of today.

CHEMICAL DEVELOPMENTS

Chemicals are the third improvement which have helped South Dakota producers. Chemical warfare has meant protection from creeping pests and clouds of flying insects which have wiped out their fields in the past. Weeds, too, are controlled by herbicides, often by aerial crop spraying. Chemicals have brought growth stimulants and fertilizers.

Weather modificiation has been made possible through cloud seeding with silver iodide. Hail suppression has met with most favor in the hail-prone northwestern area of the state where it is supported by county mill levies.

Use of chemicals has created controversy. Some have been banned because of possible harmful side effects to environment or human health. But chemicals are obviously necessary to modern production if American farmers are to

continue to produce cheap food for a hungry world. The latest chemical developments are aimed at specific plant or insect problems, without harmful side effects for other species.

SOCIOECONOMIC CHANGES

The fourth change, socioeconomic, has brought the other changes into focus. Farming became a business in which a large financial investment was needed; new skills and knowledge were required. Farmers and ranchers have had to become informed and efficient managers; they demand—and use—the best practical and scientific information they can get. They are willing to spend money to implement the changes needed for great production and greater efficiency. They welcome the new machinery, pesticides, better seed and breeding stock. They have learned to spend less time with the pitchfork and more in working out better management practices.

Dairy cows double their milk production.

Most dairies increased production; others went out of business.

Two million hogs, with increased survival of litters.

Sheep numbers are cut by price squeeze and coyote threat.

Livestock

Three fourths of the state's agricultural cash receipts come from livestock. Much of the grain produced is not sold, but fed to cattle, hogs and sheep in farm feedlots. South Dakota has a great deal of rangeland, with 53 percent of the land area in range. Big cattle and sheep ranches raise calves and lambs for eastern South Dakota feedlots.

Cattle and calves bring in nearly 70 percent of livestock receipts, with 10 percent dairy and 15 percent for hogs. More than half the remaining five percent comes from sheep and lambs, with poultry and eggs, honey, and other livestock products making up the difference.

About 80 percent of South Dakota farms and ranches have cattle operations. In 1960 this amounted to 48,000 farms and ranches out of 58,400. In 1980, with a smaller total of 38,000 farms, 29,000 had cattle. Most of these raise beef calves. Some 6000 have cattle feedlots; 6,800 are dairies.

Beef cattle numbers tend to go up and down with periodic drouth and years of high rainfall as well as market highs and lows. At present the total number of beef cows is up from the 1950 total of 810,000. In 1960 the total was 1,250,000; a peak was reached in 1970 with 1,685,000. Then a decline in numbers followed the low prices of the mid 70's and the drouth of 1980-1981.

Modern ranching involves more water and grass management than in the past. Additional water sources—through dugouts, dams, wells—give better grass usage and allow cross fencing for pasture rotation. Today's ranchers provide good winter feed and protection and follow a recommended program of herd health procedures. They cull less productive cows more closely with pregnancy testing and calf weight records.

Cattle on feed have increased greatly in the past 30 years. In January 1950, the heaviest feeding month, there were 180,000 cattle on feed. Numbers rose steadily until the peak year of 1977 when 370,000 cattle and calves were on feed in the state.

Dairy farming has seen many changes. The necessity for bigger investments in equipment has meant many small dairies went out of business. Only one-fourth of those operating in 1960 remain. Dairy cow numbers are cut in half. Yet milk production per cow has doubled, so that actually the milk production was raised from 1,463,000,000 in 1960 to 1,669,000,000 pounds in 1980. South Dakota cows now average 10,497 pounds of milk annually. Total cash receipts from dairy products are up six times what they were twenty years ago and include, in addition to milk and dried milk, butter, cheese and ice cream.

There has also been a great decline in sheep numbers in the state due to low prices and lack of effective coyote control. In 1960 sheep were at a peak of 1,207,000 ewes. That year prices hit a low and sheep flooded the market. Numbers are down to 550,000. Ewes today raise more lambs than they did thirty years ago. Then 100 South Dakota ewes averaged 88 lambs; today they have a lamb crop of 131.

Hog operations are down from 1960 when half the farms and ranches in the state raised a least a few hogs. There are about two million hogs in the state now, a number that has held quite steady for the past 20 years, on 13,500 farms and ranches. During this time there has been a small increase in litter size from seven to nearly seven and a half.

Beef cattle, above, a continual gamble with drouth and low markets. Left, numerous ranchers now have buffalo herds; some raise elk.

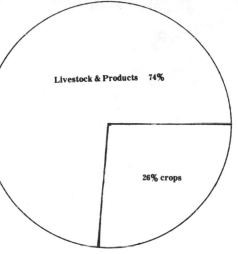

Livestock & Products 74%

26% crops

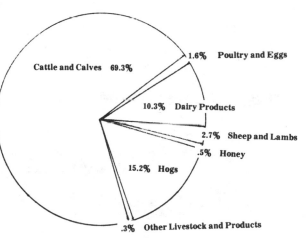

Cattle and Calves 69.3%

1.6% Poultry and Eggs

10.3% Dairy Products

2.7% Sheep and Lambs

.5% Honey

15.2% Hogs

.3% Other Livestock and Products

South Dakota's cash receipts. Above, all agricultural products. Right, livestock.

Poultry and eggs add income.

AVERAGE PRICE RECEIVED

	Dollars per 100 pounds						Cents/Lb.
	Beef Cattle	Steers & Heifers	Calves	Hogs	Sheep	Lambs	Wool
1950	23.90	--	26.30	17.30	11.30	25.80	64¢
1960	21.10	23.30	24.60	14.90	4.00	17.30	43¢
1970	27.20	28.80	35.10	21.90	6.30	26.70	36¢
1977	37.50	39.20	40.90	39.80	12.80	52.80	73¢
1978	49.40	51.30	64.90	47.40	17.00	63.00	76¢
1979	68.10	70.80	91.90	41.30	23.80	70.10	84¢

CASH RECEIPTS AND PRICES FOR WHEAT

	Total Agric. Receipts	Receipts for Wheat	% of Total	Ave. Price Per Bushel		
				Winter Wheat	Durum	Other Spring
1950	$ 508,000,000	$ 60,000,000	12%	$1.97	$2.00	$2.04
1960	603,000,000	63,000,000	10%	1.74	1.92	1.82
1970	1,015,000,000	95,000,000	9%	1.31	1.44	1.52
1977	1,528,000,000	156,000,000	10%	2.35	2.83	2.45
1978	2,080,000,000	180,000,000	9%	2.60	2.93	2.88
1979	2,287,000,000	160,000,000	7%	3.45	4.30	3.65

South Dakota usually ranks fourth or fifth in durum and other spring wheat, lower in winter wheat production.

More soybeans and sunflowers are raised.

Wind and water erosion causes serious topsoil loss.

In this cattle state hay is important, as silage, stacked loose, in round and square bales.

Cultivating a big cornfield.

Crops

In a typical year in South Dakota more wheat is harvested than any other crop except for hay. Corn and oats are in second and third place. The other crops in this order, but with much less acreage, are: barley, soybeans, sorghum, flax, rye, sunflowers.

	ACRES
Hay	4,600,000
Wheat	3,090,000
Corn	2,560,000
Oats	2,210,000
Barley	565,000

Wheat acreage has been much the same for 30 years, but production has doubled. There has, however, been a big increase in winter wheat, some increase in durum, and a reduction in spring wheat. Cash receipts from wheat have nearly tripled in 30 years, but the percentage wheat has contributed to the total commodity income has dropped slightly.

Corn for grain acreage has dropped somewhat, but more corn is raised for silage than 30 years ago. In 1950, 3,129,000 acres were harvested for grain; 95,000 for silage. In 1979, 2,850,000 acres were harvested for grain, with 520,000 harvested for silage. In a dry year more corn goes to silage. For instance, in 1980 over one million acres were made into silage, or about double the year before, with a corresponding drop in corn for grain. Corn yields have more than doubled from 28 bushels per acre in 1950 to 35 in 1960, 41 in 1970 and 74 in 1979. In 1980, yields dropped back to 53 bushels per acre. Price has fluctuated from $1.37 per bushel in 1950, to .88 in 1960; $1.21 in 1970, and $3.05 in 1980. South Dakota ranks 9th in production of corn for grain. Leading corn counties are Minnehaha, Hutchinson, Turner, Lincoln, Brookings, Brown, Union, Lake Moody, and Spink.

South Dakota is the top oats producing state with 94,400,000 bushels raised in 1979. Leading counties are Hutchinson, Brookings, McCook, Hanson, Turner.

Barley acreage has decreased somewhat, but as with other crops, there is a yield increase. In 1950, production was 16½ bushels per acre; in 1960, 30 bushels; in 1979, 40 bushels. That year South Dakota was seventh in barley production with

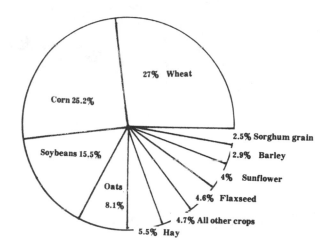

South Dakota's cash receipts for crops.

twenty million bushels. Highest barley counties are Brown, Roberts, Day, Kingsbury, Spink.

Soybean production has multiplied over ten times in the past 30 years to 780,000 acres planted in 1980. More than two and a half million bushels are harvested annually. Price has tripled from $2.41 per bushel in 1950 to $7.35 in 1980. Leading soybean counties are Lincoln, Turner, Minnehaha, Union, Clay.

Sunflowers are a relatively new crop in the United States for which the Dakotas and Minnesota have taken an early lead. South Dakota ranks third. Most sunflowers here are raised for oil with in 1979, 612,000 acres for oil and 3,000 acres of non-oil sunflowers. Total South Dakota production for 1979 was 756,300,000 pounds of sunflower seeds, a steep increase from two years before. Leading sunflower counties are Spink, Brown, Robert, Sully, Marshall.

Soil conservation is a problem throughout the state with wind and water erosion causing soil loss above tolerable limits on nearly half the cropland. This amounts to seven to fourteen tons lost annually per acre, with tolerable limits set at five tons per acre. Recent drouths have also caused some erosion loss on rangelands.

An anxious question: what's ahead for farm and ranch

Challenges For The Future

What lies ahead is an anxious question in the minds of many farm and ranch families. They do not doubt that varieties and methods will improve, that they will be producing even more in the next years.

But they are not sure they can stay ahead of the cost-price squeeze. Production costs as well as interest rates are at an all time high—and most need to operate on borrowed money. Fixed costs such as fuel, taxes, fertilizer, land leases are all on an upward spiral. Many of the high priced new machines are highly specialized, used only a few days each year, and making it expensive to change from one crop to another. Most would like more land to spread costs over larger volume, but land costs and leases have also risen steeply.

Capital investment in farming is higher than in any other business. Half a million dollars is not an unusual investment on a South Dakota farm or ranch today. Yet the returns don't always seem to justify this. As the farmer's lament goes: "You die rich. But you never have much to spend, and your kids have to go deep in debt to take over the farm."

As an example of expected returns, consider farm income in 1979, which was a good year for South Dakota agriculture. Gross income was $2,524,000,000, for an average of $66,436 per farm or ranch. But expenses were $2,329,100,000, or $61,292 each. This left a net income before adjustment of inventory of just $5,014 for each farm or ranch family. (Inventory adjust-

ment spreads expenses over higher income years to average out taxes.)

South Dakota farmers and ranchers are among the best in the world. But they often feel victimized by their own efficiency. The more they produce, it seems, the greater the surplus and the lower the price.

Producers have no control over markets. Prices for livestock and crops drop easily, are unpredictable, and bear no relationship to what production costs have been. World markets are complex, but in general the law of supply and demand works—the lower the supply, the higher the price. Yet all markets are subject to manipulation by government and private concerns. Price supports, export and import quotas and regulations, embargoes, trade deals, even labor union contracts, can affect price.

Agricultural economists at South Dakota State University say farmers and ranchers could have some difficult years ahead with record high interest rates, unstable markets, all time high operating costs. But their predictions for the future are positive. They expect a growth in world trade of more than three percent each year in oil seeds and feed grains, and one and a half percent increase in wheat. Russia, China, Japan, and Mexico will probably be big customers. They see the U.S. becoming the world's largest producer of sunflowers, with a big rise in domestic demand. Sunflowers could become a regular part of a wheat-sunflower-summer fallow rotation over much of South Dakota's winter wheat area. Rape seed, another oil producer, and dry beans will probably increase. They see a rise in forage crops and legumes used for nitrogen, with continued high prices on fertilizers. Corn will continue to be important.

Livestock emphasis will be on producing more in less time. This means higher calving percentages, larger litter sizes, heavier weaning weights, faster rates of gain, and other practices which increase the turnover rate. Economists say high interest rates mean feeders must not hold cattle, hogs, or sheep on feed longer than the optimum number of days.

They predict more livestock feedlots and processing of all foods close to where they are grown to help close the gap between raw product prices and finished product price. High

More intensive farming, better crops and, below, more finish feeding of lambs and calves.

families and their children?

transportation costs will encourage this. They expect oil seed crushing plants, alcohol plants, and more meat processing at slaughter plants, probably using the "boxed beef" concept, with products ready for retail sales.

Soil conservation will be even more important to the future, checking the wind and water erosion which is a problem throughout the state.

Irrigation will play a larger part in South Dakota agriculture, multiplying the productivity of the land. West of the Missouri, irrigation has been extensively used along river bottoms, mainly on hayland. But the Missouri River dams with their big supplies of high quality water make likely the development of large irrigation projects in the future.

Experts believe there will be less dependance on oil for energy, with more wind and solar power being used—especially here where both are abundant. Some suggest sunflower oil may be used, with 10 percent of the crop providing all the energy needed to power the farm, similar to the old custom of putting back 10 percent of the oats crop into horse power.

Transportation of farm products to market poses problems now and perhaps for the future. State leaders struggle to preserve the basic rail network; they also see needs for more central terminals and wider use of unit trains. The possibilities of barge traffic on the Missouri is under study.

High market prices must be a goal, say experts, since production costs are not likely to drop. Ranchers and farmers will become more familiar with the futures markets. Understanding and using such marketing tools, say economists, could add more than 10 percent to profits. New technology of all kinds will be used in decision making by farm and ranch families: computers, instant information, telecommunications for latest market news and production information.

Farmers and ranchers know good profits can come off their land. They know theirs are important and needed products in the world today and tomorrow. Despite the reverses which have so often come their way, most producers look to the future with optimism.

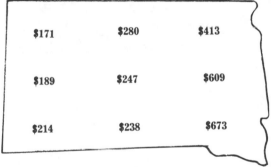

$171	$280	$413
$189	$247	$609
$214	$238	$673

Land value in the 9 crop districts, March 1981. Higher priced land is forecast.

Less reliance on the waterhole—more irrigation and pipelines.

YATES SHAFT ROSS SHAFT

CRUSHED ORE BINS

AIR EXHAUST

AIR EXHAUST

AIR IN

CAGE

CAGE

3,200 feet

4,100 feet

No. 6 SHAFT

No. 3 SHAFT

CAGE

No. 4 SHAFT

ORE POCKET

SKIP
4,850 feet

SERVICE
SHAFT

4,850

5,000 feet

SKIP

CAGE

6,200

CAGE

No. 7 SHAFT

6,800 feet

6,800 feet

SKIP

8,000 feet

8,000 feet

Homestake mine in Lead sprawls over sidehill in top photo. Below ground, simplified cross-section
shows shafts and tunnels down to 8000 feet.

9. MINERAL DEVELOPMENT

Gold has always been South Dakota's most important mineral, with rushes of excitement from time to time in the Black Hills region over silver, mica, tin, and gemstones. Oil, natural gas and uranium are potentially important for the future.

Gold mining today means Homestake, although with the high price of gold, some small family mines have also opened. Homestake produces 85 percent of U.S. gold and is the largest gold mine in the western hemisphere. Purchased by George Hearst and his partners in 1877, it became the foundation of the Hearst publishing empire.

Homestake officials say the mine has proven gold reserves of over fifteen million tons in over 8000 mining claims. Nearly 150 tons are taken annually and sold as 27 pound gold bars. In 1979 production was 250,280 ounces of gold valued at $75,084,000. It is used in industrial and electronic manufacturing as well as for gold jewelry. Three Black Hills jewelry manufacturers make the unique Black Hills gold jewelry, primarily in grapevine designs, sold throughout the United States.

Hard rock miners work Homestake's mining shafts in temperatures of 130 degrees to depths of 8000 feet—well below sea level. They break loose over one and a half million tons of ore. Twenty-car trains run below the surface in a busy underground railway system, hauling ore to the elevator shafts. All the ore is raised to the surface where it is crushed into pebbles and finally ground into powder to liberate the gold particles. Gold is separated out by several processes, one of which is cyanidation in large cyanide vats. Five tons of ore produce about an ounce of gold. Homestake employs 3000 people, hiring considerable contract work which reduces risk for the company, though unfortunately increasing it for independent workers. Hundreds more are employed in supportive industries in the Lead-Deadwood area.

Other minerals mined in this region have been silver, mica, tin, bentonite, gypsum, feldspar and manganese. Half a million dollars worth of silver is still taken out annually. But the main non-fuel minerals—other than gold, and about equalling gold in value of annual production—are sand and gravel, cement and masonry clays, and crushed and cut stone. Limestone is used extensively at the state owned cement plant in Rapid City. Red quartzite was a favorite building stone quarried in the eastern part of the state in early settlement days. Today granite is quarried near Milbank; because of its rich dark color it is much used in monuments and building stone.

Extensive exploration is going on in the state for uranium, oil and natural gas. Uranium was found near Edgemont in 1951, touching off a three year uranium rush during which more than 2000 claims were filed in that area. The boom died down, but uranium again seems potentially important for the future with several big companies involved in exploration and vying for mining permits. Company geologists have mapped out large uranium deposits in many areas of South Dakota, east of the Missouri as well as west. Protests by local citizens in regions of exploration have led to a greater awareness of possible risks. State officials insist that mining today can be controlled; new laws are more effective in making sure land is reclaimed and ground waters not disturbed. They cite as an example the regulations which have stopped Homestake's practice of dumping tailings in the creek.

Lignite coal deposits are mainly in the northwestern part of the state. In 1934, 21 coal mines operated in the area.

Oil and natural gas exploration is increasing, with several wells operating in the northwestern part of the state which is part of the Williston oil basin, extending down to Faith and Buffalo.

Stone cutting at granite quarry near Milbank.

Cyanide solution precipitates gold from ore dust in huge vats at left. At far left, miner loads ore deep underground—4,500 tons a day are brought to surface.

Sioux Falls stockyards; meat packing is big industry, promises growth.

10. BUSINESS AND INDUSTRY

South Dakota's 1980 directory of manufacturers and processors lists over 900 firms doing business in the state. Seventy-six employ more than 100 people, but most are small employing fewer than 25.

Agri-business is a big field and much manufacturing is directly aimed at serving agriculture. Equipment and supplies used by the rancher-farmer manufactured or processed here include feeds, seeds, fertilizers, agri-chemicals, fencing supplies, tools and machinery of many kinds.

At the other end of the scale is the food processing industry. Twenty meat packing and sausage plants are active, along with fifteen cheese factories, numerous creameries, poultry and egg processing, and plants for milling flour, frozen foods, baked goods, beverages and pet foods. State economists see a need for more development in this area. Vertical integration is a goal—instead of shipping raw materials to Minneapolis and other industrial centers, they urge more processing of what is raised here. This is particularly directed toward livestock, sunflowers and soybeans, but also includes other agricultural products.

The construction industry is also large and distributed throughout the state, with sawmills in the Black Hills, cement making, millwork, foundries, sheet metal work, pipe fitting, cabinet shops, mobile homes and prefabricated homes and building manufacture, furniture making for homes and offices, textile products for home and business.

Considerable commercial and newspaper printing, publishing and engraving is done in the state. Transportation equipment built here includes truck trailers, bus bodies, boats, aircraft parts. Other products include clothing, leather goods, plastics, pottery, electrical instruments, communications equipment, electronic components, surgical instruments, jewelry manufacture, sporting goods, advertising display signs.

Several movies and television shows have been filmed on location in South Dakota. Industrial development officials are encouraging more of this and presenting South Dakota as a state with nearly everything except a large metropolis. There are old towns, old trains, old mines, Indian reservations, ranches, farms, land which is flat, hilly or mountainous, with rivers, mountain streams, big lakes, wildlife, and clear air for sharp photography.

A vigorous campaign to bring in new business and industry has been waged since 1969, to help ease the state's economy and provide more jobs for young people. South Dakota's advantageous tax structure has encouraged many businesses to expand into the state. South Dakota has no corporate income tax, no personal income tax, no personal property tax, offers a tax break on new structures, and has provided 5-year tax moratoriums. Since 1969 about 60 Minnesota firms have come to South Dakota, adding 10,000 jobs.

South Dakota also claims to be the first state to view banking as industrial development. It has no ceiling on interest rates and—with interest rates soaring and consumer groups in other states forcing a clamp-down—this has encouraged New York and Minneapolis-based banks to move their credit card operations into the state.

Railroad transportation is becoming a key problem in the state. Five railroad companies now serve South Dakota. But too many unprofitable branch lines were built in settlement days, due to competition, desires for profit, and a drive to dominate settlement patterns. (Consider Milwaukee's inexplicable decision to play alternates with the north-south towns it created. As a result, Highway 12 is forever on the wrong side of the tracks, crossing no less than nine times—or every 20-30 miles—along the northern edge of the state before it overpasses into North Dakota to continue the same erratic behavior.) Today the nation's railroads face survival problems. States such as South Dakota, which need their services, are working to find effective solutions and alternatives.

Transportation is also the key to serving Asian markets from the west coast. Potential markets abound in that direction, though agriculture products have traditionally gone east to market.

Industrial development officials face such problems and are working with community leaders, present businesses within the state, and outside industry in building the state's economy. They look to the next decade as a period of expanded growth for business and industry.

Jeweler etches design on Black Hills gold ring.

Chipburning at Custer sawmill; construction business is important in state.

Aircraft parts, electronic instruments, other components for the jet age are made here.

Potter finishes bowl at Pine Ridge Pottery.

Shooting of "Orphan Train" CBS movie in Black Hills.

11. WATER

South Dakota can be severely hit by drouth, as several recent years have shown all too dramatically. Yet the state has vast water resources. Development is needed to make this supply of water usable to the people.

All plans are enormously costly, but there is renewed interest in implementing some of the possibilities long under study. They include several areas: irrigation, rural and municipal water systems, geothermal energy, industrial uses such as the coal slurry pipeline, and barge transportation proposals.

Irrigation has been the great promise held out for 50 years to the people who gave up land to the Missouri River dams, ever since Ft. Peck was built in 1932. South Dakota has 75 million acre feet of high quality water held behind four dams with a potential of irrigating more than five million acres of cropland. A proposed canal system includes irrigating in both western and eastern South Dakota, with the most concentrated system in the southeastern section.

Benefits should be higher production with higher gross income, consistently good crops without the wild swings which result from the gamble on rainfall, and increased business and industry serving the needs of more productive agriculture. For the producer it will also mean a high investment in equipment and land leveling, higher land taxes and higher priced land. Many South Dakotans are eager to get on with the plan. Congressman James Abdnor says, "We cannot further delay using our Great Missouri lakes for which we have already sacrificed a half-million acres of rich bottom land. We cannot further jeopardize future crops in a state so dependent upon agriculture. Responsibly developed irrigation holds the key to South Dakota's future prosperity."

Several irrigation projects presently operate in the state. The oldest and largest began in 1904, ditching water out of the Belle Fourche River to irrigate 54,505 acres. Smaller systems use Angostura Reservoir on the Cheyenne for 11,353 acres; Pactola Reservoir supplies 70 irrigators on Rapid Creek. About two thousand farmers and ranchers in the state now irrigate, most by individually pumping from wells or rivers.

Rural water systems for several areas are being planned. Water for domestic use has caused concern from early settlement days—especially where ground water is deep or of poor quality. One of the most ambitious proposals is the W.E.B. plan to lift Oahe water 400 feet and pipe it to nine counties in the northeastern part of the state, furnishing water to more than 3000 rural customers and 60 municipalities. Costs would be met, in part, through a conglomerate of local systems contracting for water. Rural water systems already operate in much of southeastern South Dakota.

Some of the most difficult problems with domestic water have been in the south central part of the state where wells are deep. Around Kadoka most wells are about 2600 feet; near Philip they are 3400 feet deep. This is all warm artesian water. At Kadoka a cooling tower has been used, without complete success in summer. Many ranchers rely on cisterns, hauled water and dugouts.

Geothermal heat from the deep artesian wells has been used for years in South Dakota. At Midland the school is heated with natural hot water; an early well there heated the hotel and provided hot mineral baths. Both the hotel and railroad

Irrigation holds promise for future.

depot were heated this way for years at Capa. Numerous ranches have used geothermal heat, and at Hot Springs the water breaks naturally hot from springs to keep the creek steaming all winter. Recently the U.S. Department of Energy has launched three pilot projects to study geothermal uses further. These include a Pierre hospital using 106 degree water from a 2100 foot well for heat; a ranch north of Hayes using 153 degree water for drying grain and heating buildings; schools at Philip using 170 degree water from a 4266 foot well to heat buildings, with the water being piped on to eight downtown businesses.

Industry's water needs have caused concern. Ranchers and townspeople in western South Dakota and eastern Wyoming objected when they discovered Wyoming coal company plans to pump huge amounts of ground water into a coal slurry pipeline going south into Arkansas. The water was to come from the Madison Aquifer which underlies much of western South Dakota. An alternate plan for piping water from Lake Oahe is proposed by the two states. This pipeline could also serve towns and rural water systems in the area. Officials say selling Oahe water to the coal company would give South Dakota long term rights to the water; in 50 years when it is no longer needed, it could be used for irrigation. Others caution safeguards so states at the end of the pipeline will not gain solid claims on the water through their own long use of it. They also question if the coal companies will be content with one slurry pipeline or will make additional water demands. One pipeline moving 25 million tons of coal annually would replace the need for 5000 unit train trips, more than 13 trains a day for a year, say company officials. They predict 50 trains a day could travel from the coal mines. One such coal train hauls every day 100 cars loaded with 100 tons each through South Dakota on the Milwaukee railroad to the Big Stone City electric plant.

Many experts are taking a bold look at possibilities for barge traffic on the Missouri, with the state's acute needs for transportation. They are studying ways to float a series of barges which could be emptied and reloaded at each dam. One concept is to use a closed metal container, similar to the semi-truck trailer, which could be trucked or railed to the river, and there lifted onto barges by crane. At each dam additional cranes would transfer the containers from upper barges to lower ones. This concept of a single container could include storage when needed, and would improve the quality of grain arriving at market, thus increasing the price.

Part III

History
of
South Dakota

'The history of South Dakota is closely entwined
with that of the Indian nation for which it is named'

Harry H. Anderson
DAKOTA PANORAMA

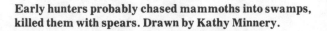

1. A LAND OF MIGRATIONS

The land we call South Dakota has been the scene of countless migrations, human movements into and out of the region, crossing and recrossing north and south, east and west. It's been the scene of changing cultures—conflicting, blending, evolving.

In some eras people came to better their condition—lured by wealth. Hunting bands raced onto open plains in pursuit of vast buffalo herds; prospectors were tempted by gold; homesteaders coveted land.

In other times, they came in retreat. Stone Age families fled glacial cold; eastern Indians came harrassed by powerful tribes; poverty-stricken Europeans escaped overpopulated lands; tough gunmen outran the law.

The open plains of Dakota offered homes and new opportunity to all. Here men and women found growing space, abundant game, rich grasses, prime farmland, gold, boom times, the unique spiritual richness that is the Black Hills.

In turn there were outward migrations. Indian tribes fled from strong hostile bands moving in, expanding their territory. Periodically drouth came. Migrating game and nourishing grasses vanished; corn withered on the stalk; boom towns died; mortgages foreclosed; hard times fell. For the miner the illusive vein of gold ran out. Today, young people search out higher salaries in another place; retirees are drawn to Arizona winters.

Human migrations across Dakota began more than ten thousand years ago and are not yet finished.

A bridge—when Oceans Fell

One of the ancient mysteries is how and when people first came into the new world.

Anthropologists believe they crossed the Bering land bridge into Alaska during the glacial ages. Typical glaciers, lasting 40,000 to 60,000 years, sucked up so much water into ice that the oceans fell 300 feet and more. This lowering of oceans exposed a 1000-mile-wide strip of land connecting Asia with Alaska.

Across this bridge traveled the big mammals. Horses and camels which originated in America, worked their way west into Asia—and later became extinct here. From Asia eastward came elephants, bison, deer, bear. Asian hunting bands followed these herds and eventually swept through two continents, populating both North and South America.

Then the ice melted. The oceans rose and flooded the bridge.

The so-called second migration across the Bering land bridge ended about 10,000 years ago—following the melt of the last ice age. Scientists speculate that a first migration came much earlier than that. Ancient scrapers and chopping tools found from the Arctic to Argentina are tentatively dated as early as 40,000 B.C.

Eskimo ancestry apparently awaited development of boat travel, more thousands of years, to come to the new world.

They hunted Wooly Mammoths

Stone Age men and women hunted big Ice Age mammals in South Dakota—wooly mammoths, giant ground sloths, arctic musk oxen. They butchered and dressed them with sharpened stone tools. Then about 10,000 years ago, these animals became extinct—perhaps in part because of the hunters' success.

Earliest evidence that these people, called Paloindians, lived in South Dakota are the Folsom points—stone spearheads—found in a few places including in Hyde and Tripp counties.

From a later time comes the oldest camp site find, dated about 8000 B.C. This is the Ray Long site south of the Black Hills. Found here were bison hunting tools, spearheads, scrapers, drills, and stones shaped for grinding as well as small circular hearths. Other sites and articles from this age have been found through the state, showing that these people ranged widely. They were probably nomadic and hunted in small family bands, living hand-to-mouth.

They killed the big mammals with spears, perhaps stalking and ambushing at waterholes.

In the later part of this period the large game began disappearing, and the smaller buffalo similar to ours were the major game. Hunters learned to use the buffalo jump, stampeding them off cliffs.

Archaic Foragers, the second culture, developed from the earlier Paloindian people. About 6000 B.C. climate changes brought hot dry weather and scarcity of game. Instead of living on the meat of big game, these people turned to a diet high in fish, plants and small animals. Reminders of the Archaic Foragers are found in several places, especially near the Black Hills and along the Missouri River, dated between 3000 B.C. and 1000 B.C. Still nomadic, still hunting in small family bands, these foragers had tools for dressing hides—scraping tools and bone awls—and were probably using hides for clothing, containers and shelter. Stone weights are evidence they probably had developed the spear thrower for hunting.

The third development came when Woodland people moved in from the east about 1 A.D., bringing with them traditions of stable communities and more reliance on farming. From this influence, evolving and blending with what was here, came what is known as the Plains Woodland tradition. These people left hundreds of domed burial mounds throughout eastern South Dakota. The largest mounds are some 50 or 60 feet across and three or four feet high. Some mounds are in clusters of as many as 50. Inside, one or more persons were buried; a Yankton mound held the remains of 16 individuals plus fragments of pottery, tools and weapons. Numerous camp or kill sites made by these people are found throughout eastern South Dakota, along the Missouri and around the Black Hills. Most lived along river bottoms and began to grow crops and make several kinds of pottery. In western South Dakota the Plains Woodland people apparently did not build mounds.

The fourth and last of the prehistory cultures, according to evidence uncovered, were the Plains Villagers. Again there seemed to be a movement of outsiders into the area to mix with cultures already here, this time from the Mississippi regions about 900 A.D. Large permanent settlements were now built with rectangular earth lodges, partly underground. Near Chamberlain four rectangular houses were excavated in a village of about 30 houses. Cache pits were found both in the floors of homes and outside, 6 feet deep, containing corn stalks and squash seeds. Other items found at South Dakota Plains

Village sites are central firepits, pottery with simple decorations, many kinds of tools and weapons, a bone bird whistle, ornaments, game disks and balls. Most villages were built near steep riverbanks such as the Brandon site on a flat ridge above the Big Sioux River near Sioux Falls. They were fortified with deep trenches and sometimes palisades on the open side away from the river. The people raised a variety of crops, principally corn.

Many such villages were located in the Big Bend region. One of these was the ill-fated Crow Creek, largest massacre site ever found in North America.

In historic times the Plains Villagers who became the Arikara lived along the Missouri River and its tributaries. Also called the Rickarees, or Rees, they expanded into a powerful and prosperous people. The golden age for the Arikara lasted into the mid-1700s. Then under pressure from the Sioux, who became increasingly more powerful, they began to draw together into larger, fewer villages.

MASSACRE AT CROW CREEK
1325 A.D.

Crow Creek was a progressive farming village located on the bluffs above the Missouri River. In the year 1325 about 1200 people lived there in 55 large earthern homes. Steep river banks protected the town from below, and across the open area, men had dug a deep trench and partly completed a wall of poles, brush and packed dirt.

In good times the villagers lived well. The women raised corn, squash, beans and sunflowers on rich bottomlands below. They stored winter supplies in deep cache pits in the ground both inside and outside their homes. Men hunted buffalo, elk, deer and antelope—without horses, but with bows and arrows and spears.

But these were not good times for the people of Crow Creek. Drouth was widespread and continued for a series of years. Corn shriveled in parched ground, producing little. Wild game moved off to better grasslands. Mothers and fathers starved and the growth of their children was stunted.

Crow Creek was not the only town on the bluffs above the Missouri. At least ten other villages were spaced out within 60 miles, with perhaps a total population of 10,000 people.

Powerful enemies were at hand. It's not clear who they were: Did neighboring towns make war on each other in competition for food and farmland in this time of drouth? Did fierce nomadic bands sweep down periodically off the plains to attack towns? Did new farming groups seek to move into the area, driving out those who were here? These questions are not answered yet, but it's clear the enemies were strong enough to amass a large force.

The attack on Crow Creek came without warning, perhaps at daybreak. Enemy warriors stormed the trenches and swept through the town—killing, looting, burning. They slaughtered more than 500 people, scalping with stone knives, hacking off heads, legs, arms, hands and feet. They took many captives that day—small children and young women. Others probably escaped down the river banks.

When the slaughter was over, the victorious army left burning homes and bloody carnage behind. Wolves, coyotes, perhaps even village dogs moved in, gnawing at the bones and eating their fill.

At dawn the enemy stormed across the trenches. By Martin Wanserski.

Days later—or perhaps it was weeks or months—someone returned to the scene. They carried the body parts of nearly 500 people into the trench and buried them there in a mass grave. Centuries passed and the trench blew level with dust and sand in some places. The village of Crow Creek vanished and the massacre was forgotten.

In the 1950's Crow Creek was excavated. Archaeologists wondered at the burned out lodges; they found a few human bones, but no hint of massacre.

Then in 1978—in one of those chance discoveries which make archaeology so fascinating—a few human bones were exposed by the falling riverbank. Erosion of the bluff had reached the bodies buried at the end of the trench. Researchers from the University of South Dakota Archaeology Lab began to dig in August, uncovering the bones from the top so soil layers could be studied. They were stunned by what they found. They had expected a burial of perhaps a dozen bodies. Instead, bones were everywhere as they uncovered what was to be America's largest known prehistoric massacre site.

On hand were archaeologists Larry Zimmerman and Richard Whitten, who wrote: "When we reach the bone bed, we see what a mammoth job lies ahead. We enlarge the excavation and then enlarge it again. The final dimensions are almost 25 feet by more than 12 feet. The floor of the pit—the old ditch—is 12 to 15 feet below ground level...At the deepest point, there are some three solid feet of human bone...The mass of bones is an enormous, confused jigsaw puzzle. No entire skeletons are present, just parts—odd pieces jumbled together." [1]

The discovery is changing the entire interpretation with which anthropologists study the Plains Village people. Says Zimmerman, "We were all pretty much overwhelmed by what we saw during the dig. The enormity of the tragedy that occurred at the village hasn't really 'sunk in' even yet."

The grim picture became more clear as the pieces were photographed, removed, recorded, studied—all with exacting care. Most of the people had been scalped; skulls bore long marks at the hairline from stone knives. Many long bones were cut through at the joints; hands and feet were severed by sharp instruments and perhaps taken as trophies,

as most were missing. Not many bones were found from young children or women between the ages of 12 and 19, indicating they were probably taken captives. Gnawing marks on the bones showed they had been chewed by carnivores before burial.

The bones produced much data about the way the Crow Creek people lived, their diet and their state of health. The bones told, too often, a sad tale of food deficiencies.

Many other questions remain. Crow Creek was probably not the only village in the area burned to the ground and abandoned in haste, as more recent discoveries suggest. A pattern of warfare is plain. The defenders were probably ancestors of the Arikara; perhaps the attackers were, too. (Sioux did not come into the area until after 1700.) Another question tantalizes: Who buried the 500 victims of the Crow Creek massacre? Did survivors return to honor their loved ones in death? Was it neighboring townspeople, doing the proper honors or perhaps irked by odor and behavior of predators? Or was it the marauders themselves, putting to rest malevolent spirits which troubled them? Excavation of other sites could bring further answers.

Archaeologists today are careful to respect the human remains they examine. When laboratory study is complete, the bones will be returned for reburial near the original site.

Scientists at the U.S.D. Archaeology Lab lament the work of looters who beat them to the Crow Creek dig—destroying invaluable evidence by carelessly chopping exposed bones from the bank in an apparent search for arrowheads. They urge all Dakotans to help preserve their heritage by reporting possible sites—rather than digging and destroying them. South Dakota archaeological sites are disappearing at an alarming rate—from flooding, plowing, mining, and other disruptions. They need to be identified before it is too late. Interested amateurs may become certified site surveyors.

1. Smithsonian Vol. II Sept. '80

Bones of 500 men, women and children lie buried in mass grave—no complete skeletons found.

2. LIFE OF THE SIOUX

Painted horses decorate Sioux tepees at Standing Rock

Sioux tribes were highly organized into clans, or extended family groupings. Several clans often camped together in bands of two or three hundred. Only on special occasions such as a buffalo hunt, trading fairs, or the annual Sun Dance, did an entire subtribe numbering in the thousands come together.

The clan was a close-knit family group. Children did not lack for attention from the several uncles they called "Father," and the various aunts called "Mother." They knew they belonged; they learned to share and to be loyal to each member of the clan.

Generosity was emphasized among the Sioux. Food was shared; homes were open and hospitable. Relatives in need -- and even strangers -- were not refused. A home though already filled, simply opened wider. A scout living with the Sioux in the early seventies said he had never found more kindness, charity and brotherhood anywhere than with the Sioux. A man could never grow rich, it was said, because he gave away what he had. Upon death, his property was given away -- so children did not inherit material wealth.

A young man did not want to accumulate wealth and be thought of by clansmen as selfish, stingy and cowardly. Instead he gained in status as he could bring glory and benefit to the entire tribe. The daring raids and war parties he rode with were partly a defensive action to keep the enemy off balance and out of the territory. If he killed an enemy or stole a band of his horses, it was regarded as honorable. It strengthened his tribe and weakened the enemy.

But in the tribe peaceful relations were important. Killing a tribal member was a dread crime; lying was disgraceful; theft was virtually unknown. When such crimes were committed, justice didn't take the European form of "getting even" by injuring the criminal. Instead it focused on helping the victim. The guilty person or his relatives were required -- by public opinion -- to make suitable restitution. Stolen property was returned with gifts. Personal injury was eased with gifts of horses or other items of value. In the case of murder, if suitable restitution could not be made to the family, the murderer might be banished from the tribe. This was severe punishment as it meant the near-impossible -- living alone on the plains -- unless some other tribe took in the murderer.

Chiefs kept the Peace

Sioux were governed in democratic ways. The clan was led by one or more chiefs respected for their deeds and wisdom. These influencial men, with leaders of other clans, sat together in council. They did not make absolute decisions, but rather came to a concensus of opinion on matters before them. This consensus was then transmitted to the people by their leaders, who were free individually to follow an agreed-upon course of action, or another which suited them better. Chiefs of the various clans acted mainly as peacemakers and advisors, not as rulers.

Thus, no single chief ruled in the European sense. (This caused a great deal of confusion and misunderstanding when whites sought a "Head Chief" to sign legal treaties binding an entire tribe.)

Personal freedom was, however, curbed by public opinion. Children and others who misbehaved were shamed, teased, and made miserable until they conformed. Private ambitions were effectively checked in this way.

A Harmony with the Land

The Sioux reverenced all aspects of nature and lived in close harmony with the land. Ohiyesa, a Santee Sioux, explained this religious harmony:

> Whenever, in the course of the daily hunt the red hunter comes upon a scene that is strikingly beautiful or sublime -- a black thundercloud with the rainbow's glowing arch above the mountain; a white waterfall in the heart of a green gorge; a vast prairie tinged with the blood-red of sunset -- he pauses for an instant in the attitude of worship. He sees no need for setting apart one day in seven as a holy day, since to him all days are God's. [1]

The Sioux spoke of living things as the two-leggeds, the four-leggeds and the wingeds. All had life and were to be treated as fellow beings, even when it was necessary to kill them. Plants, trees, and natural features of the land also had life and spirituality, as did Mother Earth from which all life emerged.

The Sun Dance

Religion took simple, everyday forms. But it could also involve complex ceremonials. The climax of these ceremonials was the Sun Dance. A time of fasting and prayer, the Sun Dance lasted several days and nights, usually during the summer buffalo hunt when an entire tribe might camp together. Individuals took part as they desired, fulfilling personal vows, asking help, giving thanks, sharing in the renewal of tribal strength.

The Sun Dance was called, in the Sioux tongue, the "Sun-Gazing Dance." Dancers faced the sun and the sacred cottonwood tree which represented the Supreme Being, gazing at the sun and the center pole offerings. They took no food or water. Some cut the flesh of back or chest, thrust wooden skewers through the cuts and tied themselves by these to the center pole, dancing and pulling on the ropes till the skin tore loose. Chased-by-Bears, a Santee-Yanktonai who died in 1915, explained why:

> The cutting of the bodies in fulfillment of a Sun dance vow is different from the cutting of the flesh when people are in sorrow. A man's body is his own, and when he gives his body or his flesh he is giving the only thing which really belongs to him ... Thus, if a man says he will give a horse to Wakan Tanka (the Supreme Being), he is only giving that which already belongs to him ... I must give something that I really value to show that my whole being goes with the lesser gifts; therefore I promise to give my body. 2

Indian women hauled goods by horse and dog travois

During ceremonies the sacred pipe was smoked, being first st offered to the sky, Mother Earth, and four directions -- east for peace and light, south for warmth, west which gave rain, north from which came strength and endurance. Typical Plains music was sung and played. This was especially well developed by the Sioux and included drumbeats and singing with pulsation and vocal tension.

'Everything tries to be round'

The circle had special significance to the Sioux. It was the symbol of eternity, of renewal and continuity of life. In large tribal encampments, each band formed its own circle and each circle had a proper place in camp. Black Elk, an Oglala born in 1863, explained that the Supreme Being always works in circles:

> Everything tries to be round. The sky is round and I have heard that the earth is round like a ball and so are all the stars ... Birds make their nests in circles, for theirs is the same religion as ours. The sun comes forth and goes down again in a circle. The moon does the same, and both are round. Even the seasons form a great circle in their changing, and always come back again to where they were. 3

The Black Hills and other special landmarks were sacred to the Sioux. Here they sought visions and direct renewal of strength from the Great Spirit. Men who had visions and gifts of prophecy had great influence and honor. Young boys learned early to seek this spiritual contact. According to Philip Deloria, the Yankton chief converted to Christianity in the 1860's, a boy was taken by his father to a high hill. An offering of food and other gifts wrapped in a cloth was spread on the ground.

> ...its four corners towards the four points from which the wind came and the offering was presented. The boy was obliged to remain in this place, without food or drink, for two days and two nights; and sometimes twice as long. Perhaps he would become so weary that he would lie down a few moments upon the sage brush; but he was supposed to stand all the time, and to call without ceasing upon the Great Spirit to help him. During such a prolonged fast, he was likely to see a vision. 4

The more menial tasks, believed to be less important, less adventuresome, less dangerous, fell to Sioux women and girls as they have in countless other cultures. Division of labor by sex was strict. Men were not to demean themselves by doing "woman's work."

Women Broke Camp

For a Sioux woman, work was truly never done. She cut wood, carried water, gathered wild plants and roots, prepared food, preserved and dried meat, cared for small children, tanned hides, made buckskin garments and the tepee in which the family lived. She grew skilled at beading and trimming with

porcupine quills and feathers. When it came time to break camp, again this was woman's work. She dismantled the tepee, saddled horses, loaded provisions and carried everything to the new location -- where she set up camp. Since a wife's work was hard, parents of a first wife might suggest a sister go to share the burden, thus becoming a second wife. Other wives might be added as time went by. When dissatisfied, wives did have the freedom to leave their husbands and return home, or remarry.

Hunting and fighting were men's work, providing two essentials -- meat and protection. On the march warrior society braves policed the long moving column, hurrying stragglers from dangerous draws and canyons. Other men scouted far to the sides and in advance, alert for enemies. Men needed to be ready to fight, it was deemed, unencumbered with laborous details of moving the enormous amounts of goods.

Cooking in camp by Rosebud creek

As they gained in power on Dakota's plains, the Sioux became known as bold and fierce warriors. Raiding parties ranged wide. The Ojibwa, who had once helped to drive them from Minnesota forests, came to fear them. An Ojibwa chief explained Sioux tactics and strength in 1789:

> While they keep to the Plains with their Horses we are no match for them; for we being footmen, they could get to windward of us, and set fire to the grass; when we marched for the Woods, they would be there before us, dismount, and under cover fire on us. Until we have Horses like them, we must keep to the Woods and leave the Plains to them.

Sioux raiding parties also threatened the walled villages of the Arikara, as well as those of the Mandans and Hidatsa farther north. They raided the villages and fields, yet at times came to trade peaceably. Raiding was a common way of acquiring horses and prestige. A young brave who led a war party successfully, stealing horses without loss of life, earned high honor. A war chief did not command; other braves followed voluntarily, even joyfully, when they trusted his ability and vision. In skirmishes, Sioux warriors fought freely on their own responsibility, trusting others to do the same.

A warrior gained prestige through his courageous exploits. Chief among these daring deeds was "counting coup." This meant being first to touch an enemy, alive or dead. A warrior might simply ride daringly into an enemy camp, touch someone and gallop off again, without hurting anyone. Coup could be counted as many as three times on the same enemy, the initial coup being the greatest. Counting coup was so important that even if someone else killed the enemy, there was a great scramble to be first to touch him. In the confusion of battle it was often unclear who deserved coup honors. Disputes were settled as quickly as possible so a warrior could add the coup to his honors to be recounted during ceremonies.

The Buffalo Hunt

Both buffalo and horses were vital to the Sioux way of life on the open plains. They hunted buffalo at first on foot by such methods as the buffalo jump and the surround. In the buffalo jump, a high steep cliff was necessary. In the surround, a kind of corral was built, preferably in a narrow canyon. The buffalo were directed toward these places of slaughter by braves springing out of hiding with flapping buffalo robes. Another method was to set the grass afire. Still another was to catch and hobble a buffalo calf, then let it jump after the herd. Instead of stampeding, the herd might stand in the calf's defense, cows and calves to the inside and bulls bellowing and pawing at the outer circle. These methods required careful timing and luck.

With horses buffalo hunting was much easier. The tribe could range farther in search of migrating herds. The great northern herd was one of four enormous buffalo herds that ranged from Texas into Canada, migrating together in spring and fall, then breaking into smaller bunches to feed on summer or winter ranges. These herds numbered 50,000,000 to 100,000,000 at the time of Columbus, according to estimates. With horses the hunters could attack from several directions, surround a small herd, and catch up with fleeing buffalo.

A large encampment of Indians, well-mounted and armed with guns, might kill two or three thousand buffalo in a day, feast and prepare meat the second day, then hunt again on the third. Success meant celebration and feasting. Delicacies such as organ meats and other choice parts were eaten on the spot.

Much meat was preserved immediately. Deftly the women cut it from the carcass in large thin sheets and hung it over sticks and pole racks to dry. When dry this meat, or jerky, was light and easy to store or carry. For pemmican the jerky was broken, or ground with berries, and mixed with hot tallow. The mixture was poured hot into stomach paunches or hide sacks where it cooled and hardened. Pemmican could be stored for years.   A winter's supply was hidden in caches. The cache was made by digging a large jug-shaped hole, as deep as 8 feet. Lined with buffalo hide and filled to the top, the cache was then covered over carefully with earth and brush so it was well hidden. Even uncured backs wrapped tightly in hides, and parts of carcasses, were cached and kept well for months, according to reports. (Both caches and pemmican were widely used by white fur traders when they learned the methods.)

Buffalo provided the Sioux with the means to a good life. Besides a year-around food supply, buffalo meant warm clothing, moccasins, and bedding. The hide was used for tepee coverings, bullboats, shields, saddles, bags, drums, halters and harness, braided ropes. Strong sinews made sewing thread and bowstrings. Bones and horns became digging tools,

Sioux winter count recorded a major event for each year. Pipe meant celebration; person with spots meant deaths from disease like smallpox; man with hat was always a white man.

spoons, needles, ornaments. The buffalo paunch was used to carry water and, with hot stones dropped into the water, for cooking meat.

A good buffalo hunt brought not only comfortable supplies for winter -- but also a rich exchange at the trading fair. Buffalo hides and robes, cured by the women, were prime items for trading.

Major trading fairs were held annually at two South Dakota sites, one near the Black Hills, the other on the James River. Here old enemies met peaceably to bargain for goods which might have come halfway across a continent. Shell ornaments from the Pacific were exchanged for Minnesota pipestones or Wyoming obsidian for making tools. Horses, guns, knives and iron kettles circulated at Indian trading fairs long before white traders entered the region. Horses stimulated this trade by providing easy mobility.

Sign language, the universal language of the plains, was widely used in trading. It was a simple but effective means of communication. Cold was shown by clenching both hands, crossing the arms over the chest, trembling. A chief was depicted by raising the forefinger, pointing it straight up, then reversing and bringing it down. Rain or snow was shown with hands at the level of the shoulders, palm down and fingers hanging down, then pushing hands downward.

Using this system a person could tell, or be entertained by, long stories. Bargaining details were carried on readily. War deeds and tribal history could be recounted.

Storytelling—A fine Art

Storytelling was a fine art among the Sioux. An early observer noted that, though a man may seem habitually grave and reserved with strangers, "he will talk himself wild with excitement, vaunting his exploits in life, war, or the chase, and will commit all sorts of extravagances while telling or listening to an exciting story." Through storytelling the young were instructed in ancient ways. Legends were handed down by elderly sages; history was kept alive. Stories were told, too, for pure entertainment. The mischievous Iktomi, who is sometimes a spider-man, figures in many Sioux stories.

The Sun Dance—a time of fasting and prayer, fulfilling of vows and renewal of tribal strength. A Catlin print.

A Woman Kills her Husband's Slayer

1. A man and his wife camped out alone while he was deer-hunting, and each day he would bring home some game, and then go off again, while his wife busied herself preparing the meat for preserving. He had just left her with more meat to care for, and gone away; so she was preparing it. But it was getting dark now; so she was covering things up and leaving them for the night, when she heard her husband unloading something, perhaps a deer that fell to the ground with a thud, on the other side of the tipi. 2. "Well, he must be home already", she thought and went around the tipi and saw him unloading so much fresh meat that she hastened to help him and chatted over nothing as she worked, but he never said a word. "Something must be disturbing him; he never was like this before. He always came home in such gay spirits," she thought; yet dreading to question him and perhaps irritate him further, she refrained from saying anything. 3. Moreover, she could not see his face; for it was now dark. So pretending she did not realize that he was not feeling like himself, she took off his moccasins, and was inwardly shocked to find the big toe missing on one foot. She gave him food which he ate hurriedly; and on finishing, he slid the dish at her without a single word. So she wiped her dish and set it away, talking all the while, and then went outside. 4. Out there she took up the task of arranging the new meat for the night, when she heard him snoring, evidently having lain down as soon as she went out. So she tiptoed in and looked at him, stretched out flat on his back, asleep. She knew now, of course, that this was not her husband, so she hastily sharpened a knife in secret and entered the tipi with it. She pretended to put the room in order, and worked with something for a minute, but that did not disturb him; so then she placed the knife against the farther side of his throat in an upright position, and quickly drew it towards her, cutting him deeply. In his sleep, he choked and gasped and then that was it. 5. Her heart beat furiously as she started out in the darkness of night and arrived breathless at the tribal camp. Immediately several men hurried out to the place in the wilderness where her tipi was, and on arriving, they lighted the tipi, and found a Crow Indian with ugly features, lying dead; there was great confusion for a few minutes while they all scrambled over the order of counting coup.1. 6. When morning came, they looked about and found the woman's husband lying dead a little distance away. As he was coming home with his day's killing the Crow evidently had slain him, taken his clothes and was wearing them. The woman he tried to trick tricked him and thus he lay, pitiable, in death.

1. Wicasa wa tawicu kicila manil tate tipi yuka talo agli nasna ake iyaya ca koha tawicu ki wakab.laha ke. Ake wana tokiyota iyaye ceyas heceya talo ota agli na iyaya cake tawicu ki hena kicayaha ke. Keyas wana htaiyakpaza cake ecekce akahpa egnakahe cu lehal wana ake hig.naku ku gliyelaka tiakotaha taku sliyela glihpeya ke. 2. Hinu tuwenigli huse,—eci natiaohomni iyaya yuka talo asukyela yuhpaha cake okiya iyakina wokiyak ska keyas ayuptesni ke. — Tokeske taku iyokipisni sece le. Tuwenis lececasni ku. Tohal ku cas woglaglak wihahaya gliyake sa ku, — eci keyas akes wiyuh aye ciha sap iyokipisniyikta-kokipa cake hehayela takeyesnike. 3. Naku ite wayakaohihisni, eci wana oiyokpaza cake he u. Hecetukeseekesni ki ab.lesesni-kus hapa kiciyuslakaha yuka sisani sipahuka wanica cake hehal iyota nihiciya ke. Woku yuka sicawaciwoti na taku eyesni waksica ki pasloha iyekciciya cake woglaglak kpakiti na mahel iyekiyi na takal ina pe. 4. Heciya ake talo ki ecekce egnakaha yuka lena wana iyuka huse itap gopaha cake nasla slal yi na aokasi yuka itukapyela hpayi na lila istima ke. Hecena wanas he hignaku ki esni ca slolkiya cake inahma se mila wa oglikiyi na yuha tima iyayi na wapikiyekus taku okuwa keyas ecacasisti ma cake lote isap agle yuzi na waksa ahiyu ke. Hecena ustima-ona gloglo na hehaya taku nisni. 5. Hecu na hehal lila cate iyapa cake inapi na wicotikakiya hahepioi yokpaze ceyas iyakahi na niyasnisni kihuni ske. Cake wicasa tona wacak manil ti ku hecetkiya natapi na el ihunipi na aozazayapi yuka Kagi wicasa ca ite ki silyela ta hpaya cake tok akinicapi ske. 6. wana apa aya ca tiwoksa atuwapi yuka wiya ki hignaku ku he kiyela ta hpaya ke. Ku hal iyahpayi na kte na tahayapi ki u na wagli keyapi. Wiya wa gnayewaci keyas iye eha gnaya cake usiya hpaya ske.

Ella Deloria
DAKOTA TEXTS

A Woman Joins her Lover in Death

1. There was a big hill, a butte, where years ago a warparty was held at bay till all the members died; and none escaped, they say. And it was there that the people stopped, on a journey, and stood looking for a suitable place to make camp, when this, which I am about to relate, took place. 2. At the foot of that butte, there was already a camp; and this group came to it and stopped, when a woman, her shawl pulled up over her head, started to sing. "There was a man I loved, alas. Can it be that I shall see him again?" With such words she stood on the hilltop, singing. 3. As the tribe fixed their attention singly on her, she started taking dancing steps backwards, and allowed herself to fall headlong over the cliff, landing, all bruised and broken, among the rocks below. She was dead. 4. So they took up her body and carried it to her tipi, but her husband, evidently jealous, did not so much as weep a tear; but said, instead, "No, do not bring her here. Take her back, she has announced that she loved him; so let her rot with him!" so they could not enter her tipi with her body. 5. Instead they took it back and left it where she fell. And they came away. So there, with him, who from all appearances was her lover, she mingled her bones, and they together in time became as dust, just as she desired in her song. 6. Then a crier went around announcing a removal of the camp. It was according to the magistrates' decision. They said, "There is no other way; we cannot stay here. We must move from this spot where such a foul deed has taken place." So, in spite of the fact that camp had just been made, they all packed in haste and moved away that same evening.

1. Paha wa taka hel ehani ozuye wa yeayewicayapi na aog.lutewicayapi cake wazini nisni iyahahci hena tapi ske. Yuka heta ca oÿate ki iglaka ayi na owakiwayak enazi cake kmu se lececa yuka ecal le ob.lakikte cile hecetu ske. 2 He paha ki ohlate ehatawicoti cake hakap lena ig.laka enazi hcehal ugna wiya wasina pamahel icomina olowa wa yawakal eyayi na — Eca wicasa wa tewahila ku, leya waweg.lakikta huse!. — eyawooazeyalya lowa pahaakal nazi ske. 3. Oyate ki ataya ekta etuwapi hcehal uzihektakta wacici hiyayi na maya ki ekta ohihpayeiciyi na ohlate iguga ota cake heciya kahlehlel g.lohpaya ca ta ske. 4. Cake taca ki icupi na ti ki ekta akipi yuka hig.naku ki atayas ceyesni ecal nawizi sake heya ske, — Hiya, lel aupisni lo. Ekta aya po he tehila keya ca kici kes atakuniktesni ye lo, — eya cake ti ki el ayapisni ske. 5. E e hektakiya ayapi na hel hihpa ya cake el ake eupapi ske. Hesupl na Ihpeya g.licupi cake hena tawicasa sece u kici hohu icicahiya atakunisni ske hecel ci keyalowa ku og.naya. 6. Hehal eyapaha wa hiyayi na ig.lakwicasi ske. Wakicuza ki hena epi ca iyukcapi ki og.naya. Heyapi ske. — Ho, takom.ni lena tipicasni ye lo Lel wicoha sica wa yaka ca ukig.lakapikte lo, — eyapi cake kitahcis ewicoti na tig.lah ko yustapi ku iyuha ig.lakapi na htayetu hake yela ataya tokel iyayapi ske.

Ella Deloria
DAKOTA TEXTS

Sioux burial scaffold.

3. EUROPEAN INVASION

The Indians living in harmony with the land, did not seek to own it. But when Europeans touched American shore they were quick to plant flags and establish sovereignty. The ultimate in this acquisitiveness had to be Balboa's claim, as he strode into the Pacific, that the Pacific ocean and all it touched belonged to Spain. In like manner, La Salle in 1682 claimed for France all lands drained by the Mississippi River. This strengthened French claims made ten years earlier in the upper Mississippi regions, including all of what is South Dakota except the northeastern corner -- which drains north. France also claimed Hudson Bay and all the lands draining into it, including the Red River Valley and that northeastern corner; but by 1713 France had to surrender this to England. Spain later gained control of the Mississippi. So this region changed ownership several times: it was French, English, Spanish, French again, and was finally purchased by the United States.

France and England both carried on aggressive fur trade here. Their traders were most likely the first white men to come into what is now South Dakota. First may have been three traders with Duluth who were sent west of Lake Mille Lacs in 1679 with a Sioux war party. Or traders under Pierre Charles Le Sueur visiting the Big Sioux Valley after 1683 may have been first. By 1700 French maps began to show clear details of eastern South Dakota rivers and Indian villages.

The first to record their travels here were the La Verendrye brothers, Louis-Joseph and Francois, sons of the noted French trader and explorer. Like their father, these brothers were in search of a waterway or easy route to the Pacific. Earlier they visited Mandan villages north of the present site of Bismarck. This second journey, lasting 15 months, took them again to the Mandans, then off to the southwest. On New Years Day, 1743, they sighted forested mountains. These were likely the Black Hills, but could have been Wyoming's Big Horn Mountains.

The La Verendrye party then returned east to the Missouri River. Here they stayed with a band of Indians for several weeks and secretly buried a lead plate on a high hill. Louis-Joseph wrote of this in his journal:

> I placed on an eminence near the fort a tablet of lead, with the arms and inscription of the King and a pyramid of stones for Monsieur le General; I said to the savages, who did not know of the tablet of lead that I had placed in the earth, that I was placing these stones as a memorial of those who had come to their country. I had very much wished to take the altitude of this place but our astrolabe had been out of service since the beginning of our journey, the ring being broken.

The location of the secretly-buried plate remained a mystery for nearly 200 years. It was not until a February day in 1913, that Hattie Foster while out hiking, kicked it out of the dirt on a hill near her home in Ft. Pierre. Fortunately the small plate of such historic significance found its way to the South Dakota Historical Society, instead of being melted down and sold for "about five cents," as was discussed by the young people with Hattie. It may be seen in Pierre, just across the river from where Louis-Joseph originally buried it.

In 1763, France ceded her western Mississippi River possessions to Spain. For the next forty years, this area was

EUROPEAN CLAIMS IN NORTH AMERICA 1700

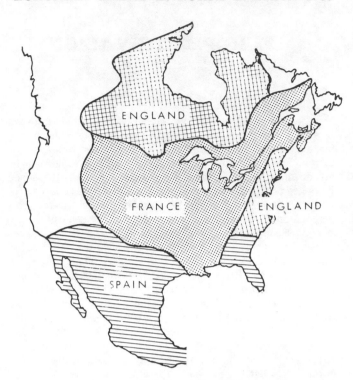

'They claim this mother of ours, the earth, and fence their neighbors away; they deface her with their buildings and their refuse ... we cannot dwell side by side.'

Sitting Bull

under Spanish control, though continually threatened by England. English traded freely here, many of their traders being Frenchmen who continued the same as when France had control of the Hudson Bay trade.

The first two permanent white settlers in what is now South Dakota were both French: Pierre Dorion and Joseph Garreau. Dorion had lived with the Yankton Sioux for 20 years by the time he met Lewis and Clark in 1804. Garreau settled among the Arikara in 1792. Both have many descendants living in South Dakota.

The Spanish formed a fur trading company to take decisive control. They hired Jean Truteau to establish trading relations with tribes on the upper Missouri. He was not very successful and his journal tells eloquently of his many difficulties and frustrations. Truteau left St. Louis in June 1794 by boat with eight men and spent the next two years trying to establish trade with the Sioux and the Arikara villages at the mouth of the Grand River.

Most Dangerous stretch of River

Truteau soon found, as did every trader to follow, that hostile Indians made this the most dangerous stretch on the Missouri. A trader going up the river had to run this gauntlet through what is now South Dakota, both on his trip upriver and on his return. Here he risked losing furs, trading goods, and his very life.

Truteau describes the situation vividly when he met a large band of Teton Sioux just above the mouth of the White River. They followed along the banks, refusing to let him go farther. "Just like a pack of wolves following a buck as he is about to land in order to devour him," lamented Truteau, as the Tetons waded out into the river and pulled his boat to shallow water.

He told them he was taking trading goods to the Arikaras and they should come there to trade.

> They replied ... that we French did very wrong to carry powder and balls to the Arikaras. That this powder would be used to kill the Sioux. That the French who had already been to the home of the Arikaras were bad French, always talking evil against them, and exciting the Arikaras to kill them ...
>
> They demanded some powder and balls in order to go on the hunt the next day, promising to give us the meat. I gave it to them. They wished to borrow all the guns of my men who let them take three ... They saw a great pirogue loaded with merchandise which it would be easy to seize through violence ... It was necessary not to rebuke them harshly. The night had come, they all assembled around our fire. My men lay down in the pirogue and kept a good guard ...
>
> The one (Yankton Sioux) who had spoken for me took me into his lodge where he caused me to eat. He told me that the Tetons were bad men; that he feared much for me and my Frenchmen; that there were so few of their nation that they (Yanktons) feared they would kill them. I encouraged him to help me in this occasion. He promised that he would do his very best, but he told me that the French would open up the bad road by giving presents, that this was the only means to pacify the Tetons, all of whom had a bad heart. 5

Eventually the Yankton Sioux did help. They urged him to give presents to each person -- men, women, children. Truteau named off his gifts sadly, "little and big knives, awls, combs, vermillion and other gifts of all kinds. I was in despair from such profusion." Later he gave more, "7 or 8 ells of cloth, a barrel of powder, balls in proportion, four carrots of tobacco, two packets of knives containing two dozen each, four white blankets, four pickaxes, four hatchets, two sacks of vermillion, flints, wormscrews, hammers."

This was not the end of his troubles:

> They brought some beaver and deer hides to me and demanded to trade them for cloth, powder and balls. They crowded around in a throng. My men had every possible difficulty in keeping off the robbers. They took from me powder, balls, cloth, white blanket, hatchet, pickax, vermillion, knives, etc., without giving me time to count their hides, yet less to settle on a price, in spite of any effort I made to resist them. This was a real pillage ...
>
> One of them called me into his cabin. While I was absent they stole two cooking kettles, and took two guns from my men. I returned immediately. I swore, I prayed, I supplicated, but all in vain ... My embarrassment and my pain was unequalled ...
>
> Some old women had warned me that they had sent couriers to warn other bands which were in the neighborhood, that they should come promptly to this place. If they arrived before my departure it would be all up with my merchandise. In order to depart it was not only necessary to secure their consent but also their aid, in order to take our pirogue out of that confounded channel, nearly dry, into which they had dragged us.

By the next summer Truteau reached the Arikaras and while trading there tried to bring about peace. But it was a time of little peace. He reports that on June 5th an Arikara war party arrived with a Crow scalp. On June 8th another war party which had gone to avenge the killing of three Arikara the winter before, returned home having killed a Santee Sioux. A few days later two Sioux brought news that three Sioux bands

THE VERENDRYE PLATE

The historic Verendrye plate was discovered by Harriet Foster of Ft. Pierre while out hiking in the hills above the Missouri River with girlfriends one February afternoon in 1913. Ironically the find has sometimes been credited instead to 15-year-old George O'Reilly, who was hunting with friends that day, met the girls and took over the leaden plate.

The story, as told by Hattie Foster, is as follows:

We girls were out walking and went upon the hill...We were standing there talking, and I was scraping in the dirt with my foot...As I was scraping in the dirt I saw the end of the plate showing about one inch above the ground cross-wise the plate as it was slanting in the ground...When I saw it, I kicked it out and picked it up. And as I picked it up it looked like a lining out of a big range stove.

I asked, "What is this?"

George said, "It is a piece of lead."

It was covered with dirt but there was some reading on it, and I asked, "What is this reading?"

George had a knife and said, "Hand it here and I'll scrape the dirt off so we can read what is on it."

I handed George the plate, he scraped the dirt off, and all that we could read was "17___" something...But George didn't throw it down, neither did he give the plate to me.

George then said, "It isn't anything but a piece of lead. I will take it to the hardware store and sell it for about five cents."

We were making light of George going to sell it. Not a member of the party knew it was of value. In a few minutes George started home, for he said he had to milk the cow...

The next day I asked George for the plate, and he said he took it home and was going to have it. He still has the plate as far as I know. (South Dakota History Col. 7)

The leaden plate is only one-eighth of an inch thick, 8½ by 6½ inches. Scratched onto the back with the tip of a knife are these words in French:

Placed by the Chevalier de la Verendrye, witnesses Louis, La Londette, Amiotte 30 of March 1743

---

were forming a party of 500 warriors to attack the Arikara village. Truteau described their fear and the defenses the Arikara had made:

The Sioux nations are feared and dreaded by all of these others on account of the fire arms with which they are always well provided; their very name causes terror, they having so often ravaged and carried off the wives and children of the Ricaras ...

The Ricaras have fortified their village by placing palisades five feet high which they have reinforced with earth. The fort is constructed in the following manner: All around their village they drive into the ground heavy forked stakes, standing from four to five feet high and from fifteen to twenty feet apart. Upon these are placed cross-pieces as thick as one's thigh; next they place poles of willow or cottonwood, as thick as one's leg, resting on the cross-pieces and very close together. Against these poles which are five feet high they pile fascines of brush which they cover with an enbankment of earth two feet thick. In this way, the height of the poles would prevent the scaling of the fort by the enemy, while the well-packed earth protects those within from their balls and arrows.

Truteau blamed white traders for causing trouble by setting tribes against competing traders and each other. Also for teaching white men's tricks and frauds.

Instead of bringing peace among the Indian nations which should be the first aim of the White Man ... these people were the cause of quarrels and dissentions among the chiefs and families with whom they lived ... Those Indians who have had little or no intercourse with us are more civil, kinder, and more humane than those whom we habitually visit, for they observe in their manner of life the laws dictated only by reason, nature, and humanity.

Certain it is that if these people whom we call barbarians and savages knew the disposition of the White Men ... Their manners and customs, their ways of living and their lack of charity for one another ... all the vile and contemptible deeds done by them for the sake of money ... the tricks, the frauds, the crimes ... they might justly apply to us the designation of savages and barbarians which we have given to them ...

It is perhaps surprising that these people ... should not be more addicted to stealing and other crimes so common to the civilized nations. But one rarely hears of robbery among them, and never of assassination or murder.

After the Revolutionary War the United States gradually extended control to the Mississippi River, though the English threatened on several fronts.

The Purchase of Louisiana

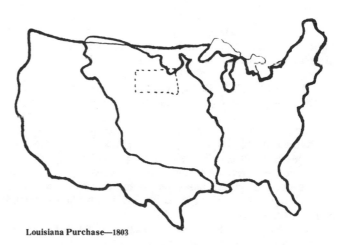

Louisiana Purchase—1803

Spain agreed, by secret treaty in 1800, to turn the Louisiana Territory back to France. But Napoleon needed money for his European conquests. He also was threatened by the power of England and, reluctant to lose Louisiana to them, agreed to sell it to the United States --- 827,987 square miles for $15,000,000.

Said Napoleon, "The English have successfully taken from France, Canada, Cape Breton, Newfoundland, Nova Scotia, and the richest portions of Asia. They shall not have the Mississippi they covet. The conquest of Louisiana would be easy, if they only took the trouble to make a descent there. I have not a moment to lose in putting it out of their reach." After selling he added, "I have just given to England a maritime rival, that will sooner or later humble her pride." [6]

4. LEWIS AND CLARK

Captains Meriwether Lewis and William Clark set out from St. Louis in the spring of 1804 to explore the vast regions purchased from France. This was a military expedition of 45 men traveling in a 55-foot keelboat and two open pirogues. They were to make peace with, and among, Indian tribes and to establish the sovereignty of the United States in the newly acquired lands.

They spent 54 days in South Dakota on the trip upriver (from August 22 to October 13, 1804), and 15 days on the return two years later. Their journals give us excellent early descriptions of South Dakota, its wildlife, its Indian inhabitants, and difficulties of travel. Their writings on wildlife include the following.

THE PRAIRIE DOG. Sgt. Ordway writes, "Shields killed a prairie dog, which was cooked for the Captains' dinner." They tried to dig out a live prairie dog, said Clark, but "after digging 6 feet, (we) found by running a pole down that we were not halfway to his Lodge. We found 2 frogs in the hole, and killed a Dark rattlesnake near with a ground rat in him. The village of those animals covered about 4 acres of ground...contains great numbers of holes, on the top of which those little animals sit erect, making a whistling noise and when allarmed step into their hole."

BUFFALO. "I do not think I exaggerate when I estimate the number of buffalo which could be comprehended at one view to amount to 3000," said Lewis in 1804. But on returning two years later, after traveling through vast buffalo ranges, Clark was amazed to see, "a greater number of buffalo than I had ever seen before at one time. I must have seen near 20,000 of those animals feeding on this plain."

MAGPIE. "A remarkable bird...long tail, the upper part of the feathers & also the wings is of a purplish variated green, the back & a part of the wing feathers are white edged with black, white belly...about the size of a large pigeon. A beautiful thing."

COYOTES AND WOLVES. "A prairie wolf, about the size of a gray fox, bushy tail, head & ears like a wolf. Burrows in the ground and barks like a small dog...The large wolves are very numerous. They are of a light color, large & have long hair with coarse fur."

ANTELOPE. "My object was if possible to kill a female antelope, having already procured a male...At rest they generally select the most elevated point in the neighbourhood, and as they are watchful and extremely quick of sight and their sense of smelling very acute it is almost impossible to approach them within gunshot. In short, they will frequently discover and flee from you at the distance of three miles. I had this day an opportunity of witnessing the agility and the superior fleetness of this animal which was to me really astonishing."

The explorers drew maps, named and described landmarks. At the mouth of the Vermillion River they visited Spirit Mound "viewed with terror by Indian tribes." They found large flocks of birds circling the mound. Clark explains the Indian belief that it was "the residence of Devils...in human form with remarkable large heads, and about 18 inches high. That they are very watchful and are armed with sharp arrows with which they can kill at a great distance...(They say) many Indians have suffered by those little people, and among others, three Mahar men fell a sacrifice to their merciless fury not many years since. So much do the Maha, Sioux, Ottoes, and other neighbouring nations believe this...(that) no consideration is sufficient to induce them to approach the hill."

Both captains paid careful attention to the details which could spell success or failure to their mission. One night the sandbar on which they were camped began to break away. Clark "ordered all hands on as quick as possible and pushed off. We had pushed off but a few minutes before the bank under which the boat and perogue lay gave away, which would certainly have sunk both...By the time we made the opposite shore our camp fell in."

Lost for 17 Days

They were frequently anxious for those who hunted. The inexperienced 17-year-old George Shannon was lost for 17 days. He and Drewyer had left the boat to look for the two lost horses. Drewyer returned, Shannon did not and in the ensuing days all four journals expressed deep concern:

AUG. 27: Drewyer came up and informed that he could neither find Shannon nor horses. We sent Shields & J. Fields back to hunt.

AUG. 28: Shields & J. Fields...joined us and informed that Shannon had the horses ahead and that they could not overtake him. This man not being a first rate hunter, we determined to send one man in pursuit of him with some provisions.

AUG. 29: Sent on Colter with provisions in pursuit of Shannon.

SEPT. 3: We saw some signs of the two men Shannon & Colter. Shannon appeared to be ahead of Colter.

SEPT. 11: Here the man who left us with the horses and has been ahead ever since, joined us, nearly starved to death. He had been 12 days without anything to eat but grapes and one rabbit, which he killed by shooting a piece of hard stick in place of a ball. This man supposing the boat to be ahead, pushed on as long as he could...The reason of his keeping on so long was that he saw some tracks which must have been Indians. He took it to be us and kept on...When he became weak and feeble determined to lay by and wait for a trading boat, which is expected. Keeping one horse for the last resource. Thus a man had like to have starved to death in a land of plenty for the want of bullets or something to kill his meat.

Tight military discipline was maintained. A trial was held for John Newman for repeatedly talking in a mutinous way. Lewis said this would not only "destroy every principle of military discipline, but also to alienate the affections of the individuals composing this detachment to their officers and disaffect them to the service for which they have been so sacredly and solemnly engaged." A court of "9 of his peers," sentenced Newman to "75 lashes on his bare back, and to be henceforth discarded from the permanent party." Next day the sentence of 75 lashes was meted out on a sandbar in the presence of visiting Arikara Indians. Clark records their reaction: "The punishment of this day allarmed the Indian Chief very much. He cried aloud...His nation never whipped even their children from their birth...I explained the cause of the punishment and the necessity—which he also thought examples were necessary and he himself had made them by death." In the spring, Newman was returned to St. Louis with the barge taking information and specimens from Ft. Mandan.

They gave Gifts and Councilled

Like the traders both earlier and later, Lewis and Clark met their greatest challenges in dealing with Indians. They had to "run the gauntlet" through hostile tribes in the South Dakota regions. But they took their peacemaking duties seriously, giving gifts, meeting with as many Indians as possible, sitting in Council, inviting chiefs to go to Washington and making arrangements for them to travel there.

The first Sioux they met were friendly Yanktons camped on the James River. "Fat Dog was presented as a mark of their great respect for the party of which they partook heartily and thought it good and well flavored." Two days were spent in

Was she Sacajawea, Sakakawea or Sacagawea?

Sacagawea—the young Shoshone (Snake) mother who traveled with Lewis and Clark to the Pacific and back—has been the subject of two long-standing controversies. The first concerns proper spelling and pronunciation of her name; the second, the time and place of her death.

The first argument has not been easy to resolve; differing state guidelines have been set up as to how this American heroine's name shall be pronounced and spelled in schools. Was she the Hidatsa *bird woman Sakakawea*, or the Shoshone *boat launcher Sacajawea*?

Lewis and Clark recorded her name 16 times, usually in syllables. Spelling varies, but basically the pronunciation is the same: Sah-ca-ger-we-ah; Sah-cah-gar-we-ah; Sah-cargar-we-ah; Sah-kah-gar-we-a; Sah-cah-gah. (*Wea* means *woman.*) The second *k* sound just isn't there; neither is an accented first syllable *sak*.

In examining the evidence and various theories, Irving Anderson writing in *South Dakota History* Fall 1978, concludes that the name is Hidatsa, meaning bird woman, but that the second *k* is more accurately sounded as a hard *g*, as was often done in the Hidatsa language. He says the spelling *Sacajawea* is inaccurate, as Hidatsa have no *j* sound. Anderson suggests *Sacagawea* as the most accurate spelling and pronunciation of the name, in line with both Hidatsa usage and Lewis and Clark's phonetic spelling. *Sacagawea* is also the spelling adopted by the U.S. Bureau of Ethnology.

As to the second argument, most historians are agreed that Sacagawea died in 1812 at Ft. Manuel in what is now South Dakota (Corson County). Popular fiction has developed other theories.

On December 20, 1812, Luttig wrote:
This evening the wife of Charbonneau, a Snake squaw, died of a putrid fever. She was a good and the best woman in the fort, aged about 25 years. She left a fine infant girl.

Clark also recorded her death. Inside the front cover of his cash book and journal for 1825-28, he lists the men of the expedition with a notation after those deceased and the whereabouts of others. On this list is "Se-car-ja-weau—dead."

But a popular story places Sacagawea's death in Wyoming at the age of nearly 100. This theory is based on the book *Bird Woman*, of which historian Doane Robinson says he could find "nothing authoritative in it. It is evidently a historical fiction and entirely imaginative." The fact that Luttig's journal was not discovered until after wide acceptance of the Wyoming story probably accounts for the continuing confusion.

Even if she had not died at a young age, it is unlikely Sacagawea would have wanted to return to her poverty-stricken family band, as in the Wyoming story. She was offered the chance to remain there by the explorers in 1805, but declined. Then upon her return to the Hidatsa in 1806 she learned of a new tragedy that befell her family band. Clark gives this report: "Charbono informed me that our back was scarcely turned before a war party from the two menetarry villages followed on and attacked and killed the Snake Indians we had seen."

The evidence seems conclusive that Sacagawea—"a good creature of a mild and gentle disposition"—died at Ft. Manuel on the banks of the Missouri River upon which she had journeyed so many miles. Historians say the "putrid fever" of which she died may have been diptheria.

council on the Calumet Bluff. The Yanktons agreed on the need for peace and asked that more traders be sent them, especially with guns and bullets for hunting. Clark was distressed to find the Sioux "are only at peace with 8 nations and, agreeable to their calculation, at war with twenty odd." He was also told the Sioux had 20 tribes, with interests so varied that some bands were at war with nations with which other bands were friends.

Three men seized the Rope

A month later the explorers came upon 2 large Teton Sioux camps of 140 tepees. Here they did not have an adequate interpreter and encountered much difficulty. Almost immediately their one remaining horse was stolen. However, they met in council, smoked together, distributed presents. In one crisis the chiefs were taken on board and as Clark took them ashore in the pirogue, three men seized hold of the rope and would not let him return. Clark's anger rose:

> The chief's soldier hugged the mast, and the 2nd Chief was very insolent both in words and gestures, pretended drunkenness and staggered up against me, declaring I should not go on, stating they had not received presents sufficient from us...I felt myself compelled to draw my sword...I felt myself warm and spoke in very positive terms. Most of the warriors appeared to have their bows strung and took out their arrows from the quiver...Their treatment to me was very rough and I think justified roughness on my part. They all left my perogue and councilled...I offered my hand to the chiefs who refused to receive it.

But the next day both captains met again in ceremonious council, and in the evening were entertained by Indian dancing.

> ...a large fire made in the center, about 10 musicians playing on tambourines (made of hoops & skin stretched) long sticks with deer and goats hoofs tied so as to make a jingling noise, and many others of a similar kind. Those men began to sing and beat on the tambourines. The women came forward highly decorated in their way, with the scalps and trophies of war of their fathers, husbands, brothers...and proceeded to dance the war dance which they done with great cheerfulness. Every now and then one (would)...come out and repeat some exploit in a sort of song—this taken up by the young men and the women dance to it.

'York—made himself more terrible'

On October 8, Lewis and Clark reached the Arikara village and passed an island covered with their fields. For nearly a week they councilled in several Arikara villages, feasting, smoking the pipe of peace, exchanging gifts, talking with two French traders who lived there. They found the Arikara peaceful, but in much dread of the Sioux. These Indians were not fond of liquor of any kind, Clark said, but were very interested in his black servant York. They "all flocked around him and examined him from top to toe. He carried on the joke and made himself more terrible than we wished him to do." Ordway adds that the children would follow York and "if he turned towards them they would run from him and hollow (holler) as if they were terrified."

The expedition continued up the Missouri River, out of present day South Dakota, spending the winter at Ft. Mandan. It was there, at a nearby Hidatsa village that they hired the Frenchman, Charbonneau, and his Shoshone wife Sacagawea as interpreters and guides.

Sacagawea unexpectedly added a heartwarming aspect to the expedition. A young mother of about seventeen, she captured the imagination of America and won for herself a place in history. She aided the explorers in many ways, in particular

by guiding them to her Shoshone family band in the Rockies and obtaining horses from them which made crossing the rugged mountains possible. She carried her new-born baby on the arduous journey to the Pacific Ocean and back. Clark called her "Janey" and her baby, "Pomp...my little dancing boy."

War Parties continued Raids

Returning through South Dakota in the summer of 1806, Lewis and Clark again visited the Arikara and the Teton Sioux. They were distressed to find neither had kept the peace as promised. Clark scolded the Arikara for letting their young men "join the Sioux in killing 8 Mandans...Their young men had stolen horses of the Menetarras; in retaliation the Mandans and Menetarras had sent out a war party and killed 2 Ricaras. How could they expect other nations would be at peace with them when they themselves would not listen to...their great father?" Of the Tetons, he writes, "I told those Indians that they had been deaf to our councils and ill treated us as we ascended this river two years past, that they had abused all the whites who had visited them since."

A few days later the exploration party was again in St. Louis, acclaimed by the entire nation. Clark remained there in government service and became active in the fur trade. He kept track of the Charbonneau family, entertaining them in St. Louis and helping to educate the two children, Pomp and a younger sister. Clark helped Charbonneau find work at Ft. Manuel where the family lived until 1812 when the trader Luttig recorded Sacagawea's death. In his 1825-28 journal, listing the whereabouts of expedition members, Clark wrote bleakly after the name Sacagawea, "dead."

Fur trading fort on Missouri. Bodmer painting.

5. THE FUR TRADE

As Lewis and Clark came downriver they met several boats of fur traders going up. The fur trade in the upper Missouri regions grew quickly. Early emphasis was on fine beaver furs; as these became both scarce and less in demand, the trade began to change to buffalo products, especially robes and pickled tongues.

By 1822, more than a thousand men were estimated to be trading and trapping in the upper Missouri regions, with 500 on the Mississippi. In 1830 they shipped into St. Louis from the country above the Big Sioux: 26,000 buffalo robes; 25,000 pounds of beaver fur; 37,500 muskrat skins, 2000 otter skins and 150,000 deer hides, according to Herbert Schell in *History of South Dakota*.

Large fur companies carried the bulk of this trade. Big money was needed to build trading posts, to stock the trading goods, to furnish transportation over thousands of miles, to hedge against the occasional disasters such as Indian attack or the sinking of a company boat loaded with furs.

Fur companies often competed bitterly with each other. Trading in liquor flourished in this competition, though it was illegal. Watered-down whiskey was used liberally in tricking the Indians, and came to be a deteriorating influence for them. The fur trade exploited the Indians in other ways: furs were valued as cheaply as possible, while trading goods came high. Yet the spirit of competition tended to keep traders honest. Samuel Pond, long-time missionary among the Sioux in the early 1800's, said they were usually dealt with fairly:

They received annually from the traders large quantities of valuable goods. Their blankets and other clothing were strong and durable, made expressly for them, and just such as they needed. The same is true of all the weapons and tools which were furnished to them. Their guns, kettles, axes, hoes, etc., were well adapted to their wants. Most of their peltries went to pay for such articles as have been mentioned, and but a small portion for ornaments.

With regard to the prices paid for these goods, the fur merchants doubtless made what profits they could, but there was no monopoly of the trade. On the contrary, there was spirited competition, and no...combination of the merchants to keep up or keep down prices...The trader was as anxious to buy a great many furs as to buy them cheap, and the Indians knew enough to carry their peltries where they could get the most for them.

As a class the men engaged in the fur trade were as honorable and fair in their dealings as the generality of men engaged in mercantile business; and, if there were rogues among them, there were also rogues among the Indians, who were quite a match for them. 7

The fur trade changed the Indian's way of life in many ways. They came to depend on the trading goods, particularly guns and ammunition; their enemies too, were well armed.

Lisa Opened the Trade

Manuel Lisa was the most successful of early traders on the Upper Missouri. He opened peaceful trading with the Indians and carried on an extensive trade until his death in 1820. He was president of the Missouri Fur Company and built many trading posts including several in South Dakota. One of these was Fort Manuel—in the northeastern corner of what is now Corson County. Chief clerk John Luttig recorded everyday activity at the post and fur shipments:

On August 30th a boat load of fur was dispatched to St. Louis with thirteen men. By October 29th the men had brought in enough fur to load another boat, and two engages, Louis Lajoie and Joseph Joyal started with it for St. Louis. The first boat made the trip in twenty-eight days. 8

Rival traders criticizing Manuel Lisa, stirred this spirited defense from him:

Before I ascended the Missouri (as sub-agent) your excellency remembers what was accustomed to take place. The Indians of that river killed, robbed and pillaged the traders; these practices are no more. Not to mention the others, my own establishment furnish the example of destruction then, of safety now...But I have had some success as a trader; and this gives rise to many reports.

"Manuel must cheat the government, and Manuel must cheat the Indians, otherwise Manuel could not bring down every summer so many boats loaded with rich furs"...Cheat the Indians! The respect and friendship which they have for me the security of my possessions in the heart of their country, respond to this charge, and declare with voices louder than the tongues of men that it cannot be true. "But Manuel gets so much rich fur!"

Well, I will explain how I get it. First, I put into my operations great activity; I go a great distance, while some are considering whether they will start today or tomorrow. I impose upon myself great privations; ten months in a year I am buried in the forest, at a vast distance from my own house. I appear as the benefactor, and not a pillager, of the Indians. I carried among them the seed of the large pompion (pumpkin) from which I have seen in their possession the fruit weighing 160 pounds. Also the large bean, the potato, the turnip; and these vegetables now make a comfortable part of the subsistence, and this year I have promised to carry the plough. Besides, my blacksmiths work incessantly for them, charging nothing, I lend them traps, only demanding preference in their trade. My establishments are the refuge of the weak and of the old men no longer able to follow their lodges; and by these means I have acquired the confidence and friendship of these nations, and the consequent choice of their trade. 9

War of 1812

As Indian agent during the War of 1812, Manuel Lisa did a great deal to hold the loyalty of the Sioux. This second war with England caused much unrest on the Dakota frontier. The British had trading interests deep into South Dakota. Robert Dickson, who had a trading post on Lake Traverse, was appointed British agent to the Indians. He enlisted as many Indians as he could. By 1813, it was said that a quarter of the Sioux on the Mississippi were ready to march with the British under Major Dickson. Lisa's loyal Sioux were able to influence a major defection, and the British were defeated in the Lake Region. If it had not been for this defeat, the U.S.-Canada border would probably have been much different than it is today.

Of Dickson's forces, 22 Sisseton Sioux came from the South Dakota area. Under the leadership of Red Thunder and his son, Wanetta, they fought with the British at Fort Stephenson in Ohio. After the war, Dickson joined with Joseph Renville and formed a trading company with posts at the mouths of the Vermillion, James, and Niobrara rivers, and probably also at Aberdeen and Flandreau. A number of rival traders also operated in this boundary lakes region.

Fur traders obtained their pelts from three sources. First, Indians—usually trading independently. Second, company trappers hired for the purpose. Third, independent hunters and trappers, trading where it was most convenient or where they could make the best deal.

'Mountain Men'

The trappers were called "mountain men," even though they worked in plains or badland country rather than the mountains. They were hardy and courageous men. They had to know the land, the weather signs, the Indians of the region, and the animals they hunted. They needed to be constantly on the alert when, for instance, spending the winter alone in hostile Indian country. Many died alone and far from help. Many were killed, their furs stolen and traded at some distant post.

Hugh Glass was one of these hardy mountain men. He was not a young man and had probably been on the plains for some

years when he joined the Ashley and Henry fur trapping expedition. Traveling up the Missouri by keelboat, the party stopped at the Arikara villages on the Grand River and traded for horses to travel overland. The Arikara seemed friendly during trading. But in the night they attacked, killing 13 men and wounding ten or eleven more. The trappers retreated and soon sent the wounded downriver in the keelboat.

When the wounded men reached Ft. Atkinson, Col. Henry Leavenworth decided to punish the Arikaras. He started out with a force of 250 men. These were soon joined by 60 men from the Missouri Fur Company, which had also been attacked and robbed. They added Yankton Sioux at Chamberlain, and 200 Hunkpapa Tetons. Later they were joined by other large bands of Sioux warriors, eager to fight their old enemies. When they reached the Ashley and Henry trappers, these men also joined the forces.

A mixed Army

Over 1000 fighting men in this mixed army attacked the two Arikara villages on August 9, 1823. The defenders, with a population of 3000 to 4000, battled fiercely for three days then surrendered to Leavenworth's peace efforts. They agreed to restore the property taken from the Ashley-Henry trappers and to live at peace with traders on the river.

But they returned very little stolen property. Both the Sioux and the trappers were furious with Col. Leavenworth for his weak agreements, and demanded restitution and vengeance. That night, fearful of revenge, the entire population of the two Arikara villages escaped unnoticed. When this was discovered, Leavenworth gathered his forces to return south. As they began the march, he was angered to see the villages in flames. Whether they were burned by the fur traders or the Sioux was not discovered, but it forced the Arikara out of their secure fortress at the mouth of the Grand. They returned only briefly, were found some years later living in western Nebraska, and about 1835 moved farther north on the Missouri to settle near the Mandans. They were hard hit by smallpox in 1837 and never regained their former strength.

Hugh Glass—mauled by a Grizzly

Hugh Glass continued up the Grand River with the trapping expedition. They were attacked by the Arikara and two men were killed. Shortly after, near the forks of the North and

Uneasy encounter between trappers and Indians, 1887 drawing by H. Farney.

South Grand, in a heavily wooded area, Hugh Glass was attacked by a grizzly bear while scouting ahead. The grizzly clawed and tore his body so badly that he lost consciousness for 5 days and hovered near death. He was too badly wounded to move, so Henry left two men to guard him until death came.

But Glass did not die. He lay unconscious with his terrible wounds as the days passed. The two trappers grew increasingly anxious to join the rest of the party. At last, certain that Glass would die soon, they took his gun and left.

When Hugh Glass revived, he began to crawl back the way he had come, his leg badly maimed. He traveled at night, watchful for the Arikara. As he recovered strength, he was able to find enough food to stay alive, chasing wolves from a carcass, catching small animals and birds. After weeks of painful effort he reached Ft. Kiowa, near Chamberlain, 200 miles away. He joined a party of trappers going up the river, eager to return to his trapping. Legend says he swore revenge on the two who had left him alone without a gun, and was looking for them. The trappers Glass joined were attacked by Arikara warriors and killed.

Glass escaped and was taken by friendly Mandans on horseback to Ft. Tilton. From there he again pushed westward and joined Henry at winter camp near the mouth of the Yellowstone River. Some months later, Hugh Glass came through western Nebraska bound for Ft. Atkinson. Again the Arikara ambushed the trappers he was with and killed all but Glass. He escaped to Ft. Kiowa. Legend has it that he finally found the two men who deserted him at Ft. Atkinson and forgave them. For the next ten years he continued to hunt and trap on the upper Missouri. Bruce Nelson in *Land of the Dacotahs* says Hugh Glass was killed the winter of 1832 by his old enemies the Arikara as he crossed the ice on the Yellowstone River.

'Worth $4 in trade'

In the trade a buffalo robe—hide dressed with the hair on—was the common standard of currency. It was valued at $4 at Boller's trading post in 1858.

"For example," Boller explains. "You want to buy a horse from an Indian—he will, if a 'buffer' horse ask 30 robes for him; you pay him in goods from the store, to the value of 30 robes, estimating each at 4 dollars, altho' the actual St. Louis cost of the goods would not be more than 30 or 40 dollars." Four cups of sugar, coffee or tea equalled the price of a robe.

More than 100 trading posts were established at one time or another in South Dakota, say historians. These were scattered from the eastern lake country to the Black Hills, some quite temporary, with the largest ones being located along the Missouri River.

After the death of Manuel Lisa, Pierre Chouteau, Jr. became the most active trader on this stretch of the Missouri. He took over the western branch of the American Fur Company, brought up the first steamboat, the *Yellowstone*, and built several trading posts. The most important post in South Dakota at Ft. Pierre was named for him.

By 1850 white hunters had joined the Indians in the slaughter of huge numbers of buffalo every year. The Indians protested, but to no avail.

"Our country was changing fast," said Chief Plenty Coups, a Crow, "Anybody could now see that soon there would be no buffalo on the plains and everybody was wondering how we could live after they were gone."

6. STEAMBOATS

The colorful era of steamboats on the upper Missouri began when Pierre Chouteau's fur trading boat *Yellowstone* came upriver as far as Pierre in 1831. The era ended when railroads crossed the Missouri and took over northern plains traffic a half century later.

During those eventful years, steamboats stocked fur trading posts with goods and returned loaded with fine furs, buffalo robes and buffalo tongues. Steamboats supplied gold mining camps with miners, picks, flour, dried apples—and carried away a fortune in gold with men and women made wealthy by gold. Steamboats brought soldiers, arms and ammunition to military forts and supplied fighting armies from the riverbank. Steamboats hauled annuity goods to treaty Indians and transported entire Indian tribes to new reservations.

At its peak season seventy-one steamboats were on the upper Missouri. That same year, 1867, a record of thirty-seven went all the way to Ft. Benton, Montana. Profits were high, except when disaster struck. At the height owners could expect $10,000 to $40,000 in profits from each steamer that made it all the way to Ft. Benton and back. The *Luella* reportedly carried a cargo of $1,250,000 in gold dust from Montana gold fields in 1866.

A shifting Channel

But the Missouri was difficult to navigate. The river was continually shifting and changing channels, with a channel so twisting that it doubled the mileage between many river points. Riverboat pilots called her, with affection and exasperation, the "Big Muddy" and "the Misery"—a river like no other. Piloting required great skill and was better paid than on any other American river. In 1866, for instance, pilot wages on the Ohio River were $175 monthly, while on the Missouri they were $725.

In dry seasons the riverbed surfaced in broad sandbars. In flood stage, the water surged with floating logs. George Catlin, the noted painter who came upriver on the *Yellowstone's* second trip, called the Missouri a "Hell of waters" and the "River Styx." He described the logs and snags:

> The shores of this river (and, in many places, the whole bed of the stream) are filled with snags and raft, formed of trees of the largest size, which have been undermined by the falling banks and cast into the stream: their roots becoming fastened in the bottom of the river, with their tops floating on the surface of the water, and pointing down the stream, forming the most frightful and discouraging prospect for the adventurous voyageur. Almost every island and sand-bar is covered with huge piles of these floating trees, and when the river is flooded, its surface is almost literally covered with floating raft and drift wood; which bids positive defiance to keel-boats and steamers, on their way up the river. 10

The water, said Catlin, was the color of "a cup of chocolate or coffee, with sugar and cream stirred into it." He conducted an experiment to see how opaque it was and found, by dropping a white shell into a glass of river water that the shell could not be seen through one-eighth inch of water.

In addition to the submerged snags and sawyers in the channel were soon the hidden hulls of steamboats which had burned or snagged and sank. Experienced pilots on other

The *Rosebud* in 1880's from Yankton to Pierre, probably carrying load bound for Black Hills.

rivers traveled at night, but they found this nearly impossible on the Missouri except in clear moonlight.

Low water caused the biggest problems. Usually the river was high in spring after ice break-up. It dropped through May, then ran bank-full as spring and early summer rains brought on the June raise. Water levels then dropped to a late summer and fall low. But there is wide variation from year to year in rainfall and snow cover in country drained by the Missouri, so each year was unique and unpredictable. Riverboat captains might find high water and excellent shipping through August and September one year—and "scraping and thumping" from sandbar to sandbar around every turn in June of the next.

Henry Boller, the young fur trader, made these notes on the trouble encountered from the sandbars when he traveled here in 1858 on the steamer *Twilight*:

> MAY 29: At 11 p.m. we grounded on a bar again and did not succeed in getting off until the spars had been put in operation for nearly two hours. Missouri River and all western boats are provided with heavy spars to pry off with when they get aground.
> MAY 31: We have made today scarcely a dozen miles, being almost constantly on the bars. The old mountaineers on board shake their heads ominously & say if the June freshets don't arrive soon, we will be pretty much high & dry for perhaps months.
> JUNE 1: Boat has made very poor progress.
> JUNE 2: We got on a bar & a floating tree, & between the two it was nearly evening before we got off.
> JUNE 3: Landed on a sand bar and sent the boat ahead to sound for the channel—she was gone 2 or 3 hours. We consequently laid here all night. We amused ourselves meanwhile by running races on the bar, jumping & c. & c. until we could hardly move.
> JUNE 4: About 11 o'clk in backing off a sand bar, the rudder was badly broken; laid to, & the rest of the day was spent by the carpenters & blacksmith in repairing it. The oxen were led out to feed on the willow shoots.
> JUNE 7: We have just had a tremendous thump on a sandbar—we have a dozen every day but this is the hardest yet.

> JUNE 13: The boat got along very well until noon, when we struck a sand bar which we could not cross until the boat was lightened. All of us, soldiers & voyageurs included, also, the 12 oxen & 2 horses, were landed, and after a 2 hours struggle the boat got across, when she signaled us to come aboard. 11

Boller notes the frustration of passengers with some amusement. "One says he would pay $500 cash down to be back in St. Louis, & out of this 'cussed barren country.' Others because no game has been killed...A couple of young Englishmen are on board, and poor fellows, they are homesick, and completely disgusted with Indian life and Indian scenery. Altogether, there are 8 or 10 passengers not connected with the fur company (of 200 on board), and they are one and all heartily tired of their trip."

The noisy little engine used for sparring, or "grasshoppering," off sandbars was a further annoyance. Dan Scott, a trader on the *Western* says when this loud rattling engine was used almost continuously, one passenger overturned his breakfast plate and began to whistle. Another could no longer stand it and left the boat to continue his trip on foot.

'Rusted, crusted and busted'

Ideally, Missouri River boats were shallow draft, dropping not more than 3 or 4 feet into water when loaded. The *Chippewa Falls*, one of Chouteau's mountain boats, drew only 12" when lightly loaded. Side-wheelers were considered more graceful and balanced on other rivers, but the narrower stern-wheelers proved better for the narrow, snag-filled channel of the Missouri.

Yet nearly every kind of craft was used here. The first steamboat, *Yellowstone*, was built especially for the Missouri River fur trade—but was a side-wheeler, 160 feet long, drawing six feet of water when loaded.

The steamboats burned cottonwood and used muddy river water in the boilers. Iron boilers—in the words of rivermen—were soon "crusted, rusted, and busted." Sometimes a boiler or furnace explosion burned the ship, destroying it in minutes.

Fuel was always a problem. The steamboats burned 25-30 cords of wood in 24 hours running time, or about a cord an hour. Boller notes that the *Twilight* crew went out two or three each day to cut wood. When they had to, they burned green cottonwood and driftwood. As river traffic grew, "woodhawks" began to cut and sell wood along the riverbanks. The woodhawks, who were often Indians, part-Indian, or traders who lived with Indians, charged up to $8 a cord for the wood, with the higher prices farther up the river. Woodhawking was dangerous work, as they were easy targets for marauding war parties.

Steamboats, too, were sometimes attacked when they stopped at a woodyard or to cut timber. Most boats were armed and the pilot house was often plated with boiler iron. At any point above Ft. Randall, an attack or ambush could be expected, particularly where the channel swung in close to a high bank. Just north of what is now the South Dakota border, the mate of the *St. Johns* was shot and killed in the pilot house by Sioux warriors waiting at a bend in the river. Two years later the son of the captain of the *Silver Lake* was wounded in the same area.

Wrecked on the Ice

Ice and ice break-up posed another threat to shipping. At Yankton during the spring flood and ice jam in 1881, several docked steamboats were totally destroyed. Robert Karolevitz describes the wreckage in *Challenge, the South Dakota Story*:

> ...the crushing bergs smashed against the sides of the steamboats on the ways. The previously damaged

Western smashed in ice gorge at Yankton, 1881.

Western was virtually reduced to kindling; the *Butte* was broken in two; the *Helena* was twisted and badly gouged; the *Black Hills* was similarly battered. As the icy water rose, the giant hawers of the *Peninah*, the *Nellie Peck* and the ferryboat *Livingston* were snapped like store-string, and all three vessels were lifted out of the riverbed and deposited grotesquely and brokenly on the shore. [12]

Wrecks were all too common. The Missouri River took a toll of 450 steamboats, according to Robert Thompson in *Dakota Panorama*. Thompson says twenty steamboats were wrecked in what is now South Dakota. Eight of these hit snags, three burned, one hit a rock, one ran aground, three were smashed in ice, and the other two were destroyed by unknown causes. The *Leodora*, valued at $25,000 burned in the river below Yankton in 1866; the same year the *Pocahontas* sank above Ft. Randall.

River rivalries flourished. Crews vied for speed and companies fought for contracts—especially the fat government plums for hauling Indian annuities and military supplies.

In 1863 Pierre Chouteau got the federal contract to move Santee Sioux and Winnebagoes down the Mississippi and up the Missouri to the new reservation at the mouth of Crow Creek. Chouteau agreed to use enough boats to provide "ample space for comfort, health, and safety." But when the *Florence* stopped in Yankton, observers noted she was loaded with 1,400 people and "there was not an Indian on board that could be said to be free from some malady." The *Florence* returned for a second load, and the *West Wind* brought 800 Santee. In the three trips, Chouteau moved 3,251 people at $25 each.

Freight and passenger rates varied greatly depending on ship lines, competition, and type of contract. Cost for cabin passage from St. Louis to Ft. Benton varied from $100 to $200 in the 1860's. In 1863 the *Shreveport* charged $125 for stateroom fare to Benton, or $50 for deck passage (without food.) In 1867, 10,000 steamboat passengers paid a total of $1,500,000 in fares on the upper Missouri.

Freight rates ranged, in 1865, from 10¢ a pound to 18¢, St. Louis to Ft. Benton. With more boats on the river, prices soon dropped. Government contracts paid $1.50 per 100 pounds from St. Louis to Yankton, $2.00 to Pierre in 1863. The next year a similar contract raised that amount to $2.00 per hundred pounds to Yankton, $3.00 to Pierre.

General Sully used 15 different steamboats for hauling men and supplies in his 1864 campaign against the Sioux. He blamed river conditions for many of his frustrations:

> Had the Missouri River commenced to rise in April, as it generally does, instead of June, the boats from St. Louis would have got up...sooner; the command would have been in the field sooner, boats would not have stuck on sand-bars, freight would not have been unloaded and loaded, whereby much of the stores were badly damaged. Had not two of the boats sunk and one become disabled, more supplies would be on hand. [13]

Steamboat season was short at best. A boat could make only one trip a year to Ft. Benton. Only twice were there exceptions, both undoubtedly during years of high water. Light draft ships could hit forts between Dakota Territory and St. Louis several times during the season.

The last steamboat usually left Ft. Benton by the first part of July. So hundreds of gold miners came floating downstream in the fall in an assortment of small boats, rafts, and mackinaws. The mackinaws, a favorite craft, were like low boxes, flat-bottomed with a pointed bow, 40 to 75 feet long and about 10 feet wide. The mackinaws were built at Ft. Benton and sold, usually for lumber, when miners reached St. Louis. They could travel 100 miles a day, but if the ice on the river caught them they had to stop. Many stopped in Yankton, sold their boats, and continued by stagecoach. This traffic into Yankton was especially heavy in October and November of 1866 when some 2000 miners from Montana gold fields arrived there.

High water meant an easy, profitable trip.

7. WAR AND RESERVATION

Tensions ran high in Indian country by mid-century. Boller wrote that war parties were everywhere in Dakota. "All the bands of the Dahcotahs and the Riccarees are very much exasperated at the Whites, and upon the slightest encouragement will break out into open war...Living in Indian country is now more dangerous than it has been for very many years."

Indians were angered at the intrusions of whites; at the way they were being pushed westward by ever-increasing settlement; at the well-traveled roads through their best hunting lands as wagon trains made their way to gold fields in Montana and settlements in Oregon; at the thinning-out of the buffalo herds, and at the broken treaties. Indians retaliated by raiding settlements and attacking travelers.

In 1855 General Harney led a force of 1000 men south of the Black Hills to punish the Tetons for raiding the emigrant trail. He found Chief Little Thunder's camp of Brules at Ash Hollow and destroyed the camp, killing 86 men, women and children. In addition to punishment, this was to be a warning against further attacks.

Returning, Harney led his forces up the headwaters of the White River and across to the Cheyenne, but found no more Indians. He continued up the Bad River and wintered at the Ft. Pierre military post. Unfortunately his big campaign did nothing to ease tensions, but rather increased them.

1862 Uprising—'a bloody harvest'

The big blow-up came in Minnesota in 1862. Starving Santee Sioux, when refused food guaranteed them by treaty, went on a bloody rampage, killing some 360 settlers. Many of them then fled westward into Dakota Territory to join their buffalo-hunting Sioux relatives, bringing white women and children captives with them. In Minnesota thirty-eight Santee were hanged in a mass execution. Others were kept captive in big stockades and brought the next year by steamboat to newly-established reservations in South Dakota. Although this happened in Minnesota, it had violent repercussions throughout the northern plains for many years stirring excitement and renewed hostilities through the entire Sioux Nation.

The next 15 years brought, in the words of one general stationed in Dakota Territory, "a bloody harvest (of the)...vice, injustice, bad treatment sown by whites."

Dakota Settlers Fled

Indian scares were frequent in frontier settlements. When news of the Santee slaughter reached the South Dakota settlers, they fled their homes in terror. All settlements but Yankton were abandoned. After a time some people returned and built stockades at Vermillion, Brule Creek and Elk Point. Sioux Falls was completely deserted for two years; most of the buildings were burned by Indians.

Santee war parties were frequently seen along the Vermillion and James Rivers, with the Yanktons rumored ready to join them in open warfare. Judge J.B. Amidon and his sons, William were killed in the hayfield about a mile from Sioux Falls. Two freighters were attacked at the ferry near Yankton, one killed, the other seriously wounded. Five children in the Wiseman family at St. James on the Nebraska side of the Missouri were killed while their father was gone to fight with General Sully. The trail of their Indian killers led up the James, then toward Sioux Falls. The stage was attacked and one man killed. A man haying in the Brule Creek settlement was killed by a small band of Santees.

Even where war parties were not seen, they were all-too-vividly imagined. Rumors flew and people demanded military protection. The Yankton Dakotian called for vengeance for all who had seen "their wives and husbands, fathers, mothers and children, butchered before their eyes..."

Voluntary militia groups were formed. Cavalry troops were finally sent to patrol the deserted settlements, but returning settlers were dismayed by their foraging activity. Moses Armstrong, a Yankton journalist, wrote:

> **Nearly all the farmers in the country have left the fortification and removed back on their premises, and they now complain, not so much of the Indians, as of the depredations of the roaming squads of cavalry scouts committed on their fields and gardens, and pigs and chickens and fences. Rails are used for firewood, chickens are bagged by the sackfull; corn, potatoes and vegetables are confiscated for Uncle Sam's use.**

Ransomed Captives

News of the captives began to reach Dakota settlements. Some were ransomed and traded for many years; others were killed vengefully during military attacks. Many were rescued through efforts of friendly Indians.

In a famous Dakota case, eleven young Sans Arc Tetons, called the Fool Soldier Band, rescued Mrs. Duly and Mrs. Wright with six white children in the Mobridge area. These young men traded their possessions to pay ransom for the captives and delivered them to an infantry troop near Ft. Pierre. The soldiers took pity on the captives and, having just been paid, took up a collection of several hundred dollars for them. But the young Indians who had paid ransom went unrewarded and are regarded as heroes in South Dakota history. Led by Martin Charger and Swift Bird, they included Kills Game and Comes Home, Four Bear, Mad Bear, Pretty Bear, One Rib, Strikes Fire, Sitting Bear, Red Dog and Charging Dog.

The Shetek captives above the Grand River were discovered and aided in rescue by the Eagle Woman Who All Look At, a Yanktonais Sioux and the wife of Major Charles Galpin. For this and other services in tense times, she is known as Potter County's most distinguished daughter.

Heroic ride by Sam Brown

The epic ride of Sam Brown is another story of South Dakota heroism in the dangerous '60's. Brown, a half-breed, was chief of scouts at Ft. Wadsworth in the Coteaus. One day in April 1866, he learned of suspicious Indian movements and wrote a note to Ft. Abercrombie warning of hostiles advancing on their settlement. The note was to be sent by messenger next morning. That evening Brown rode 45 miles to a James River scout camp. There at midnight, he discovered his mistake: the suspicious Indians were not raiders but runners, sent to Indian camps to explain a peace treaty. Unwilling to let his false message go out, Brown decided to immediately ride back, although a blizzard had come up. Riding through blowing snow, bitter cold and darkness, he lost his way and rode far to the south. When at last he reached Ft. Wadsworth he was nearly frozen. Both his legs were permanently paralyzed and Sam Brown never walked again.*

The Army Attacked

Large military expeditions went twice to punish the Santee Sioux and all who gave them aid, in 1863 and again in 1864. First was to be a two-pronged attack with General Sully coming up the Missouri with 200 men and meeting Henry Sibley marching west from Minnesota with 2800 men. The two forces never found each other. But Sibley fought three battles in northern Dakota, destroying a large Indian camp with all its winter supplies. Sibley had trouble with his steamboats. Finally he left them and traveled by wagon up the James River into northern Dakota where he found a camp of Sioux. His troops killed about 150 Sioux, destroyed their horses, tepees, and 200 tons of dried buffalo meat. In his second attack the next summer, Sully fought a large band of Sioux in the Killdeer Mountains.

Sully's attacks were intended to "settle the Indian question for all time." Instead they had the opposite effect. The injustice of punishing innocent bands for crimes of certain Santee deeply embittered the Sioux.

To cope with fierce hostilities, military posts were built at several South Dakota locations. Ft. Sully was built below Ft. Pierre in 1863 (later moved east of the Missouri and 30 miles north.) Other posts were at Ft. Sisseton, Ft. Pierre, Ft. Dakota near Sioux Falls, on the James near the mouth of Firesteel Creek, Fort Randall and at several points between Brule Creek and Yankton Agency.

Red Cloud's War

In Wyoming three military posts were built protecting the Bozeman Trail. These posts especially angered the Sioux as the trail cut through their best hunting grounds which were between the Black Hills and the Big Horn Mountains. The Oglala Sioux under Red Cloud mounted determined attacks on these forts and on the wagon trains—in what became known as "Red Cloud's War."

A peace commission at Ft. Sully in 1865 tried to settle the troubles. Nine treaties were signed with the Teton and Yanktonnais Sioux. The treaties pledged peace and freedom for whites to travel through Indian country in exchange for annuity payments. The only problem was that the treaties were signed by friendly bands at Ft. Sully and not by those involved in raids.

Three years later the peace commission was able to end Red Cloud's War. They met this time at Ft. Laramie, determined to obtain peaceful guarantees for the Union Pacific railroad to build through Nebraska and Wyoming.

The Laramie Treaty of 1868 was signed by most of the hostile bands that spring. In return for peace in building the railroad, the commission agreed to a number of concessions, including giving up the three forts and abandoning the Bozeman Trail. Red Cloud refused to sign the treaty until the

Peace commission meeting to settle 'Red Cloud's War'—signed the 1868 Laramie Treaty.

forts were actually vacated, and burned by his men. He answered the commissioner's message to come at talk, with this one: "We are on the mountains looking down at the soldiers and the forts. When we see the soldiers moving away and the forts abandoned, then I will come down and talk." 14

Southern Dakotans were angry with the terms of the Laramie Treaty establishing a Sioux reservation in the entire western half of what they considered their state. It was a sell-out of Dakota for peace in Nebraska and Wyoming, they charged.

A new Agency - Reservation System

The Laramie Treaty established the Great Sioux Reservation in western Dakota Territory with these boundaries: the Missouri River on the east, the Nebraska line on the south; the 46th parallel on the north; and 104 line of longitude on the west. (These last two lines ultimately became South Dakota's borders with Montana and North Dakota.) In addition, a large neutral hunting area was defined to the west in which no white person was supposed to go without Indian consent. These were the noted buffalo ranges between the Black Hills and the summit of the Big Horn Mountains, north of the North Platte River, and south of the Yellowstone.

The Sioux agreed to allow the Union Pacific railroad to build south of this region unmolested. They agreed not to attack travelers who were outside the reservation or neutral lands, nor to ever "kill or scalp white men, nor...capture, or carry off from the settlements, white women or children."

In return the government promised to set up agencies and issue annuities, especially food, for four years. By the end of the four years, Congress fully expected that the buffalo-hunting Sioux would be transformed into self-supporting farmers. Instead—with problems brewing at the agencies, broken promises, increasing shortages of buffalo on allowed ranges, raids and retaliations—the northern plains was by then ready to explode into full scale war.

The Great Sioux Reservation agencies were at first under the military control of General Harney. General Harney built three agencies on the west side of the Missouri, at the mouths of the Whetstone, Cheyenne and Grand rivers.

Earlier a reservation had been set aside for the Sisseton and Wahpeton tribes of Minnesota Santee in 1867 at Lake

Fort Thompson Agency, 1865.

Butchering at Lower Brule on beef issue day. Below, drying the meat in camp.

Riding the ferry across river. Below, children at Pine Ridge day school are dressed in their best 'white clothing.'

Traverse. Crow Creek Reservation had been established at Fort Thompson on the east side of the Missouri, for Minnesota Santee and Winnebagoes. These two groups were now moved to Nebraska and replaced by Brule and Two Kettle bands of plains Sioux.

The first Indians moved forcefully into the new agencies were from Wyoming; military experts said they lived too close to the new railroad. Spotted Tail and his people were loaded into government wagons and hauled to Whetstone Creek. There whiskey traders and food shortages demoralized them and they were later moved under Spotted Tail's urging. The first winter was bitterly cold. Over one hundred died from cold and starvation, mostly children and old people.

'Hills covered with graves'

Problems were soon widespread at all three new reservation agencies. The treaty Indians had signed away rights on the promise of food and provisions. But the food they needed was often lacking because of inefficiency and corruption. There was also the problem of non-treaty Indians moving into the agencies expecting to be fed, either by their relatives or the government.

The winter of 1874-75 brought heavy snow and bitter cold. Rations were delayed. The Brule on Bordeaux Creek ate their horses to survive and by spring "the hills were covered with graves of their children."

Supplies frequently failed to arrive on schedule. When they did, Indians were often cheated of the full shipment. There were—as Flying Bird put it—"many rats between here and the Great Father's door." Another Sioux, Fast Bear, said that for each steer they received, two were counted. Traders and half-breeds at Whetstone sold the same flour and other supplies twice, it was discovered. A clothing supplier, Wannamaker & Brown of Philadelphia, showed a fine sample for the bid, then shipped items which were cheap and flimsy. Agents often conspired in the fraud; many received a cutback. It was commonly accepted that agents grew rich at their jobs. The Indians on the Missouri had a saying that agents came in canoes and left in steamships.

'Only honest agent' took Half

Dr. Burleigh, the agent at Yankton between 1861 and 1863, claimed he was "the only honest Indian agent. I gave the Indians half and took half myself." Investigation showed he kept Indian cattle at his farm near Bon Homme. His herdsman testified that a beef animal was killed from this herd once a week and the meat sold to Indians. The herdsman was also told to keep the Indian cows "until we get a calf or two apiece from them."

President Grant's term of office, from 1868 to 1877, was notorious for corruption, though he himself was said to be honest, but weak. The Indian Service was a prime example of the corruption Grant allowed. A so-called Indian Ring, involving officials at all levels, was known to influence Indian affairs for the financial benefit of insiders.

Low salaries of agents encouraged both corruption and incompetence. One investigator said the high cost of living on the frontier made the $1500 annual salary only equal to a New York wage of $500.

Few agents bothered to learn anything of Sioux language or culture. One listed the refusal of Indians to learn English as a major problem of his agency. Frequent turnover of agents made dealing with them difficult for Indians. Col. Hazen pointed out problems this caused:

> One set of civil officers in good faith undertakes an experimental policy, good enough of itself, but as soon as anything is done on the new plan, with all of its in-

variable pledges and flattering promises fully conceived and begun, a new administration begins, with equally good intent, an entirely new policy, unintentionally violating all the promises and efforts of its predecessors and its agents. The savage cannot comprehend this and naturally calls it a lie, the white people a nation of liars. 15

The Grand River agent was patient in regard to work: "The only way to overcome the deep prejudice to laboring is good advice, judicious management and liberal help and encouragement from the Government." But at Yankton, Agent Gassman said bluntly, "Make them work or starve." Another admitted frankly that the more he learned of Indians and their problems, the more he had to change his opinion.

Grant tries 'peace policy'

At first the military had charge; surplus officers from the Civil War were offered agency posts. Then in 1870, Grant decided to cut corruption by giving the churches control of running the reservations. Under this Peace Policy, or Quaker Policy, reservations were now divided up among the churches. A single church was given sole responsibility, not only for mission work and schools, but for hiring the agent there. South Dakota's reservations were mostly assigned to the Episcopal church. Episcopal assignments included Crow Creek, White River, Cheyenne River, Yankton and Whetstone-Spotted Tail. The Catholic church had Grand River, later called Standing Rock; the joint Presbyterian-Congregation mission effort was assigned Sisseton.

All this was changed in 1881, with exclusive rights abruptly removed. The Indian Service administrator next year said he had never heard of the Peace Policy.

'The ration issue is without system'

For their part, agents dealt with staggering problems, whether honest or dishonest, competent or incompetent. Supplies were typically short and of poor quality. At Whetstone the sugar was said to be black and dirty and the flour filled with maggots.

Agencies were thrown into turmoil by unassigned Indian bands moving in to spend the winter. Local Indians were caught in the middle and often requested the newcomers be fed even when it meant scarce supplies for themselves. The agent at Whetstone had orders not to feed Red Cloud's band one winter; Washington officials said this would force them to move back to their own agency. The Whetstone agent replied by telegram that if these people were not to be fed, Washington had better send guns and ammunition—so his Indians could protect themselves. Whetstone was a favorite winter place because the winter was mild and military forces far away.

Rations were given at first to tribal leaders who divided them somewhat unequally among their members. Not always was there food for older widows or Indian women with half-breed children deserted by white fathers. Commissioner Brunot objected:

> The ration issue is without system and both irregular as to the time and amount, with no census of of Indians being taken, although easily possible. The issues are made to the headmen in bulk, who gives them out as he seems to please, but the Indians take them, although the proportions are unequal, with apparent satisfaction. 16

A major goal of the reservation system was to change the Indians into self-sufficient farmers. In Congress this seemed reasonable. But on the Great Plains during the 19th century, it was an impossibility. Except for river bottoms, the plains had never been farmed and there were no known techniques or crop varieties for dryland farming. Nevertheless at Yankton,

Tree burials like these were soon outlawed by the government.

in 1873, the agency farmer broke 40 acres on "the high land" and planted wheat. But the agent Gassman reported his failure to get wells on the high land and to persuade the Indians to move up there. Even on bottomlands, Sioux farming efforts were mostly unsuccessful as drouth and grasshoppers often took the crop.

Every agent stressed the great improvements made in his reports. Information discrediting his efforts was omitted, or blame laid to outside forces. Each agent proudly noted the number of new acres broken every year, acres under cultivation, acres seeded, and bushels harvested; not infrequently the number of bushels harvested was less than acres seeded. Indians could not have had much confidence in a system that put more seed in the ground than was harvested in the fall.

Worse, the Sioux did not want to farm. Men considered farm labor degrading and beneath them. Among the Arikara, Mandans and Hidatsa, planting corn had been a way of life. But such work was traditionally looked down upon by the buffalo-hunting Sioux warriors.

As a result, women and the agency farmer did much of the work.

To make farming even more difficult, many agencies were moved after much plowing, fencing and building. Farming efforts were abandoned and begun anew. Standing Rock, originally called Grand River Agency, was moved twice. Whetstone and Spotted Tail were relocated numerous times.

The constant shifting and state of uncertainty was demoralizing for the Indians. They had either to submit to every erratic decision and draw rations—or travel west to join the hostiles and live off the diminishing products of the land. Many chose to leave.

Harney City—haven for Whiskey Traders

Whiskey was another demoralizing force, particularly at Whetstone. There a shanty town was built called Harney City, which became a haven for white and half-breed whiskey traders. One night a raid there netted 8 barrels of whiskey. (Other agency reports of "no problem with spiritous liquors," were not necessarily accurate. The liquor trade was lucrative for many agents, so they discouraged close scrutiny by falsifying reports.)

Liquor was outlawed on reservations, but most agencies were on the Missouri so traders had only to cross the river and travel up and down it by boat. A number of whiskey traders set up on the east bank across from Whetstone. In winter they crossed the ice in wagons and peddled liquor in wooded areas. One trader ran the ferry boat from his mile-and-a-half long claim on the east riverbank and did a brisk business in whiskey as he made his crossings. Two steamboat owners, Durfee and Peck, carried whiskey up and down the river to Indians and soldiers. Whiskey traders clustered around army posts such as Ft. Randall and Ft. Sully to get the soldier trade. When Indian agencies were set up conveniently near, they quickly expanded trade.

Many traders were part Indian and when occasional arrests were made they pleaded successfully that as non-citizens they could not be prosecuted by civil authorities. Others were able to buy off officials.

Spotted Tail objected strongly to the boldness of the whiskey traders and drunkenness among his people. Where previously his band had been tranquil, he said there was now fighting, murder and conflict. Through the night shouting and singing could be heard in Harney City. Indian men; old and young, traded their rations at $30 worth for a $1 bottle of whiskey.

'the land of his fathers'

Spotted Tail went to Washington in 1870 to explain to the President why his people should be moved from Whetstone. Grant listened and agreed to a move up the White River. But relocations proved frustrating for both Indians and a succession of agents. The Interior department selected Hidden Buttes, only 20 miles from the Black Hills. Brule chiefs held out for Little White Clay, which happened to be in Nebraska. Agent Washburn said there was not enough timber, grass or water there and began building at Big White Clay. Then while he was away on a trip, the agency farmer and white traders moved the buildings to Little White Clay—hoping to benefit from being closer to the impending gold rush to the Black Hills. In 1872 a new agent moved the agency to Big Beaver Creek. This time an investigation uncovered fraud: too many civilians were hired; more goods were claimed than hauled; Indians and goods were hauled at government expense even when they had their own transportation; vouchers claimed 70 to 90 miles instead of the 36 miles actually traveled.

A later move in 1875 put the Whetstone agency at the west fork of Beaver Creek. That year the government began urging Indian tribes to move into the unsettled area of Oklahoma. Spotted Tail went to Oklahoma to look it over but on his return declared it was bad country. He would remain in the land of his fathers, he said: His father's country was his country; it was the whites who did not belong.

School was a shock

Education of children was considered an important means of subduing the Sioux. Early reservation schools were run by mission churches with federal funds. The Episcopal church and the joint Presbyterian-Congregational missions established Indian schools in the Missouri River area in the early 1870's. Catholic mission schools began in the mid 1880's. By the turn of the century government policy changed. All financial aid was withdrawn from mission schools and young people were urged to go to Indian Bureau schools instead.

First schools were called day schools, meaning the students lived at home. Attendance was usually poor. Agents complained that parents sent their children erratically so that schools would be empty one day, overflowing the next. Many felt boarding schools were the only solution. One investigator reported: "The day school burnt down and was a failure, as are all day schools where the Indians rove...a boarding school would be a great improvement."

Dr. Nicholson, superintendent of Indian Affairs, believed not only in boarding schools—but that they should be far from home:

> Schools should be established at a distance from the tribes. Put them where the climate and soil are favorable, where they can live after their schooling is over; let them intermarry and they will lead lives of self support...If the children are educated and then leave the school (returning to the tribe) there is a strong tendancy to go back to the old habits. The people of the tribe laugh at them for their short hair, their civilian clothes, call them 'squaw,' etc. The result is the boys let their hair grow, get their bow and arrow, jumps on his horse and is again an Indian.[17]

School was a terrific shock for Indian children. Suddenly they had to cut their hair, wear stiff clothing and hard shoes, sit indoors, and submit all too often to severe physical punishment. They were used to a free outdoor life and to being taught in the manner of example, shaming and teasing. Indian parents, seeing their children so unhappy in school, did not force them to go.

One visiting senator complained he could not see any progress with: "a school of 10 or 12 in a whole tribe of Indians where there are 1000 children."

At first the government urged teachers to teach in Sioux, and a Nebraska teacher was cited as a bad example for having taught her pupils to spell, read and write "wonderfully" in English, though they didn't understand one word of what they said. Yet in just a few years all teachers and students were forced into this. Speaking "Indian" was forbidden not only in the classroom but everywhere on the school grounds. Children heard speaking their native Sioux were severely punished.

'A coward—cuts his hair'

Mission churches also pressed civilization on the Sioux. The first services in what is now South Dakota were preached by Stephen Return Riggs who came to Ft. Pierre in 1840 from his Congregational-Presbyterian ministry to the Minnesota Santee. He spent a week holding services for 500 Yanktons and Tetons, saying of this experience, "We gathered a good deal of information...communicated to them something of the object of our missionary work, and of the good news of salvation."

Later Father DeSmet, the noted Catholic missionary, began traveling through Dakota, visiting Sioux bands, speaking from the deck of a steamboat and often baptizing from the boat great numbers of Indians who thronged the banks.

In 1872 Thomas Riggs, the son of Stephen Return Riggs, founded the first mission for Sioux west of the Missouri, near Ft. Sully. He spent the next half century in this region.

Riggs willingly learned from the Sioux. "One part of my education, perhaps the most valuable, was in learning to see life from their point of view, to understand their mental reactions and, in short, to think as they did, no longer a stranger or outsider, but as one of them," he said. The Riggs family pioneered in developing the written language of the Sioux. They had printed dictionaries, Sioux Bibles, textbooks, and by 1875 were publishing a monthly newspaper "Word Carrier" in Sioux.

Native missionaries and ministers were important to the missions. At Sisseton in 1874 the missionary reported six churches, five with native pastors and one with a native "licentiate." At Ft. Sully that same year, Martha Redwigg became the first Indian woman to serve as missionary. In 1873 the Episcopal mission at Yankton under Rev. William Hare had a membership of 450 with about 300 attending church and 250 attending three Sunday Schools.

Most missionaries were intensely concerned that the moral life of the Indians conform to white standards. To become a baptized Christian it was usually necessary for a man to cut his hair and put on "citizen's dress."

Philip Deloria (Tipi Sapa) became Episcopal missionary and teacher at Standing Rock after his conversion to Christianity in 1870. He is described as a born leader with great energy, force and ability by Sarah Olden in *The People of Tipi Sapa,* but he told her of his reluctance to accept the outward appearance of Christianity that was required.

> "You are to cut your hair short, dress like a white man and go to school," (said the missionary). I replied, very decidedly, "No!" Again and again he asked me, and as often I gave him the one answer. In their teachings my father and mother had said so often: "A scalplock of beautiful long hair is a most desirable thing for a warrior to possess. Take care of your hair. Be brave, and if an enemy gets your scalplock, die like a man. He who dies uttering a cry is not a man, and is a disgrace to his people." I wanted to keep my hair long and beautiful as became a warrior. It was far from easy (afterward) to go back and face my people, many of whom were disappointed and jeered at me. "Coward! He fears warfare." "See, he chooses an easy life," and many similar taunts were flung at me.

Marriage was an especially sore spot. Indian marriages were not considered valid, and had to be done over again by the missionary. More than one wife was forbidden, so to be baptized, Indians had to "put away" extra wives. Thisba Morgan describes the difficulty in making this decision:

> Chief American Horse wanted to become Christian but was told he could have only one wife. He went home to think about it, returned and replied: "I took my wives according to the custom of my people. They have been with me in my joy and in my sorrow; they are the mothers of my children. They are now old and I cannot throw any of them away, but if a time ever comes when I have but one wife, I will join your church."

Thomas Riggs gives similar examples:

> Stephen Yellowhawk...had two wives who were sisters. When the time came for him to decide between them, he showed more than the wisdom of Solomon, for he entered them upon a contest of skill, promising to marry the one who first became skillful in the white women's ways, in cooking, washing and ironing. One became so proficient that she was known as "Little Ironing Woman." He married her, "putting away" the sister. Later, Little Ironing Woman died and he married the put away sister.

One agent complained his efforts were hampered by constant visits from the "lawless and idle Indians (who) destroy and demoralize those who have done well in the new order...It is known of young men who have been laboring for over a year performing all things required of them, to leave everything, resume their Indian costume, and disappear from the Reservation under this influence."

Thus tension and dissatisfaction were widespread even among the peaceful agency Indians. They were often torn between the hostiles and the government. Troops would be sent in to keep order when they needed protection from whites or from hostile bands.

It was through the heart of this newly-formed Great Sioux reservation, tense with bitter rivalries, disappointment, starvation and broken promises that, in 1874, George A. Custer led his large military expedition into the Black Hills.

Custer—on an expedition 'to dazzle the eye.'

8. CUSTER INVADES THE BLACK HILLS

On July 2, 1874, four columns of men, wagons and supplies set out from Ft. Lincoln at Bismarck to explore the Black Hills under the command of Colonel Custer. (He was Brevet Major General of volunteers, and usually referred to as General Custer.) Included was a vast train of 150 wagons pulled by 900 mules; 1000 cavalry horses; 2000 men including civilians; and a herd of 300 cattle for beef.

The purpose was ostensibly peaceful, "exclusively in the interest of science," said the St. Paul Pioneer; the troop would simply make some studies and return without effecting any change. Scientists with the party would make maps, study geological formations and wildlife, and collect fossils.

But two other purposes were clear—though not officially stated. Both threatened the sanctity of the Sioux rights agreed to in the Laramie Treaty, sealing off the Black Hills to whites. The first of these purposes was to locate the site of a possible military fort. (Three sites were ultimately suggested: one near Harney's Peak, another at a point on the Little Missouri River, and still another near Bear Butte—where Ft. Meade was later located.) The second purpose, widely acclaimed, was to find gold. Custer himself played down the gold angle; his reports of gold discoveries seem understated. Yet he was prepared by bringing along two experienced gold miners—and a number of newspaper reporters to ensure any gold reports would be well publicized. (News stories written by these reporters, and Illingworth's photos, are collected in *Custer's Prelude to Glory* by Krause and Olson. Reports here are from this source.)

Gold seekers were elated that their hopes would be confirmed. A frontiersman interviewed in Chicago gave this statement:

> They would never have sent General Custer to prove the existence of gold there unless they wanted miners to rush in and work up the country. Besides, how

Four columns of wagons pulled by mules, 300 head of beef cattle, 1000 cavalry horses, 2000 men—moved south to explore the Black Hills.

are they going to stop them? Miners would laugh at any edict to keep them out of the country like this. Depend upon it, my idea is correct. The expedition is sent for a set purpose. Money is scarce, and the country needs gold...the Black Hills will be opened, and pull us through. 29

The Custer expedition moved slowly through often difficult terrain, but when they reached the Black Hills they were awed and delighted at the scenery. Newspapers in Chicago, New York and St. Paul soon ran long columns extolling the natural beauty and wonders of the hills.

CUSTER PARK: Evening found us encamped in one of the most charming and lovely natural parks in the world...We have spent four days in this delightful retreat, have gone up, down, and across it, and yet its graces have not been half revealed...Expressions of admiration are heard from all. No one ever saw anything to equal it.

HARNEY PEAK: But around us, for miles and miles away, what a waste of mountains. Naked granite everywhere. Ridges, walls, pinnacles all around us. Gen. Forsythe says: "This is the Switzerland of America."...On the top we ate our lunch, and from cool canteens we all drank to General Harney's health.

FLORAL VALLEY: The whole valley was a nose-gay...numberless little springs, and a rapid, rocky trout stream, as clear as crystal and cold as snow, which singularly grew deeper and wider as we neared its source, until it became a dashing mountain torrent, booming over a bed of rocks...The greed for gold was forgotten. We ceased to look for the nuggets which would make us suddenly rich. Beauty for the time seemed the only wealth, and men who had never picked a flower since their childhood days bent and paid the long-neglected homage. Cavalrymen and teamsters decorated their horses and mules; infantrymen plumed their hats; officers gathered nosegays...There was something almost affecting in seeing rough, coarse men softened and refined by the sweetness of the flowers, taking out worn, tobacco-scented pocketbooks and putting in a flower or two "just to send to the old woman." For once grumblers against camps and country were hushed by their own confession. I know no more powerful testimony to the charm of the valley.

In this place they called Floral Valley, Custer added his own report: "It was a strange sight to glance back at the ad-

vancing columns of cavalry and behold the men, with beautiful bouquets in their hands, while the head-gear of the horses were decorated with wreaths of flowers fit to crown a queen of May."

The officers saw and killed considerable game—elk, antelope, deer, cougar, bighorn sheep, black bear, two grizzly bear—though well supplied with beef on the hoof.

Messages of peaceful intent had been sent in advance to Indian camps, yet everything was in readiness for attack; no one strayed far from the column without armed escort. Rumors of an impending attack by a large force of Sioux were frequent and, at one point, it was announced in the press that the expedition was attacked by 4000 Sioux warriors.

Ree scouts wanted Revenge

Instead they found only one small band of Indians (although they found many signs of recent camps and trails.) This band of no more than 27, included five men with 30 to 40 horses. Soldiers and scouts quickly surrounded the secluded Sioux camp.

The Indians were terrified by the Arikara scouts who, they quickly understood, were bent on vengence for a recent bloody Sioux raid on their villages. The 60 Ree scouts had amazed and alarmed reporters, even before leaving Ft. Lincoln, with their war dances and obvious hopes for the chance to battle the Sioux.

At every hint of fresh Sioux trail the Rees had made ready. One reporter described how a Ree prepared for battle at full gallop:

Firstly he lashes his horse to the length of his speed, with a stinging little cat-o'-nine tail he carries, then, guiding the animal with his knees, he commences to "peel." As fast as he removes the superflous clothing, he hangs it on his saddle, somehow, somewhere, unknown to the civilized mind, unbraids his hair, and throws it back upon his shoulders, gathering a few of the front locks in what the ladies call a Grecian coil above his forehead, in which he places a cluster of painted feathers. Then, taking a little buckskin bag from some mysterious place, he dashes a coat of vermillion over his face, arms, chest, sides, and limbs...and he is ready.

Custer assured the little band of his peaceful intent, trying to keep his Sioux scouts in the fore and his Ree scouts in the background. He asked that one man come to guide them for a few days. Though frightened, the Indians agreed to come to the base for provisions urged upon them—coffee, sugar, pork and hard-tack.

In a few hours three men did come and were given these supplies. But they seemed uneasy—one rode off quickly. The other two were held. One struggled with a soldier over a gun, was shot in the leg and escaped. The other, an old man named One Stab, was captured. Meanwhile the women and children had broke camp and fled. They left behind whatever might slow their flight—but destroyed for use. Chopped tent poles, kettles with holes cut in them, ruined dried meat.

One Stab was kept as guide several days, while the Ree scouts eyed him "murderously," according to reporters—who eyed the scouts.

Then One Stab was quietly released one night, given five days provisions and "passed beyond our lines about nine or ten o'clock, so that he might put at least a nights travel between himself and the danger from our blood-thirsty Rees...When our Rees found that he was indeed gone and out of their reach, they were moody and silent...the Chief, Bears Ears, went to Gen. Custer and, after expressing his displeasure, resigned his office as one of the guides...Mad Bull (appropriately named) made a great speech, showing that he and Bears Ears should have been allowed to take out and kill and scalp the poor, old, emaciated, disarmed, unoffending captive...Bloody Knife and his men were out five hours or more, but returned scalpless, having been unable to follow the trail in the dark, and there were howls of disappointment, and anger around the Indian camp."

Gold!

Gold was found and the long-awaited news was taken out by scout riders and printed in newspapers across the nation:

In this valley gold was at last found, and though bed-rock has not been reached, the most skeptical must be convinced that it is here...I saw a prospect taken from one pan of earth which yielded fifty pieces of gold the size of pin heads...Gold was found in the grass roots, and in the earth, in paying quantities, to the depth of eight feet. Miners estimate that gold to the extent of one hundred dollars per day to the single man, can be secured...

Our miners...There are two of them—old veterans in the craft—who have been worth fortunes as many times as they have toes, and who know the names of every gulch west of the Rocky Mountains. Ross and McKay are their names.

"Now, by gosh," says McKay, taking a fresh quid of tobacco, "it begins to look like something." And he went at work, with his pick and pan, every time the train stopped long enough for him to unstrap them. It wasn't very satisfactory prospecting, to leave a lead as soon as they got "the color" and they got it frequently, but the expedition hurried on, and it was not until we went into camp here that a fair test was made. The farther north we go, they say, the better are the indications, and by the time we get to the plains again, I expect we shall be loaded down with nuggets...All the camp is aglow with the gold fever.

After a dozen pans or more had been washed out, the two persevering men who will be the pioneers of a golden State came into camp with a little yellow dust wrapped carefully up in the leaf of an old account book... At daybreak there was a crowd around the "diggins," with every conceivable accoutrement. Shovels and spades, picks, axes, tent pins, pot hooks, bowie knives, mess pans, kettles, plates, platters, tin cups, and everything within reach that could either lift dirt or hold it was put into service by the worshipers of that god, gold... The most excited contestant in this chase after fortune was "Aunt Sally," the sutler's colored cook, a huge mountain

'The whole valley was a nosegay— cavalrymen and teamsters decorated their horses and mules'

BUCKSKIN JOE, THE MULE WHACKER

"Under that old slouch hat," said an officer friend to me one evening, pointing to an old mule driver, "I think you will find a romance." The man we were looking at took an old gray slouch hat from his bushy hair to wipe the perspiration from his forehead, and it was like lifting a curtain from a picture. "That's Buckskin Joe," continued my friend, "the oldest man on these plains, I believe...His wife ran away and married a Congressman some years ago."

"In '55," said (Buckskin Joe) quietly, "I went out with (Harney), and our trail was fifty miles south of this—we went around the foot of the Black Hills and up the Cheyenne." And in answer to other questions he told me briefly and politely that for forty-one years he had been between the northern Mississippi and the Rocky Mountains. His language was pure, grammatical, and well-pronounced; his voice was soft and musical.

"You don't know how it is, my friend; the open air and a team of mules is as much to my taste as your city home to you. I couldn't breathe in a city. I have been on the plains forty-one years, and now and then I have vowed that I would quit it, but before my team was unharnassed I'd be anxious to get off again...Yes, I'm old—64 last January—but I am tougher now than most of the young fellows...I ran away from my home in Philadelphia when I was 9 years old, and went into the western part of the state, and worked for nigh seven years; then I went back home and worked under the very same roof with my mother, she tending dairy and I doing chores, and she didn't know me all that time. I stayed there a year or two, and then I came West, and hereabouts I've been—at Sioux City, Fort Dodge, and all around—teaming and trading with the Indians ever since, and I couldn't leave it now...

"I have no family, but I was married once. I lost my wife some years ago," and he rubbed his eyes, saying something about smoke and alkali dust. Then he got up and moved around restlessly, took the kettle off the hooks, and lifted the lid. The old man had dug down into his memory as far as he dare go. He did not sit down again, but kept busying himself in the preparation for his meal, and I hadn't the heart to ask him any more questions.

One is continually meeting such men in frontier life—men who have found the civilized world too small for them, too crowded.

William Curtis
Chicago Inter-Ocean

of dusky flesh, and "the only white women that ever saw the Black Hills," as she frequently says.

A gold company was formed listing Ross as discoverer and setting aside 4000 feet for individual claims of company members "as soon as peaceable possession can be had."

But even as members of the Custer expedition washed for gold and laid plans to return, General Sheridan was issuing warnings to would-be gold miners. His orders to the St. Paul military post were:

> Should the companies now organizing at Sioux City and Yankton trespass on the Sioux Indian reservation, you are hereby directed to use the force at your command to burn the wagon trains, destroy the outfit, and arrest the leaders, confining them at the nearest fort.

Custer did not escape criticism as glory-hunter, charges leveled against him in the past and destined to be renewed in the future. The New York Tribune made this accusation:

> It evidently is hoped that these roseate stories of gold and silver discoveries will condone the sheer independence of the commander of this aurilerous hunt, at the cost of the Government, and so dazzle the general eye as to make accusation and criticism seem harsh and unwelcome in the universal gloating over the newly discovered treasure...General Custer knew why he was going there before he started. He did not march off in that direction to suppress Indian hostilities so much as to invest his name with the charm of being a discoverer.

Some even questioned whether gold had really been found. Lieutenant Fred Grant, son of President Grant, first agreed to gold reports but later disclaimed them. "We had several miners along," he said, "who had nothing to lose and everything to gain; they all lived together and could concoct any plan they wished...they came each day and showed specimens and would say 'I got this from one pan of earth today' and I noticed that they showed the same pieces every day. Then they told about what could be produced saying that one man could get from 10 to 100 dollars a day. I saw about all the gold that was produced in the hands of the different miners, and I don't believe there was two dollars all put together and that they took out there with them."

Grant's statement was clouded by the report that he was "drunk nearly all the time," and was at one point arrested by the teetotaller Custer for drunkenness. Reportedly their former friendship had cooled before the expedition was finished.

Two who panned gold with the expedition were convinced there was gold. Both Ross, the discoverer and veteran miner, and Aunt Sally returned to become long-time gold hunters in the Black Hills. Ross died there, a pauper.

Upon his return from the Black Hills, Custer issued the statement: "I shall recommend the extinguishment of the Indian title at the earliest moment practicable, for military reasons."

9. LAST STAND OF THE SIOUX

Among Indians there was widespread anger and apprehension over the Custer expedition to the Black Hills. At the peaceable Cheyenne River agency, the agent said it did "visible harm in causing dissatisfaction and discontent even among those who have hitherto been most friendly and appreciative." Custer's route became known as "the Thieves' road." The Sioux were all too aware the expedition threatened their hold on the Black Hills, so recently guaranteed by the Laramie Treaty.

The gold craze spread. Prospectors invaded the Black Hills that fall and winter, although the military tried hard to keep them out. Twenty-six people built a stockade at French Creek, but were routed next spring by the cavalry. A second group was also intercepted; 29 wagons filled with provisions were burned near Gordon, Nebraska. But by the summer of 1875, 800 miners were in the Hills. A government geological group under Walter Jenny, spent the entire summer examining minerals there.

Most area newspapers encouraged the miners and called for ending Sioux ownership. The Chicago Inter-Ocean put it this way:

> The Sioux must leave their hunting grounds in the Black Hills...There is gold in the hills and rivers of the region, and the white man desires to take possession of it. What, to the roaming Yankee, are the links that bind the red man to the home of his fathers? He is but an episode in the advance of the Caucasian. He must decrease that the newcomers may grow in wealth.

The word was spread that Sioux seldom visited the Black Hills and had no use for them.

Sioux refuse to Sell

Pressured by the gold craze, the government met in council on the White River to seek "relinquishment of the Black Hills." The Sioux came in force, with 15,000 to 20,000 people. They were angry and in no mood to sell the Black Hills, much less cede their hunting grounds on the Yellowstone River and Powder River as requested. The commission suggested a lease, offering $400,000 annually for mining rights in the Hills; after the gold had been taken the land would be returned to the Sioux. They offered $6,000,000 to buy the Hills outright.

The Sioux refused both terms. They said the Black Hills were sacred to them and a last refuge. One leader stated, "You have driven away our game and our means of livelihood out of

Where there was no crossing they made a road—'the thieves road'—the Sioux called it.

the country until now we have nothing left that is valuable, except the hills that you ask us to give up." Another demanded payment for damages already done and said, "The white man is in the Black Hills just like maggots, and I want you to get them out just as quick as you can. The chief of all thieves made a road into the Black Hills last summer, and I want the Great Father to pay the damages for what Custer has done." [18]

The commission went home admitting failure. Forcing relinquishment of the Black Hills was not to succeed until Custer's defeat at Little Big Horn swept public opinion against the Sioux. But the government called off troops from the Black Hills and let the miners sweep in unhindered.

Fears of Indian War Spread

As Indian tensions rose, rebellious bands broke away from the agencies and fled west to join hostile Sioux and Cheyenne bands. There was much angry talk among them about making a "last stand" against the whites.

Fear of a full-scale Indian war spread across the northern plains. In December 1875 the commissioner of Indian Affairs sent out orders for all Indians to report to their agencies by the end of January. All who did not were to be considered hostile. This was a harsh order. The Sioux were in winter camp. Ordering them to break camp and travel perhaps hundreds of miles, transporting their goods through deep snow and bitter cold, was quite unreasonable. Hostile bands such as Sitting Bull and his Hunkpapas, who had never signed a treaty, made no attempt to comply.

Three-pronged attack is Planned

The military gathered to move against them. A three-pronged attack was planned. General Crook set out from Wyoming in the spring with 1300 cavalrymen. Colonel Gibbon would come down the Yellowstone River with a force of infantry from Fort Ellis, near Bozeman, General Terry would come from Fort Lincoln at Bismarck with 1000 men; 600 of these were 7th Cavalrymen under Lt. Col. Custer.

At the head of Rosebud Creek on June 17, Crook met the Oglala warriors of Crazy Horse and the Cheyennes of Two Moons. The Indians attacked with such force that Crook retreated, built fortifications and sent for help. Elated, the victorious Indians left him and hurried on to the large gathering of Sioux and Cheyenne camping on the Little Big Horn River.

A week later Custer, unaware of Crook's defeat farther up the same creek, led his 7th Cavalry up the Rosebud and over the divide toward the Little Big Horn. Many Indians ahead—reported his scouts. Custer pressed on eagerly, impatient to surprise the hostile bands before they could disperse into the badlands and mountain foothills. It was clear that Gibbon and Terry, coming from the north, were at least two days away. Indian strength was estimated at about 500 to 800 fighting men.

But in the big Sioux and Cheyenne encampment which stretched for three or four miles along the Little Big Horn, were closer to 3000 warriors; probably a total of 10,000 people. (Many had left the agencies and joined the hostiles when they heard of the impending military moves into Sioux hunting lands.) Sitting Bull was the main spiritual leader. Though not a war chief at this time, he had a reputation for prophecy and making strong medicine. He prophesied the Sioux would score a great victory over the soldiers somewhere near the Big Horn rivers. To insure victory, he made medicine continuously. Many believe that Sitting Bull watched through visions as Custer and the 7th Cavalry rode out of Fort Lincoln and across many miles of badlands and plains.

The large camp was not pitched for war, being sprawled, but it was a camp of famed war leaders: Gall, Black Moon, and Crow King of the Hunkpapas; Crazy Horse, Big Road, He

'A camp of famed war leaders—Gall, Black Moon, Crazy Horse, Crow King—'

Dog of the Oglalas; Lame Deer and Hump of the Minniconjous; Two Moons of the Cheyenne. They knew their strength greatly outnumbered that of the approaching soldiers and were confident in Sitting Bull's prophecy of victory. Yet women bundled together their belongings to prepare for flight if it became necessary.

At noon on June 25, with the large camp just ahead (although it could not be seen because of hills and river bluffs), Custer decided not to wait for the infantry of Terry and Gibbon. He divided his forces to attack from three points, in a strategy he'd used with success before. His own force of some 200 men, he led down a long draw—right into the hands of hundreds, perhaps thousands, of Sioux and Cheyenne warriors. Too late he realized his mistake, sent back a desperate message for help, and tried to take command of the crest of a small knoll.

The Battle of the Little Big Horn was fought one hundred fifty miles west of the South Dakota border. But its repercussions—which included the forced sale of the Black Hills and the atrocities at Wounded Knee—were probably felt more keenly here than anywhere else. Virtually all of the thousands of Sioux who were camped that day by the Little Big Horn came to live within the Great Sioux reservation of Dakota.

Mrs. Spotted Horn Bull, a Hunkpapa of Standing Rock, gave this account of what happened that day:

> From across the river I could hear the music of the bugle and could see the column of soldiers turn to the left, to march down to the river to where the attack was to be made. All I could see was the warriors of my people. They rushed like the wind through the village, going down the ravine...Soon I saw a number of Cheyenne ride into the river, then some young men of my band, then others, until there were hundreds of warriors in the river and running up into the ravine. When some hundreds had passed the river and gone into the ravine, the others

Sitting Bull, spiritual leader, prophesied great victory.

who were left, still a very great number, moved back from the river and waited for the attack. And I knew that the fighting men of the Sioux, many hundreds in number, were hidden in the ravine behind the hill upon which Long Hair was marching, and he would be attacked from both sides. And my heart was sad for the soldiers of Long Hair, though they sought the lives of our men; but I was a woman of the Sioux, and my husband, my uncles, and cousins, and brothers, all taking part in the battle, were men who could fight and plan, and I was satisfied...

I cannot remember the time. When men fight and the air is filled with bullets, when the screaming of horses that are shot drowns the war-whoop of the warriors, a woman whose husband and brothers are in the battle does not think of the time. But the sun was no longer overhead when the war-whoop of the Sioux sounded from the river-bottom and the ravine surrounding the hill at the end of the ridge where Long Hair had taken his last stand. The river was in sight from the butte, and while the whoop still rung in our ears and the women were shrieking, two Cheyennes tried to cross the river and one of them was shot and killed by Long Hair's men. Then the men of the Sioux nation, led by Crow King, Hump, Crazy Horse, and many great chiefs, rose up on all sides of the hill, and the last we could see from our side of the river was a great number of gray horses. The smoke of the shooting and the dust of the horses shut out the hill, and the soldiers fired many shots, but the Sioux shot straight and the soldiers fell dead.

The women crossed the river after the men of our village, and when we came to the hill there were no soldiers living and Long Hair lay dead among the rest. There were more than two hundred dead soldiers on the hill, and the boys of the village shot many who were already dead, for the blood of the people was hot and their hearts bad, and they took no prisoners that day. [19]

News of the outcome of the battle arrived at the Cheyenne River mission at Oahe the next day, even though it did not reach the outside world for two weeks, until the night of July 5 when the Far West reached Bismarck with the wounded. Missionary Thomas Riggs writes: "On the day following the battle, some of the Indians on Peoria Bottom came to me and told me that 'Yesterday the Long Hair (Custer) and the soldiers with him were all killed. Some of the other soldiers were killed, but most got away.' As you will see this report was received at a point fully a thousand miles away, within twenty-four hours of the time the battle occurred...How the Indians sent this message in such detail, I do not know. I know that they used smoke signals, fire signals and reflected sun's rays in their signalling." [20]

Stripped of Horses and Guns

Indian victory was short-lived. The army moved determinedly against them. The various bands scattered and foraged for food. Some returned to their agencies. Sitting Bull and a large group of Hunkpapas fled to Canada. Others were hunted down in a series of skirmishes. General Crook attacked a small band under American Horse at Slim Buttes on September 8, well within the Sioux Reservation. He destroyed the camp, but was in turn attacked next morning by a large war party under Crazy Horse, who had been camped within ten miles. Crook withstood the attack, but turned south toward the Black Hills. Army rations ran out and the men were forced to eat horsemeat and wild berries until supplies reached them after crossing the Belle Fourche.

Crazy Horse and many of the Sioux spent the following winter in Powder River country. Finally, discouraged by food shortage and harrassment from the army, they were persuaded to come into the agencies and surrender.

The army was determined to weaken the Indians permanently by forcing them to surrender their guns and horses. At Cheyenne River and Standing Rock, both were taken from all the friendly Indians as well as the new arrivals. Spotted Tail's Brules, who had helped persuade the hostile bands to come in, were allowed more leeway in keeping their property. At some agencies, favored chiefs were allowed to keep one horse. Unjust discrimination against those at Cheyenne River was noted by Riggs. He said the taking of arms and horses "was said to be a necessity and perhaps it was. It is, however, remarkable that at the Cheyenne Agency where there were very few of the hostiles, the war measure was so severely enforced; while with the followers of Spotted Tail and Red Cloud the merest pretense was sufficient." Riggs further objected because 3072 horses were taken at Cheyenne and replaced by only 1200 cows, though the Indians were promised a cow for each horse taken.

When they learned they would be stripped of horses and guns, many hostiles fled west again or joined Sitting Bull in Canada. It was 1881 before Sitting Bull and the last of these returned to Standing Rock.

'Long record of broken faith'

The commission to purchase the Black Hills moved swiftly in the heat of public anger over the Custer tragedy. The Sioux must not only give up the Black Hills and their hunting lands west to the Bighorns, it was decided, but also a fifty mile strip at the western edge of Dakota Territory. In the agreement, most Sioux were required to move east to the Missouri River. The agreement was viewed as a supplement to the Laramie Treaty, so the new requirement for signatures of three fourths of adult males was ignored. In September of 1876 the commission met with chiefs at the various agencies. Beaten, discouraged, without horses or weapons, utterly dependent on the rations the commission threatened to withhold, the chiefs made their marks to the agreement.

But the commissioners listened again and again to Indian recounting of their wrongs, and were moved to add to their report:

We hardly know how to frame in words the feeling of shame and sorrow which fills our hearts as we recall

the long record of the broken faith of our Government...
There are too many graves within our borders over
which the grass had hardly grown, for us to forget God is
just...The Indian...believes in the immortality of the soul.
He has a passionate love for his children. He loves his
country. He will gladly die for his tribe...A great crisis
has arisen in Indian affairs. The wrongs of the Indians
are admitted by all. Thousands of the best men in the
land feel keenly the nation's shame...Unless immediate
and appropriate legislation is made for the protection
and government of the Indians, they must perish. Our
country must forever bear the disgrace and suffer the
retribution of its wrong-doing. Our children's children
will tell the sad story in hushed tones, and wonder how
their fathers dared so to trample on justice and trifle
with God. 21

Spotted Tail, long-time friend of the white man, said,
"When my people are to receive anything from an agreement
of this kind, and we sign a paper as we are asked to now, it
always turns out we don't get the things that are promised...It
has been said to us that there is no deceit in touching the pen to
sign a treaty, but I have always found it full of deceit."

There were objections to moving to the Missouri River,
where demoralizing elements were strong, and where whites
had cut down most of the trees. The words of a chief at the
earlier council were recalled: "I hear that you have come to
move us. Tell your people that since the Great Father
promised that we should never be removed, we have been
removed five times." 22

Crazy Horse in 1877 brought his band into the agency and
was told to go to Fort Robinson, Nebraska, to surrender. There
he was taken prisoner and, in a struggle, stabbed by an Indian
policeman, Little Big Man, a fellow Oglala. Major Lemly
recorded his dying speech:

We had buffalo for food, and their hides for clothing and we preferred the chase to a life of idleness and
bickerings and jealousies, as well as the frequent
periods of starvation at the agencies. But the Gray Fox
(Crook) came out in the snow and bitter cold, and destroyed my village. All of us would have perished of exposure and hunger had we not recaptured our ponies.
Then Long Hair came in the same way. They say we
massacred him, but he would have massacred us had we
not defended ourselves and fought to the death...Again
the Gray Fox sent soldiers to surround me and my vil-
age; but I was tired of fighting...I came here unarmed,
but instead of talking, they tried to confine me, and when
I made an effort to escape, a soldier ran his bayonet into
me... 23

Then writes Lemly, Crazy Horse broke into "the weird and
now-famous death song of the Sioux. Instantly there were two
answering calls from beyond the line of pickets, and Big Bat
told me they were from Crazy Horse's old father and
mother, who begged to see their dying son. I had no authority
to admit them, and resisted their appeal, piteous as it was, until Crazy Horse fell back with the death-gurgle in his throat."

In the government's relentless efforts to break down tribal
culture, dances, feasts and religious customs were forbidden
in 1883. Agents stripped traditional chiefs of power and
elevated other more submissive Indians. Control was also
achieved through food supply, since rations were the only food
available to the Indians. Food was withheld as punishment and
coercion, and the supply declined with corruption throughout
the 1880's.

'Surplus lands' taken

Soon pressure built again to force the Sioux to give up
more land. For awhile they resisted successfully. But in 1889
the Great Sioux Reservation was divided into five separate
reservations. About half the reservation lands—so-called sur-

Top picture shows sweat lodge on Rosebud reservation. Below, a grand council circle of friendly and
hostile chiefs at Pine Ridge in 1891.

plus lands—were taken in this move and opened for settlement.

Wild West Shows were a bit of excitement that entered
these reservations of despair in the early 1880's. Sioux Indians
were recruited to go on tour. Sitting Bull toured fifteen cities
with the Colonel Allen Indian Exhibition in 1884. The next year
he traveled with Buffalo Bill Cody's Wild West Show, where he
was a popular star and signed autographs for one dollar each.
Two years later Buffalo Bill toured Europe and invited Sitting
Bull along, but the old chief declined. Short Bull and Kicking
Bear went instead, succeeding him as chief attractions. Other
features were two very small children, later pupils of Thisba
Hutson Morgan's at Pine Ridge. The brother and sister rode
for the Czar of Russia; one of their proudest moments was
when he complimented their riding ability and called them
back to ride again. Many of the best dancers and riders in the
Wild West Show came from Pine Ridge, according to Morgan.

But discontent and hopelessness kept spreading through
the shrunken Sioux reservations. Drouth and grasshoppers
took the crops. Rations were short and of poor quality.

A new Hope for Indians

Then in 1890 a new hope spread among the Indians. A new
religion born in Nevada offered a peaceful and happy return to
the old ways. The religion which became known as the Messiah
Movement or Ghost Dancing, blended Christian precepts with
the teaching of traditional tribal prophets. Short Bull and
Kicking Bear went with five other Sioux to Nevada to learn
more about the new religion. On his return Kicking Bear
reported:

My brothers, I bring to you the promise of a day in
which there will be no white man to lay his hand on the
bridle of the Indian's horse; when the red man of the
prairie will rule the world and not be turned from the
hunting grounds by any man. I bring you word from your
fathers the ghosts (the dead), that they are now marching to join you, led by the Messiah who came once to live
on earth with the white men, but was cast out and killed
by them...And the Great Spirit spoke to us saying, "Take
this message to my red children...I have neglected the
Indians for many moons, but I will make them my people

now if they obey me in this message. The earth is getting old, and I will make it new for my chosen people, the Indians...I will cover the earth with new soil to a depth of five times the height of a man and under this new soil will be buried the whites and all the holes and the rotten places will be filled up. The new lands will be covered with sweet grass and running water and trees, and herds of buffalo and ponies will stray over it, that my red children may eat and drink, hunt and rejoice..." 24

The two men said if the Indians faithfully danced the Ghost Dance, white people would disappear in two seasons and dead relatives would be restored to life. Dancing was forbidden, but wearing of "Ghost shirts," brightly painted, would protect them from bullets of white men who tried to stop the dancing.

Throughout the Sioux reservations the Ghost Dance was performed in remote camps in a frenzy of excitement and hope. Whites grew increasingly nervous. An uprising seemed likely, even though Indians were disarmed. At Pine Ridge a new inexperienced agent tried one day to break up a Ghost dance and was chased away. He called for government troops and troops were then sent to Pine Ridge, Rosebud, Cheyenne River, and Standing Rock reservations. The largest force, including survivor's of Custer's 7th Cavalry, went to Pine Ridge; some charged they were bent on revenge. Indians retreated into the badlands and continued dancing with more fervor then ever.

Death of Sitting Bull

At Standing Rock, Agent McLaughlin began to fear a return to power of the old militant leader, Sitting Bull. He sent out his Indian police under Lieutenant Bullhead to arrest him. The police arrived at the camp in the early morning on December 15, 1890, and broke into Sitting Bull's log house. The arrest was peaceable enough until Sitting Bull was ridiculed by his son for submitting. The camp became excited and other Indians urged Sitting Bull to resist. A scuffle followed and a shot rang out. Lieutenant Bullhead fell, shooting Sitting Bull as he went down. In the flurry of shooting that followed, six policemen, Sitting Bull, and seven of his followers were killed.

Some of Sitting Bull's band then fled into the badlands and joined Big Foot's people who had left the reservation and were traveling to Pine Ridge. Troops were sent out to order their return. But Big Foot's band evaded the soldiers and continued south, going down the badlands Wall over what is now called Big Foot Pass. Orders were sent to the 7th Cavalry in Pine Ridge to intercept them.

Big Foot was ill with pneumonia, riding in the back of a wagon when the 7th Cavalry found him. He surrendered under a white flag and his band was escorted to Wounded Knee Creek. There they camped in uneasy truce for the night.

Next morning, on December 29, the camp was surrounded by the 7th Cavalry and Hotchkiss guns were trained on the camp from the hillside. The Indians were ordered to bring out their weapons. Tepees, wagons and their persons were searched, but the pile of confiscated weapons was pitifully small—a few old guns, knives, axes.

Hunted down and Killed

Suddenly, as the soldiers continued their search, an unexplained shot was fired. Perhaps, as reported later, it was fired by an Indian struggling for possession of a gun. At any rate, it was the signal for the cavalry to empty their guns into the ragged band of defenseless people. Some ran to touch the white flag of truce; others ran in three directions from the camp. The Hotchkiss guns trained a deadly fire on those running away. Some reached the safety of a nearby ravine, but were hunted down and killed. Killed at the scene were 84 men, 44 women, and 18 children. About 50 wounded, almost all women and children, were rescued from the field when the killing was finished. As many as another hundred reportedly died; some bodies were found two or three miles away. The 7th Cavalry had exacted its revenge, if such was its motive, but 31 soldiers were killed, many apparently in their own crossfire.

News of the massacre swiftly reached surrounding Indians. Short Bull led a raid against the Mission, but was held off by the cavalry. A few skirmishes followed.

The wounded Indians were taken to the Episcopal mission church, still decorated with greenery for Christmas. Pews were taken out and hay spread on the floor. There Bishop Hare found them bleeding and groaning. "Above, the Christmas green was still hanging," he said, "a mockery to all my faith and hope."

'The child was choked with blood'

The following eyewitness accounts were given years later at a Congressional hearing in which victims of Wounded Knee asked compensation (not granted).

STATEMENT OF AMERICAN HORSE: "The men were separated as has already been said from the women, and they were surrounded by the soldiers...When the firing began, of course the people who were standing immediately around the young man who fired the first shot were killed right together, and then they turned their guns, Hotchkiss guns, and so forth, upon the women who were in the lodges standing there under a flag of truce, and of course as soon as they were fired upon they fled, the men fleeing in one direction and the women running in two different directions. So that there were three general directions in which they took flight.

"There was a woman with an infant in her arms who was killed as she almost touched the flag of truce, and the women and children of course were strewn all along the circular village until they were dispatched. Right near the flag of truce a mother was shot down with her infant: the child not knowing that its mother was dead was still nursing, and that was especially a very sad sight. The women as they were fleeing with their babes on their backs were killed together, shot right through, and the women who were very heavy with child were also killed. All the Indians fled in these three directions, and after most all of them had been killed a cry was made that all those who were not killed or wounded should come forth and they would be safe. Little boys who were not wounded came out of their places of refuge, and as soon as they came in sight a number of soldiers surrounded them and butchered them there...

"I stood very loyal to the government all through these troublesome days, and believing so much in the government and being so loyal to it, my disappointment was very strong, and I have come to Washington with a very great blame on my heart..."

STATEMENT OF DEWEY BEARD: "I would like to tell you gentlemen today that there was no reason at all that the United States troups massacred the Big Foot band...and that the United States must be ashamed of it, or something, because they have never offered to reimburse us or settle in any way.

"At that time we stuck up our white flag, and they took our guns away from us. When we were bare handed they cut loose on us. The children did not know what was going on. We always had been told that when the white flag was stuck up there would be no trouble, and the people believed in that white flag. All at once they cut loose on us, and at that time I was shot in the leg, and up till today I never found out why they did that to me...But still they shot me down....

"My wife and I had a baby of 22 days old, and right at the time when the firing started I missed my wife, and later I found out that she was shot through the breast. The little 22-day-old baby was nursing from the same side where the mother was wounded the child was choked with blood. A few days afterwards the little boy died. I saw on that field small children like that lying by the side of their mothers, and I saw four or five of them lying there frozen to death.

"After that—they knew I was wounded and helpless, and they came and shot me all over again, in the breast. I was lying off there to one side, right by the camp side, and the soldiers

At right the Episcopal Church of the Holy Cross; inside, a make-shift hospital with hay on the floor—'the Christmas green was still hanging.'

were going through the field, and the men and women were wounded and could not help themselves, and the soldiers came over there and put the bullets through them again." [25]

Thisba Hutson Morgan, who was teaching at the government boarding school in Pine Ridge, describes her view from the school:

"On this same Christmas Eve, there had been set up in the little Protestant Episcopal Church at the Agency, the Church of the Holy Cross, a huge Cedar tree reaching to the ceiling. It was lighted by candles and a large star at the top. It was festooned with yards and yards of strung popcorn and little bags of fruit, candy and nuts. Colorful scarfs and handkerchiefs for the boys floated from the branches, and beautiful French dolls for the girls peeped like fairies from everywhere. The two hundred pupils attending the Oglala Boarding School were having their Christmas celebration that the beautiful story of the Christ Child might be impressed upon them and the joy of Christmas be theirs. The lovely French dolls, one hundred of them, had come from the missionary-minded women of Christ Church in New Orleans. It was heartwarming to see the faces of the Indian children brighten and their eyes sparkle as they examined and caressed their gifts, never forgetting the quiet decorum so carefully instilled into them by their grandmothers that was so often mistaken by the white people for indifference or vacuity.

"This was the first of a series of such services. Each day during the Christmas octave, the tree was to be redecorated and each night the Indians from the outlying districts, where the Church had sub-missions, were coming in their turn to the Mother Church for Christmas gifts...Five times the tree had been laden with gifts. Four times the beautiful Christmas service had been given in the Sioux language; then on December 29th, like a thunderbolt, came news of the terrible battle of Wounded Knee, stunning the peaceful Indians and the whites alike.

"...We were sixteen miles away but news of it rapidly reached us at the school. It was the noon hour and the children were scattered over the grounds at work and at play, awaiting their call to dinner, when the first runners from the battlefield reached the Agency. The children were the first to get the news and report it to us, because they could understand and interpret the sign language of the runners as they reached the knoll behind the school house, outstripping the Army couriers, swift though they were. The children were panic stricken as more news came in for many of them knew that their parents must have been in the fray...

"The holiday scene within the little church changed...The tree was taken down. The altar, organ, and pews were removed and stored, and the place was ready for the Indian men, women, and children as they were brought in from the battlefield. Hay was put over the floor and the wounded placed in rows upon it. Some were placed in tents nearby. I went to give aid with Miss Goodale, who could talk with the wounded in Sioux. Their situation beggars description...

"For three days following the battle of the Wounded Knee, the weather was bitter cold and many of the dead remained where they had fallen. The soldiers could not reach them because the Indians were there brandishing their clubs, wailing their death song, the most blood-curdling sound that can issue from the human throat. They were marking the few spots from which they had been able to remove their dead by driving a stick into the frozen ground and attaching to it a rag or wisp of hair to which they could come again to wail.

"On January first, some twenty or more soldiers volunteered to go with picks and shovels in big army wagons drawn by four horses over the rough hard frozen road to bury the remaining dead. While some stood guard, swinging their arms and stamping their feet to keep warm, others dug a long deep trench, and still others gathered the hundred and more stiff frozen corpses from over the field, loaded them into the wagons to be piled like cordwood in the long trench. Among them was the old medicine man in his ghost dance shirt. Every night the Indians came to the trench to wail; and the coyotes howled about it for months." [26]

The next year 18 Congressional Medals of Honor were awarded to cavalrymen who participated in the massacre at Wounded Knee.

For the next two generations the Sioux were controlled by a bureacracy that allowed no self-determination and tried to destroy every detail of Indian culture and indentity. Native language, dress, foods, religion, ceremonies, scaffolding of the dead, were all forbidden. Sioux lands continued to disappear. Yet despite all this, much of the traditional culture was retained; tribal ties remained strong.

Gathering the frozen bodies for burial at Wounded Knee—'Indians came to wail and coyotes howled for months.'

'This old Indian Trail over 100 years old was used by many Indians taking children to Pierre Indian School from the Cheyenne Reservation past Lindsay over Lindsay Buttes north of Standing Buttes over Yellow Hawk Buttes—Each fall and spring caravans a mile long of Indian wagons, lots of kids, ponys, dogs was a familiar sight.'

Old inscription marking trail
north of Ft. Pierre

This picture shows taking children to school in the fall over Broken Arrow Trail 65 miles west of Pierre.

At the Indian Boarding School
1890 - 1895

During the last few days of August the acting Indian Agent would send his policeman out over the Reservation to notify the parents the time had come again for the boarding school to open. Some of the children would be ready and anxious to return...still others would have to be arrested and brought in by force.

All had to be taken by the school matrons directly to the two large bathrooms, one for the boys and one for the girls, where they were lined up outside the school house to await their turn at the bath. The stationary wash bowls and the unusually large bathtubs had been filled with water as hot as could possibly be used, and in it had been put a generous amount of kerosene, scrubbing brushes, and plenty of yellow soap. The older pupils who knew the routine would take the scared little newcomers in charge and commence the liquidation of the myriad insect inhabitants of the prairie and the tepees which the children unwittingly had brought along with them. The results were unbelievably effective...

The girls' hair was carefully dried and braided in one braid. The boys had to endure the humiliation of having their long hair cropped. They felt immodest, indeed quite naked...They were now ready to be dressed in the school uniform...All this was nothing to the suffering their poor little feet were to endure when they were taken out of their soft flat-soled moccasins and put into the awful brogans furnished by the United States government. They limped and shuffled about trying to learn to walk in the heavy things that were blistering their feet, some leaving bleeding sores which often became badly infected.

This ordeal completed, they were given an English name by which they were to be known at the school...

The Head Matron then employed in the school placed great importance upon the girls braiding their hair in one braid. She thought changing the mode of hair dress broke one more thread that bound the Indian girl to her camplife, so she made it an offense for a girl to comb her hair camp style, which was a part down the middle of the head from the forehead to the nape of the neck and braid each half tightly from behind the ears, framing the face as she thought most becomingly when it lay upon her chest. As a variant, a girl would often be seen braiding another's hair using four, five and sometimes seven strands. It was one of their native skills and it tended to soften the discipline of the one braid.

Another offense was for the girls to pluck out their eyebrows. This gave a decided Mona Lisa expression to their faces that they thought also added much to their good looks. As a result of this over-emphasis on the unimportant, when something at the school had really gone wrong, and the girls felt a spirit of rebellion within them, they would manage not to be seen doing it, nor heard protesting, but would suddenly appear with their hair in two braids and their eyebrows plucked.[27]

Thisba Morgan
Teacher at Pine Ridge government school
(where 200 children lived in two three-story
dormitories, heated by Franklin stoves and
lit by kerosene lamps.)

SCHOOLS FOR
INDIAN CHILDREN

Boys at Pine Ridge learning the printing trade; below, girls sewing class.

The girls...would set up camps in the several corners of the playground, complete with tepees made of unbleached muslin, about two feet high for the families of Indian dolls made from sticks, covered with brown cloth, with beads for eyes and real hair clipped from their own braids. Their dresses were cut Indian style, decorated with the tiniest of belts and necklaces and moccasins. Wagons would be made of the boxes and spools, to convey them and their belongings when on visits to a camp in a neighboring corner. There a feast would be prepared from scraps brought from the kitchen. One could see as many as fifty tepees at one time. One group would be encamping, another decamping, and another moving their heavy laden wagons.

Teepees in the playground.

Sometimes another touch of reality would be added to the camp when a travois would be seen near a tepee, a tiny horse or dog, moulded from the sticky gumbo with twigs for legs and dried in the sun, would be between the poles.

Frequently there could be seen a dozen or more braves squatting on the high ground looking down upon these miniature camps with nostalgic interest. They said it reminded them of their camps in the hills.

Thisba Morgan

'Exclusively in English'

The following order was issued in 1887:

The instruction of the Indian in the vernacular is not only of no use to them, but is detrimental to the cause of their education and civilization, and no school will be permitted on the reservation in which the English is not exclusively taught.

The order was protested vigorously by teachers, missionaries, agents and Indian leaders:

In its present shape it is tyrannical and officious... because it is a wanton measure, uncalled for and unjustifiable by precedents...a great hindrance to the enlightenment of the Indians. (Bishop Hare)

When the children hear Dakota they open their eyes and listen. But now you say we must not teach them anything but English. This makes my heart sad. It takes them long time to learn English good, but soon learn to read Dakota...The boys near forts learn English, but these words are very bad; they are most all swear words. In Dakota we do not have swear words...I hope you can let us teach Dakota for some time. When General Grant was president, we taught Dakota. (Catika, Left Handed, Sioux teacher)

All this controversy had one good good effect. It stirred the Indians to a greater appreciation of their Dakota Bible and many parents began to teach their children at home to read Dakota. The result was exactly what the Commissioner had tried to prevent, as it gave the Indians a stronger attachment to their own language. (Thomas Riggs)

In spite of objections by many educators, Indians report cruel punishments by others were meted out to them for speaking Sioux out of the classroom as well as within it.

Generations of Sioux children have gone to boarding school, both government and mission schools. With the assimilation policy in mind, many of the schools were set up off the reservation. One of the most famous of these was the Indian school established in Carlisle, Pennsylvania in 1879. Some of the first students were 84 boys and girls from Pine Ridge and Rosebud, including five of Spotted Tail's children. They were to stay three or four years without returning home, spending their summers living in white homes to strengthen the white influences. Agents soon protested that the skills these children learned were not useful on the reservation; parents objected to distant schools that kept their children so long and where, in fact, many died of tuberculosis and other diseases. The children were often terrified. Chief Luther Standing Bear, an Oglala, went to Carlisle at the age of eleven and returned to teach on the Rosebud reservation:

I remember when we children were on our way to Carlisle School, thinking that we were on our way to meet death at the hands of the white people, the older boys sang brave songs, so that we would all meet death according to the code of the Lakota—fearlessly...At Carlisle School where the change from tribal to white man's clothing was sudden and direct, the effect on the health and comfort of the children was considerable. Our first resentment was in having our hair cut. It has ever been the custom of Lakota men to wear long hair, and old tribal members still wear the hair in this manner. On first hearing the rule, some of the older boys talked of resisting, but realizing the uselessness of doing so, submitted. 28

Creating and Reducing
THE GREAT SIOUX RESERVATION

The American people need the country the Indians now occupy.

Bismarck Tribune
June 1874

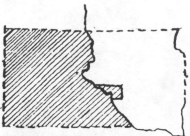

LARAMIE TREATY—1868
Created the Great Sioux Reservation from all South Dakota lands west of the Missouri River.

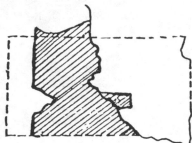

BLACK HILLS AGREEMENT -1876
Removed Black Hills and 50-mile strip from reservation.

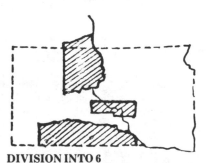

DIVISION INTO 6
          RESERVATIONS—1889
'Surplus' lands between these reservations opened to homestead settlement.

The utmost good faith shall always be observed towards the Indians; their land and property shall never be taken from them without their consent; and in their property, rights and liberty, they shall never be invaded or disturbed, unless in justified and lawful wars authorized by Congress; but laws founded in justice and humanity shall from time to time be made, for preventing wrongs being done to them, and for preserving peace and friendship with them.

Ordinance for Territory of the United States northwest of the river Ohio, 1789

SUBSEQUENT AGREEMENTS
made additional reservation land within these six areas available for settlement. Land openings held in 1904, 1907, 1909, 1911 and 1915.

Deadwood in 1876 was a roaring gold camp. In picture at far right, three Rockerville miners work a sluice box.

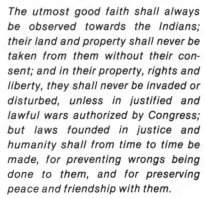

Madam Canutson, lady bullwhacker, brings freight into Black Hills.

At left below is wagon issue for Crow Creek Indians. Settled in localities, many Sioux lived in houses—but built open-air leaf-shaded bowers for summer living as did these Brule.

2356. "Gold Dust." Placer mining at Rockerville, Dak. Old timers, Spriggs, Lamb and Dillon at work. Photo and copyright by Grabill, 1889.

10. THE GOLD RUSH

The first prospecting party to enter the Black Hills the fall of 1874 built a strong stockade against the Indians and spent the winter there in six cabins within the stockade. Annie Tallent, a Black Hills historian and first white women in the Hills, was with this party. But in the spring they were evicted by military patrol.

All the next summer miners filtered into the many hidden valleys, gulches and caves of the Hills while the military pursued them. In the fall when the commission met with the Sioux to try to buy the Black Hills, General Crook requested the miners cooperate by getting out while the council met, in an effort to gain Sioux good will. Many miners responded and left for a time; others did not. Captain Pollock was left in charge of capturing the remaining miners. The miners deeply resented Pollock's strenuous efforts. They said he corralled them in "bullpens," tied them up, hanged some by their thumbs for hours, and used abusive language. (One might imagine the miners used abusive language in return.) Pollock marched his captives out of the Hills, but most came back.

With the commission's failure to deal with the Sioux, the government withdrew all troops from the Black Hills. Miners and Indians were left to work out their differences, as gold seekers poured in by the hundreds. By spring there were 10,000 miners in the Hills.

'All ded but me'

As miners swarmed through the hills and gulches, they began to find evidence of earlier miners. Rusty tools at the bot-

tom of what seemed to be a mine shaft; an iron chain deeply imbedded in a large tree; the broken stock of a rifle pocked with bullet holes, evidence of a bitter fight; the clothed skeleton of a white man. An old Colt pistol was found 16 feet deep on bed rock in a placer mine in what appeared to be a drainage ditch—the gun, said the Black Hills Times, was made in 1853. The Times also reported the discovery of a marked trail leading to an "old drift, 12 to 15 feet deep, which judging from a blazed tree standing at the mouth of the drift and whose age can be clearly determined by its circles, was made in 1865...adding one more to the many indications that the Hills were visited by adventurous miners years ago."

Most intriguing was the 1877 discovery of the Thoen Stone, found by Louis Thoen near Lookout Mountain. The date 1834 and the names of seven men were carved on a slab on sandstone with this cryptic message:

> Came to these Hills in 1833 Seven of us All ded but me Ezra Kind Killed by Ind. beyond the high hill Got our gold June 1834 Got all the gold we could carry our ponys all got by the Indians I have lost my gun and nothing to eat and Indians hunting me.

No trace of these miners or their gold was ever found; it was assumed Ezra Kind met the same fate as the others. The stone seems to be authentic. Most of the seven men were traced by letter, with relatives replying that the men had gone west and were not heard from again. The Thoen Stone is displayed in Deadwood.

Gold Strikes

The gold rush first hit Custer City in the southern Hills. By early 1876, Custer was a town of 6000 filled with saloons, gambling houses, dance halls and tent stores—sadly lacking in merchandise. A hastily built log hotel offered a cot on the ground and hard tack for the price of $10 a week. Most people camped in wagons, tents, or shelters of brush and poles.

Mining camps sprung up wherever a rich strike was made. Hundreds of people crowded in every day—by horseback, on foot, in wagon trains. Many came with dreams of finding rich claims and handfuls of golden nuggets. Others came with the quick instinct of getting rich off the gold others found. They came from other gold mining camps—in California, Colorado, Montana—expecting to strike it rich today and doubly rich tomorrow. In gold camps it was easy come, easy go, for throngs of miners, gamblers, saloon keepers, outlaws, dancehall girls, gunfighters, young people seeking adventure.

Even in the roaring mining camp atmosphere there was great fear of Indians. War parties and traveling bands of Sioux

Bear Gulch—only a trickle of water, well used.

Sluicing on Two Bit Creek.

skirted the Black Hills; many were on their way to join Sitting Bull and Crazy Horse on the Powder River. They ambushed the routes into the Hills, struck boldly at outlying mining camps, and raided settlements for horses. There was much fear of a full scale attack against whites in the Black Hills, and frequent appeals for troops—which were not granted until after the final Black Hills treaty.

Frequently travelers were ambushed in the Red Canyon area and around Spearfish. The Black Hills Pioneer reported "considerable trouble with Indians around Rapid City," in early September 1876. "Three men were killed on Thursday of last week and two more on Saturday." In October James Irion, hired to watch for Indians, "on account of his courage and skill as an Indian fighter," was killed by Indians in False Bottom.

The next summer the raids continued. A letter printed in a Deadwood paper pleaded:

> It seems to me that we should have some protection. The Indians are within three miles of us at this

Many rode into Deadwood on the stage from Spearfish.

Old Spearfish and Deadwood Stage Coach, Black Hills, S. Dak.

time burning hay and everything before them. I am worn out and other men here are the same...Have had four hours sleep in the last forty-eight. Yours in haste, W. L. DeMoss

The Black Hills Times reported on the same episode:

> Tom Overfelt and the eleven men who went out to fight the Indians are reported to be slaughtered, 20 miles from Deadwood. Wallace Kapinger's house and hay stacks have all burned and his five field men slaughtered not six miles from Deadwood.

Two hundred head of stock were run off at Centinnial by Indians, and the owners organized a posse of 20 men to go after them. At Belle Fourche a "large herd" of horses was stolen; a pursuing party recovered all but 20. The Black Hills Pioneer warned in February 1877: "It is no longer a matter of doubt, the Indians are upon us and prompt action is the only thing that will save us further loss of life and destruction of property."

Feeling against the Indians rose so high in the Black Hills that a proclamation was issued in July 1877 offering a reward of $250 for any Indian captured dead or alive in Lawrence County. The stated purpose was "to secure protection for our citizens from the depredations of the marauding savages, and to punish them for outrages already committed."[30]

Indians were blamed for 52 killings during the first three years of white settlement in the Black Hills. However, there is little doubt they were credited for somewhat more than their share of both killings and horse stealing.

Preacher Smith, the wandering Methodist minister who preached on street corners in Deadwood, was killed as he walked to Crook City to hold a service. Indians were blamed, but there was much local speculation and rumor that gambling interests had paid $300 to a certain killer to get the preacher off their backs. A local historian on the scene said this was an extravagant claim as the killer mentioned "would have shot his own grandmother for $30."

Hang them or set them Free

Another sensational ambush and murder involved five members of the Metz party traveling in Red Canyon. Although Indians were blamed, and the killings added to the intensity of Indian scares, many believed it to be the work of white outlaws. A favorite trick for outlaws such as Persimmons Bill and his gang, was to dress as Indians, using black horse tails for long flying hair.

Stagecoaches carrying gold were favorite targets for outlaws; some carried as much as $200,000 in gold. Four main routes left the Black Hills—to Cheyenne, Sidney, Bismarck, Ft. Pierre. All four offered tempting canyons, gullies and hilly curves for ambush. The Black Hills Pioneer reported wryly on one such ambush:

> Coach from Deadwood was stopped again last night near Cheyenne River. Both treasure boxes were taken. The passengers were not molested. The Road Agent sent word by the driver to the manager of the stage line to send them a pair of gold scales. They say dividing the dust with a tablespoon is not always satisfactory. (June 28, 1877)

Stealing horses was another profitable crime. Horses were rare in gold camps and could be sold for high prices. But the risks were high also. After one rash of horse stealing, a Homestake bookkeeper called Lame Johnny—known for his fine taste in horses—was arrested and taken by the deputy in the stage coach for Rapid City. But a posse of his victims stopped the coach at Buffalo Gap and Hung Lame Johnny to a nearby tree.

Potato Creek Johnny, above, found the largest nugget

At Hangman's Hill in Rapid City, three other victims of a lynching were strung up for stealing horses. The youngest of the three, Kid Hall, died protesting his innocence, saying he had joined the others shortly before they were caught.

Other miner courts were more lenient. A miners meeting in Custer City found two horse thieves guilty and debated whether to hang them or set them free. The decision was merely to exile them from Custer.

Miners who struck gold had to be on their guard. S. M. Booth was robbed of over $1000 of gold dust he had hidden in his boots, plus his shirt studs, sleeve and collar buttons. Shortly before, Booth lost $3400 in a holdup.

Loose Gold—Hard Gold

Loose gold was scattered in flakes, grains and nuggets in streams and old creekbeds where it had been washed down from veins of gold-bearing rock. This was the gold mined by placer methods. Loose gold was poor man's gold; all that was needed to get rich was a pick, shovel and pan. The romance of prospecting has always been in loose gold.

Hard gold was quite another matter. This gold was held in gold-bearing rocks and quartz, and was the source of all the gold in lower creeks. The quartz had to be crushed and treated for the gold to be extracted. Quartz mining was expensive and required capital and hired labor. But experienced miners searched for these rich veins where the percentage of gold in quartz was high. Most of all they dreamed of finding the "Mother Lode," the center from which the richest veins evolved.

Loose gold was the easy, first gold taken from the Black Hills. For it, miners dug their "pay dirt" in old gravel creekbeds, banks and places they judged promising. Then they panned the dirt in waters of a nearby creek. Since this was slow and tedious work, most miners soon built a sluice box. The sluice was a long sloping trough, built of lumber with cleats nailed to the bottom. As water and sand or mud were directed through the trough, gold and the heavy black sediment slid along the bottom and were caught by the cleats and riffles. Occasionally the water would be shut off and the material collected in the riffles panned out in the creek.

Sluicing required a good water supply, and usually the labor of two or three people. The dirt or gravel to be washed might need to be hauled some distance from the claim to the stream. It was sometimes hauled on a dried cow hide or carried in gunny sacks. Wheelbarrows and wagons of various types were also used. Three partners carried their pay dirt a half-mile—and made $2000 in one summer.

When water was scarce, as it was in Rockerville Gulch, the rocker was used. This was a kind of wooden box on rockers. It required two people—one to shovel in the pay dirt, the other to pour water and rock. Several hundred rockers were sometimes going at once in Rockerville. Water was often so scarce that even with this method mining could only be done in the spring.

The two richest places for loose gold, or placer mining, were Deadwood and Rockerville. Attempts were made to bring more water to Rockerville; one company spent a quarter of a million dollars on a 17-mile wooden flume, but the costs were not recovered in gold. Eventually the loose gold ran out; most placer mining was over by the 1890's. Placer mining was also wasteful—only about 65% of the gold was recovered through panning.

Hard gold meant digging deep shafts and tunnels, and bracing them with huge timbers. Other requirements were a means of blasting loose the ore, hauling it above ground, and extracting the gold. By 1876 there were already more than 150 of these quartz mines in the Deadwood area. Three years later over 4700 quartz mines were recorded. The miners used candles and lanterns to light their way. In the bigger mines, horses would haul the ore cars.

Ore was crushed by various methods, depending on the financial investment of the miners. Stamp mills were in common use, ranging from the little one-stamp mills to the eighty-stamp mill brought in by Homestake in 1878. The crushed ore was further crushed, then gold particles separated out by melting and formed into gold bars. Again this was wasteful with the primitive methods available. Only high grade ores were worth the costs of processing.

Homestake primed the Pump

Homestake, the richest gold mine of them all, was discovered by two brothers, Mose and Fred Manuel, with Henry Harney. These prospectors discovered a rich quartz vein in 1876, added the Old Abe mine, and took out $5000 in gold the first summer. The next year they sold their three mines—Homestake for $70,000, Old Abe for $40,000, and Terra for $35,000. But the company they sold to was not able to make expenses and resold to Hearst, Haggin and Tevis. Thus laid the foundations for huge Hearst fortunes.

Homestake acquired several other mines and improved methods and efficiency. As one observer noted, it takes a lot of money to prime the pump and Homestake always had the money when it was needed. Miners were paid $3.50 a day, with foremen and skilled miners earning up to $6 by 1889. Shrewd management, strong financial backing, and the fact that they seemingly had the Mother Lode meant success for Homestake. Numerous other big mining companies were formed in the Black Hills, operated for a time and then closed, usually due to financial difficulties.

Accidents were not infrequent in mining camps with deep mining. Three men were killed in a cave-in at Gayville; an explosion in the High Lode Mine killed three more. The Black Hills Times reported in 1886, "An explosion of powder on the 300 foot level of the Calendonia Mine in Terraville killed four miners and injured many more. Blood, dust, and powder were everywhere."

'A curse and a plea'

Disappointments were daily for the miners who hoped to strike it rich in the next shovel full. The days and weeks of hard work without seeing "color" discouraged many. One bitter miner wrote home with a curse, "Bad luck to this country!" and a plea, "If you have a grin of charity in your soul, send me $25." At Custer, the mayor had this terse comment: "Those coming here expecting to find it setting around in bags labelled with their names, or nuggets chasing them around begging to be picked up, generally go right back, cursing their mother for weaning them so young."

But as the loose gold played out in one canyon, a new report would come in of a gold strike in another part of the Hills, and the rush would be on again. Mining camps were deserted overnight.

When gold was discovered in Deadwood Gulch, everyone left Custer City. Only 14 people remained. What had been a booming city of 6000 one day, was suddenly a ghost town with 1400 empty buildings, abandoned diggins, broken sluice boxes.

Chinatown—Colorful, Sinister

Each new mining camp was a melting pot of fortune hunters from distant states and nations. Deadwood had at one time a large Chinese section called Chinatown, which thrived for 25 years. Chinatown was a colorful place with customs which seemed strange and sinister to the average westerner. There were gaudy ceremonies, feasts of roast pig, long burial processions to Mount Moriah, food placed on graves, bones later disenterred and sent to China. Secret Tong societies battled for power in Tong wars within the Chinese community. Whites sought to control the sinister opium dens. The Black Hills Times reported the ineffectiveness of one raid:

> It is a fact, not generally known, that the smoke houses are just as numerous as before the raid was made upon them, but are not so open. Only the initiated have access to the pipes of peace—and death. (Sept. 6, 1879)

Bull Teams supplied the Camps

Supplies came into the mining camps by wagon train—long lines of wagons hitched together and hauled by many teams of yoked oxen, mules or horses. As more and more people thronged into the hills, freighters brought enormous amounts of supplies: flour, food, furniture, mining equipment, mail, whiskey, goods of all kinds to supply the stores. A bull team—usually eight yoke of oxen—could haul four tons. Several of these teams made up the bull train.

Freighters were noted for their pungent language and frequent use of the long bull whip. The whip cracked like a rifle shot above the heads of the oxen, and was applied liberally to hides in getting through a mudhole or break in the road. Dakota gumbo was a big problem for freighters in rainy weather. The gumbo balled around wheels and built up in huge clumps on the hooves of oxen. Many times the bull trains were stranded and had to stop until the trails dried out.

In the mining camps food was often scarce; prices jumped with scarcity and dropped when several bull trains arrived with fresh supplies. In Deadwood during January 1879, eggs sold for 60¢ a dozen, onions 10¢ a pound, butter 50¢ a pound, apples 10¢ to 20¢ each. Live chickens were from $12 to $15 each, though they were selling in Yankton for $2.50 a dozen.

Deadwood was described as exciting but peaceful by the Black Hills Times in 1877:

> In the evening the miners employed on day shifts at the different mines begin to pour in Deadwood City. The streets are thronged, and the multitudes are regularly regaled with music from one or both of the theaters. Fifty cents will buy an admission ticket with a coupon tacked on, redeemable at the bar...The card halls are usually crowded with the anxious and delighted throngs, some intent on the progress of the various games, while others are attracted by the music of the orchestra found in these places of amusement...All this until the wee hours when out of the gaslight, out of the dazzle, the hardy miner wends his way to his cabin on the hill.

Crime and Passion

But a Chicago reporter described Deadwood as a cruel place where a man or two was killed every night, blaming the killings on the crimes and passions of claim jumping, high gambling stakes, jealousy of the heart, robbery, and hard drinking.

The rowdiest section of Deadwood was known as "the Badlands." At one time it contained 76 saloons, according to Gold-Gals-Guns-Guts, the Deadwood/Lead history edited by Bob Lee, "The Gem was one of the most popular variety show places with curtained booths where ladies entertained 'hellbent for fun' miners above the dance floor, bar and stage...Crowded audiences were delighted with ministrelry, ballad singing, banjo whacking, bone rattling scenes, sketches and refrains, acrobatic acts, dancers, can can girls and trapeze artists."[31]

The first wagonloads of dance hall and "upstairs" girls came to town in the Colorado Charlie Wagon Train the summer of '76, says the history. "Wherever the miners uncovered new diggings, the sporting population was not far behind."

The men and women in mining camps were "a Ruff crowd," in the words of a Custer pioneer. Famous and notorious characters of the west came to the Black Hills: Sam Bass, Doc Middleton, Texas Charley, Laughing Sam, Lame Johnny Reddy, Modoc Bill, Long Yank, Wyatt and Morgan Earp, Bat Masterson, Poker Alice Tubbs, Madame Canutson—female bullwhacker, Wild Bill Hickok, and Calamity Jane.

A people's law prevailed—some mining camps drew up rigid rules. Yet violence was common. There were 96 deaths in the Lead-Deadwood area in 1878, 16 of them murder, 6 suicide.

Fly Speck Billy was lynched one night on French Creek for killing a freighter. Photo is from Custer pageant.

Prospectors coming to the gold fields were known as 'a ruff crowd.'

The "Yellow Doll," a young and beautiful Chinese girl, was found chopped to bits with a hatchet in one unsolved 1877 murder. John Hinch of Nevada was killed at his claim after a gambling argument in which he had accused John Carty and Jerry McCarty of cheating. The two men were captured, tried and found guilty of assault and battery. James Farrell was killed that fall in a Deadwood restaurant in an argument over a bill; Harry Varnes was killed in nearby Gayville in Hanley's Saloon over a card game.

There is the story told by Ben Casey in *The Black Hills* of the male piano player who came to Deadwood with a pretty young singer. One night they were performing in the theater—she singing beautiful sad songs for homesick miners—when a man rushed in and fired twice at the piano player. He swung around on the piano stool, fired cooly and dropped the intruder. The singer screamed, wrung her hands and sobbed, "Oh John, he's killed you." The dying man called for a priest. "She's my wife," he said hoarsely. "She ran away with this man. And I don't want to cash in my chips till I know she's going to be properly married." The priest arrived, administered last rites and stayed to marry the widow to her husband's killer.

Bummer Dan was killed in a case of mistaken identity with Slippery Sam.

Kitty LeRoy was a pretty entertainer, the toast of the mining camp, who had left her first husband and child in Michigan, danced in Texas and California. Her new husband Samuel Curley objected to her continuing her profession in Deadwood and left for Denver. A few months later he returned, broke into Kitty's at the Lone Star House, shot her and killed himself. A local account lamented Kitty's loss: "There in all her subtle beauty and youthful loveliness she lay dying. And close by was the body of her poor, mistaken scoundrel of a husband, with the top of his head blown off."

Ruby Tucker who ran the Ruby House in Keystone was killed in a gunfight between Lecherous Leo the Lawman and Wildman Ed, over her affections.

The first killing in Custer City occurred when two partners, Tom Milligan and Alex Shaw were contesting their shooting skill. Since both were drinking excessively, Milligan settled the contest by shooting Shaw instead of the old bucket they used as a target. A lynch mob decided against a hanging and instead fined Milligan $25 for shooting his gun within city limits.

The people were not so generous in the case of Fly Speck Billy Fowler, a freckled faced two-bit outlaw who got drunk in

'Oh John, he's killed you'

Custer and shot his empty gun at Abe Barnes, a freighter who had given him a ride into town. His second shot spun a bullet out of the chamber and Barnes fell dead. The sheriff arrested Fly Speck Billy and held him in a cabin. Later that night a lynch mob surrounded the cabin, dropped a loop over Fly Speck Billy's neck and dragged him to a pine tree on French Creek. The hanging was unneeded, it seemed; Billy had been dragged to death. The Custer Chronicle of January 8, 1881, reported the sheriff gathered a posse to retrieve his prisoner:

> The posse followed the tracks of the mob across French Creek, and there they found Fly Specked Billy hanging from a pine. Judge Lynch had executed his inexorable sentence cleverly and secretly, and Fly Specked Billy, with his hands warm with the blood of his inoffending victim, had paid the penalty. And his soul, if such as he have souls, had fled to the tortures of an eternity of punishment. The body was cut down and brought into town...The body of the murderer will be buried today. Mr. Barnes will be kept waiting for the arrival of a brother.

The Dead Man's Hand

By far the most famous killing in the Black Hills was the shooting of Wild Bill Hickok by Jack McCall. Wild Bill was a famous gunman when he arrived in the Black Hills, having cleaned up the tough town of Abilene as its marshall. He came to the Black Hills the summer of 1876, and had only been there a few months working some diggings and playing poker when he was killed. Historians agree he did little of importance in the Black Hills, except to die there. But his death was quite enough to insure immortality in Deadwood's colorful history not only for himself but for Jack McCall and Calamity Jane as well.

On the fatal night, Wild Bill was playing poker with three friends in Saloon Number 10, when a drifter named Jack McCall came in, walked behind and shot him in the back. Hickok's cards fell to the floor—a pair of black aces and three eights, ever since known as the "dead man's hand."

The killer was tried in an informal people's court; since there was no law in Deadwood—everyone was there illegally—there could be no official court. Jack McCall was found not guilty when he claimed Wild Bill had killed his brother in Kansas. Later in a drinking bout in Cheyenne he boasted of killing the biggest gunman in the world, was arrested and taken to Yankton for trial. This time he was silent on the claimed killing of his brother and it was apparent he had never known Hickok; the motive seemed to be in his boast of having been tough enough to kill a fast gun. McCall was found guilty and hanged.

> IT IS REPORTED from Sturgis City that Calamity Jane walloped two women at that place yesterday. Calamity can get away with half a dozen ordinary pugilistic women when she turns loose, but she never fights unless she is in the right, and then she is not backward to tackle even a masculine shoulder hitter.
>
> **Black Hills Daily Times**
> **February 8, 1879**

Wild Bill was buried above Deadwood, "starting the graveyard." His friend Charlie Utter inscribed this message on his wooden tombstone: J. B. Hikok killed by the assassin Jack M'Call in Deadwood, Black Hills, August 2d, 1876. Pard, we will meet again in the happy hunting ground to part no more. Goodbye, Colorado Charlie, C. H. Utter.

Subsequent actions of Calamity Jane showed her motives not unlike those of Jack McCall in linking her name to that of the famous Wild Bill Hickok. She declared he had died in her arms, murmuring she was the only one he'd ever loved. As Calamity Jane told it, in an autobiographical pamphlet she sold during the last years of her life, "I at once started to look for the assassin and found him at Shurdy's butcher shop and grabbed a meat cleaver and made him throw up his hands, because through the excitement of hearing of Bill's death having left my weapons on the post of my bed."

Other witnesses say a posse found McCall in an empty barn across the street. Also questioning Calamity's claim are two letters from Wild Bill to his bride of three months, a talented circus bareback rider living in Cheyenne. On July 19 he wrote:

> **My Own Darling Wife Agnes: I have but a few moments left before this letter starts...My friend will take this to Cheyenne if he lives. I don't expect to hear from you, but it is all the same; I know my Agnes and only live to love her. Never mind, Pet, we will have a home yet, and then we will be so happy. I am almost sure I will do well here...Goodbye, Dear Wife**

Twenty-seven years later, when Calamity Jane died, conveniently near Deadwood, her wish to be buried beside Wild Bill Hickok was granted, even though the truth seems to be that she did not really know him in life.

Despite this striving for second-hand fame, Calamity Jane is a legendary figure in her own right, She is easily the most famous woman in South Dakota history. A strong and colorful woman, she was notorious for her loud, profane language, and apparently deserved her reputation as a hard drinking, loud mouthed, gun slinging tough. She boasted that she "never went to bed sober or with a penny in her pocket," and her favorite speech upon entering a saloon was said to be, "I'm Calamity Jane—and this drink's on the house."

Roundups threw together great herds. Largest gathered 45,000 cattle at the head of the Bad River in 1897 roundup.

Rough in his ways? Yes,
  But kind and good-hearted;
There wasn't a flaw
  In the heart of Wild Bill.
And well I remember the day that he started
  That graveyard on top of the hill.

Captain Jack Crawford
Poet Scout 1879

11. EARLY RANCHING

Cattle kingdoms and the long Texas drives which are so much a part of South Dakota history began with the opening of two markets: Indian annuities and supplies for Black Hills mining camps.

Cattle had come into Dakota Territory much earlier, however. Before 1820, there were cattle at Manuel Lisa's trading post. Military expeditions and army forts were supplied with live beef herds. Pioneers brought cattle into the first settlements—in fact, cattle often transported the pioneers and their goods. Herds of beef cattle ranged early on the James River near Yankton. The 1870 census showed over 12,000 cattle in Dakota Territory.

But when western markets opened, the long drives began. At first southern cattlemen filled contracts for Indian beef. The 1868 Laramie treaty agreed to issue a pound of meat per day for four years for treaty Indians. Most was Texas longhorn beef—almost more horn than beef, it was said. Later requirements called for part of this issue to be filled with heavier cattle from Oregon or the east.

By 1876, beef herds were trailed into the Black Hills to feed the miners. Some were pastured, with the Centennial prairie and Spearfish Valley as favored grazing lands. Work oxen were grazed there for freighters at $2 each per day under guard from Indian attack. The first ranchers, such as the Deffenbach brothers, settled in this area.

'Last Chance' Grew Bigger

Short grass ranges proved to be excellent pasture. Though seemingly scant, the grass was nutritious and cured on the stem, making its own winter hay. Snowfall was normally light, so steers could be turned loose on the open range and left winter and summer with little care until ready to market as five or six year olds. It was a recognized fact that steers turned out on the hardy northern ranges grew 200 pounds heavier than they did in the south. Even the horses began to grow—and some said the cowboys, too.

Ike Blasingame, a Matador cowboy from Texas on the Cheyenne River reservation, tells of his surprise one day upon seeing a large fine-looking horse which seemed strangely familiar. "Sure enough, I had broken him in Texas," he says. "And because he was so sorry and scrubby looking I named him Last Chance. He still had the name, but he had developed and filled out to twice his former size."

In good years profits ran high for the big cattle companies. But a hard winter hit them with heavy losses because they provided no hay or feed. "Through" cattle suffered most—cattle recently arrived from the south and not acclimated to cold winters.

After the Black Hills treaty, white cattlemen had a 50-mile strip of public land at the western edge of South Dakota in which to graze, plus a somewhat wider area around the Black Hills. In 1889 this was enlarged as the Sioux reservation was cut back to five smaller reservations. But until 1902, no white cattlemen used reservation lands legally; the only cattle supposed to be there belonged to Indians or whites married to Indians.

In the western edge and along the Hills, many small stock ranches grew up. Some were started by freighters and miners; others by cowboys who had come with beef herds from the south. After the Sioux were settled, big outfits moved in, trailing steers north by the thousands. Each spring new shipments of longhorn steers took the place of those marketed the fall before, and those lost over winter.

Longhorns were Spooky

Texas longhorns were wild and spooky. They'd stampede at the flick of a rope and chase any moving object. A newsman who watched cowboys work four days to cross a big Texas herd to the Whetstone Indian agency, wrote that any bravery he'd seen previously in the west was pale before "the actions of Morrow's herders who are constantly among the immense herds of wild Texans who, almost every day, charge upon and overthrow both man and horse in their mad career...I saw several instances of this kind while watching the efforts to get the herd across the river, and must say that I would greatly prefer attempting to handle a wounded and enraged buffalo bull, rather than some of the Texans now here."

The days of free open range were soon numbered. Pioneer farmers began to settle in the outlying valleys of the Black Hills. They fenced off waterholes and trails. The Herd Law passed by eastern Dakota settlers required all stockmen to fence their animals in or be responsible for damages caused to gardens and fields. When the Herd Law was enforced around Kadoka in 1910, one widow gave up and quit ranching; her children were not able to herd the cattle out of small patches of homesteader corn, so settlers would pen up her cattle and charge her one dollar a head to get them back.

Stockmen countered by pushing through an amendment to the Herd Law allowing county choice. This kept several predominately range counties exempt for years until a new wave of dryland homesteaders objected.

Cattlemen purchased land where they could. Since it was not practical to fence single sections because of water and lay of the land, many fenced in public lands with the private.

Small ranchers were ignored when reservation grazing opened. These rich grasslands, virtually ungrazed since buffalo times, were leased only in huge blocks to the big outfits. Matador leased the entire east half of the Cheyenne River reservation—about 48 miles square—at three cents an acre, then re-leased the southern half to the Turkey Track. Several big outfits came directly from the south to their new reservation leases, without having ever run cattle in Dakota before.

Ed Lemmon, noted South Dakota pioneer who first came to the Hills in 1877 with 100 steers for a cavalry detachment, engineered the first reservation lease when he went to Washington with a cattlemen delegation. The stockmen went to ask President Roosevelt not to enforce the law forbidding fencing of public lands. Teddy Roosevelt knew these men and understood their problem; during his brief Little Missouri ranching days he had been active in helping them organize stockmen's associations in Dakota and Montana. But he did not budge from his stand. "Gentlemen," he said "the fences will come down."

'World's Biggest Pasture'

Lemmon did persuade the president it was time to lease South Dakota Indian reservation lands. As manager of the L7 he arranged the first lease of over 865,000 acres on Standing Rock and fenced it with 270 miles of three-wire fence—the largest fenced pasture in the world.

Many of the big cattle outfits were foreign financed. Both the Turkey Track (called 'The Tracks' by the cowboys) and the Matador were owned by English and Scotch. The Turkey Track built up to 45,000 head in 1890; the Hash Knife ran 50,000 head; Oelrichs had 65,000 cattle at their peak; Triskill of the TXT brought 3000 longhorns north each year till they had 30,000 to 36,000 grazing the Belle Fourche region.

Murdo MacKenzie, for whom the town Murdo was named, managed the Matadors and expanded that company into one of the greatest cattle empires in the world with huge herds in Texas, Wyoming, Canada and South Dakota. He ran 60,000 cattle on the northeast quarter of the Cheyenne River reservation. MacKenzie was a "great cowman," in the words of cowpunchers who knew him. President Roosevelt called him the "most influential of the Western cattlemen...a leader... far-sighted and enlightened." Other big outfits were the VVV, the

Z Bell, the Bar T, the 101, and the Sword and Dagger (called 'Daggers'). Big Indian ranchers were Marcisse Narcelle; Bill Benoist; who owned 2000 head of cattle and many bands of horses; the La Plant family with 3000 head on the Cheyenne River reservation; the Claymores; Fred Dupree.

Despite the domination of huge cattle companies, the vast majority of ranches were individually owned and ran from a few hundred to one or two thousand head of cattle. Some, such as the big JA were run by women—Mrs. Adair had 10,000 cattle on the Belle Fourche. Many girls and women were excellent riders and top hands at handling cattle.

Ed Lemmon tells of two girls, Edna and Inez Moses, ages seven and nine, who did most of the riding for several hundred range cattle and a big band of horses. One day Lemmon said their father was worried because the girls had been gone five hours chasing a band of wild horses which had stampeded from the corral that morning. But, says Lemmon, "while we were talking...here they came, fogging the band of wild horses right into the corral...those little girls didn't seem to think chasing that bunch of horses thirty-five miles to Coyote Holes and back again was anything unusual."

Spearfish became a place where many ranchers headquartered or wintered and a number built showplace homes there.

By 1884, there were 700,000 to 800,000 cattle in western South Dakota. But with the opening of the reservations in 1902, the totals leaped much higher.

On the Reservation

Running cattle on the reservation entailed special responsibilities. Cattlemen had to agree to handle all the Indian cattle run on their lease the same as their own, branding and rounding up for shipping. Each Indian owner could run 100 head free, and paid one dollar a head over that number.

The roundup cook was usually willing to feed visiting Indians, and gifts of beef were sometimes given. Ike Blasingame writes in *Dakota Cowboy* that Matador cowboys were encouraged to show good will by attending Indian celebrations. He describes the pretty Indian girls at a Christmas Eve gathering he attended:

> They had sparkling stuff in their black hair—bits isinglass (mica) from the hills, which shone like diamonds when they moved their heads. They wore beaded bands, fitted with gay feathers and beautiful beaded capes covered their shoulders, and their moccasins and white buckskin clothing was heavy with beadwork. A colorful, shining sight. And around the maidens clustered the young bucks, like honeybees around their queen, laughing and showing off.

Many cowboys came to sympathize with the Sioux distress at being forced to bury their dead; their traditions were to place the body high in the air, not to force the spirit to fight out of "the darkness of a hole in the ground." Blasingame says

Cowboys 'take grub' at roundup camp

Many ranchwomen broke and trained their own horses.

they would sometimes hide the bodies in trees, but these were usually discovered and a burial forced by the Indian agent. Not always were dead babies found, however. One day, he says, he and another cowboy found a blanket-wrapped bundle tied high in a tree containing a baby's dried body. They did not report it, but thought of the squaw they had heard howling from the hill at midnight. If she "was happier in her little buck high in a tree near her, instead of mouldering in the grave as the white man insisted, then she could have him there...But we remembered whenever we rode by the old elm or when we heard the squaw keening in the darkness."

Each spring thousands of cattle arrived at the railhead towns east of the Missouri, such as Evarts and Chamberlain. All had to be dipped for ticks, scab and lice. Evarts had two long vats, 80 and 150 feet, filled with fuming solutions of nicotine, lime and sulphur. Cattle plunged through the vats as they ran down the chutes to the ferry. In the highwater of spring, cattle crossed the river on ferries built with pens like a floating stockyard. An entire trainload of four and five hundred thin Texas cattle could be loaded on the ferry at Evarts, says Blasingame.

Locating the wild cattle could be tricky. Bill Hill who trailed 3000 head from the Texas Panhandle north to the Moreau River, said he and the other cowpunchers had to hold them there a month and a half waiting for the boss to send another thousand located cattle to mix in. "The cattle would walk clean out of the country in bunches of 50 to 500 unless you stayed with them till they got located, or could mix them in with local cattle."

Stolen Beef

Rustling cattle was a continuing concern of stockmen. Indian rations were often slim—and the mining camps infested

on the Belle Fourche in 1887.

with lawless men—so cattle were a frequent target of both hungry Indians and outlaw bands.

The Z Bell which ranged near Pine Ridge during the troubled times of the Wounded Knee Massacre, lost so much beef it began closing out in 1893. Beef rations had been reduced by the government in efforts to force Indians to farm. Indians were traditionally meat eaters; with the wild game gone, the promised rations reduced and eroded away by fraud, they felt justified in butchering the beef they needed now and then.

Cattlemen were angered as their losses increased, blaming the government for forcing them to make up the difference. Some of the cattle companies with Indian contracts were not above short counts of their own. Ed Lemmon mentions the "run them around the hill" trick of an acquaintance, in which counted cattle were recounted after disappearing from sight. Sometimes weights were averaged, with a few of the heaviest steers weighed and that figure multiplied by the total number.

Much stolen beef ended up in mining camp butcher shops. In at lease one instance, in August 1877, cattlemen got together and dealt with cattle thieves who were furnishing butcher shops in a final way. They had been losing cattle in Spearfish Valley, and one day discovered a beef had been butchered in the timber. A vigilante group of Spearfish ranchers caught Beans Davis and George Keating, who ran a butcher shop in Central City, sleeping at the foot of Lookout Mountain with the stolen meat. The vigilantes woke the two men, dragged them to a tree and hung them, in the first recorded hanging for cattle rustling in Dakota Territory.

Ed Lemmon describes a near-lynching near McLaughlin in his book *Boss Cowman*. Angry cattlemen who had been losing many cattle got together one night in a darkened schoolroom with the long-time suspect, now caught red handed. Some argued for hanging, but in the end cooler heads prevailed and the rustler was tried and convicted in court.

But convictions were hard to get. Known rustlers usually went free. Jack Sully, called the "prince of cattle thieves," was arrested many times over a period of seven or eight years. The last time he was jailed near the Rosebud reservation, but escaped and was shot by a posse.

Cattlemen organized to deal with the problems of rustling, wolves and roundups. A blackball system was used, so only those ranchers approved by everyone could join the association. Small ranchers and others crowding onto range where they were not wanted were often kept out and denied benefits of roundups and brand inspection.

In South Dakota from the beginning, much association money was spent on detectives and brand inspection. One of the able stock detectives hired was Sam Moses. One day Moses set out to catch Spokane Augher, a cattle thief known to be selling beef to railroad construction crews. With Ed Blakely, sheriff of Fall River County, he watched through field glasses as Spokane and a young helper roped and shot a steer. Just as they rolled it on its back to begin skinning, Moses and Blakely rode down, shouting for them to raise their hands. Spokane grabbed in the grass for his six-shooter, threw himself behind the carcass and began firing. The lawmen were better armed with rifles, and shot right through the carcass. Spokane stepped out, dripping blood and surrendered. He served two years.

Roundups

Roundups were held spring and fall, lasting a month or more. The Black Hills Livestock Association issued the following instructions for their first spring roundup in 1881: the northern to begin May 10 north of Bear Butte, follow up the Belle Fourche River into Wyoming, then up the Little Missouri and swing back toward the Slim Buttes; the southern roundup to start May 15 at the southern end of the Black Hills going

This 1887 roundup photo shows both the working herd (background) and the holding herd of a particular brand. Cattle were milled clockwise in working herd while the reps rode among them.

down the Cheyenne to the mouth of the Belle Fourche, then up that river to the point near Bear Butte where the northern roundup starts.

All creeks, watersheds and plateaus in the region were combed for cattle with some cowboys riding the inside draws, and others the outside. An elected wagon boss took charge. Big outfits sent their wagons and cowboys; smaller ones sent one or two "reps," men representing their brand. Over 100 men worked the spring roundup of 1885.

Roundup days were long. Cowboys spent 18 hours in the saddle; they rose for breakfast at 3:30 a.m., went to bed at dark, and stood a two-hour stint of guard duty during the night. Still, roundups were a time of excitement, sport and practical jokes. A reporter with the first roundup said there were many kinds of contests, especially horse racing, "As there is no lack of good horses and good riders, some very fine races take place." Green-broke horses nearly always bucked first thing in the morning.

Some roundups gathered herds of thousands before any brands were cut out, especially in fall when beef herds were gathered. Others worked with smaller herds, cutting out from day to day. Ed Lemmon, who bossed what has been called the largest roundup of all time, says that 1897 roundup threw together 45,000 head of cattle on Peno Flat at the head of Bad River. These cattle were gathered by five separate roundups with nearly 300 cowpunchers.

Lemmon's method of working the big herd was to work about 500 at a time. This more manageable herd was circled to the left, clockwise, as 60 reps moved among them cutting out the brands they were looking for. Each rep turned his cattle out at his cut, or designated spot, where other cowboys held stock with that brand. Lemmon, who was known as a fast and competent cowman, says, "By working five herds a day, three in the forenoon and two in the afternoon, we finished the job in three days."

Other big roundups followed the hard deep-snow winters of 1902 and 1907 when starving cattle traveled far off their ranges, across drifted fences and down onto the breaks of the Missouri. For their 1907 spring roundup on the Cheyenne River reservation, the Matadors had 60 reps come to ride with them from as far away as North Dakota, Wyoming and Montana. What many found instead of live cattle were thousands of dead carcasses carrying their brand. The worst winter of all time was 1886-1887; cattle losses were great with heavy snow, continuous blizzard conditions, and cold temperatures. After the hard winter of 1907, the L7 began closing out; so did the Sword and Dagger.

Hard winters caught big cattle outfits unprepared. The cured grass they depended on for winter feed was under deep drifts of snow. Overgrazing during dry summers also left little margin for long cold winters.

Expert cowboys were highly valued to work the big herds of wild cattle. Many of them were Indian. Charlie Bearheels,

who rode in the last big roundup in White River country, explained that many of them were good ropers because they learned to rope wild game when ammunition was short. "When we first went on the reservation we could not have any guns. Even later when we could have guns we had little cash. Bullets were not to use unless no other way. I used to rope deer and wolves from running horses." said Bearheels.

In fall it was important to handle a beef herd right so as not to run off weight. Bird Rose of the L7 was known for his easy manner of handling wild stock. In *Dakota Cowboy* Blasingame tells how Rose would leave a touchy steer alone until after he quieted. "He would ease up to the cattle and just sit around on his horse...He took time to let stock get acquainted with him and see what he looked like."

But Blasingame admits it was more fun to work roundup with Ed Lemmon. "His horses were fast, and so was he, and those of us young fellows who were a little on the 'wild cowboy' order enjoyed working with (his) outfit...Ed Lemmon slapped a roundup together fast."

In his own book, Lemmon recalls his pleasure in one time inheriting a crew of eight top cowhands, as wagon boss for the WG. These were the dependable cowboys who had each filed homestead claims for WG at strategic locations. They were placed under the popular leadership of Lemmon because they were in "a mighty independent position" and had to be treated well. The handling by this top crew of a cattle shipment in Valentine, Nebraska drew open-mouthed admiration from watching cowmen, says Lemmon.

On returning from cattle deliveries at Middle Creek stockyards, Lemmon usually let his crew stay over in "Scoop Town" (Sturgis), because of their fondness for "booze and painted dance hall women."

Sturgis was just one of the lively cowtowns that edged the open ranges. Rapid City was another all time favorite. Belle Fourche was the world's largest primary cattle shipping point in the 1890's and a popular spot for cowboys. Evarts and La Beau were lively centers for reservation cowboys. La Beau was especially popular with Matador cowboys until a quick series of events spelled its end in 1909. Dode MacKenzie, son of Murdo MacKenzie, was shot and killed in a saloon there. When the killer was tried and found not guilty, Matador cowboys shunned the town. Two fires soon finished the once-lively cowtown; even the tracks were torn up over which Matador had shipped so many cattle.

Stampeding Longhorns

During roundups and trail drives cattle were held on the bedground at night to keep them bunched and quiet. Longhorn steers were easily spooked. Thunderstorms especially alerted the cattle and got them on their feet, ready to run. Every cowboy had his favorite story of the worst stampede, set off by something as harmless as a cough or as explosive as fiery lightning balls leaping along the backs of wet cattle.

Blasingame says his worst stampede started from a

yellow slicker tied onto a staked horse to keep the saddle dry. Thunder crashed in the night, the horse jerked loose and plunged into the horse remuda. Lightning flashed; the yellow slicker popped and flapped like wings from the saddle. The loose horses spooked through the middle of camp, taking the picketed night horses with them. All of them ran through the 2000 head of gathered steers. Horses and steers ran most of the night; few cowboys even had a horse to ride. Next morning cattle and horses were scattered for miles and roundup began all over again.

One fall night a big stampede mixed 6000 steers in several beef herds being held for shipment on the west bank of the Missouri near Evarts. The cowboys worked all next day to separate them, and had just finished when a man on a pinto horse with a dog at his heels came trotting down the trail. Cattle which have run one night are more likely to do it again and the L7 steers lifted their heads, snorted and ran for two hours.

Beef herds were usually brought into Evarts 1200 at a time, for three trainloads of 400 steers. Each outfit was allowed to fill just one train a day during busy season. These were shipped on Monday, Tuesday and Wednesday to arrive at market the first three days of the following week. Evarts was one of the largest shipping points in the United States at that time. At the height of the season, a full train of steers left Evarts every hour.

Thousands of steers were held on the west side of the Missouri waiting their turn to cross. Corrals led onto the pontoon bridge which was used in fall with low water, anchored with cables to the riverbottom. Steers were loaded from ten chutes off the bridge directly into boxcars.

Beef from northwestern South Dakota was trailed down "the Strip" to Evarts. The Strip was a six-mile-wide lane leased by the Milwaukee railroad through the Cheyenne River reservation. It was 80 miles long and provided with watering places about every 12 miles.

Horse Ranches

Horse ranching had a parallel development with cattle. Good horses were so essential to cattle ranches that many cattlemen raised a band of horses on the side. A strong horse market developed, with heavy settlement east of the Missouri, and some ranchers began specializing in horses.

Horses raised in short grass country became known for their bone, muscle, wind and heart; the U. S. Cavalry purchased many of their best horses from this region.

California Joe, a scout with Custer, started a horse ranch on Rapid Creek as early as 1876. But he was raided by Indians so often he gave it up. Soon after Reiley brought brood mares to Spearfish Valley and Gammon to the False Bottom ranch. The valley at St. Onge became known for its excellent horses; horse racing was common there in the 1880's with betting by local sportsmen. Star and Bullock raised standard-bred trotters on the Belle Fourche and the Wells horse outfit located at the mouth of Rabbit Creek with 700 horses. The famed JB horse ranch near Slim Buttes, running up to 3000 head of Percherons, was started by a freighter who also tried his hand at panning gold. South Dakota had 469,000 horses by 1900, and reached an all time high of 832,000 by 1920.

Sheep meant Profit, Conflict

Sheep ranching was well adapted to the open range country. In 1878, a stockman named Hale moved 3000 sheep onto the range near Bear Butte. Other sheepmen soon became established in that region and south of the Black Hills. As with beef, quick profits could be made. In 1884, Ed Stenger trailed 2400 sheep into the Black Hills and—though more than half died the first winter—sold them in spring for more than he'd paid for the herd. With 85,000 sheep in the area, sheepmen

Green broncs showed cowboys plenty of 'blue sky' each morning. Below, calves are roped and branded.

Wintering a horse band.

formed an association to protect their interests. By the turn of the century there were over 500,000 sheep in the Hills region, and this number increased sharply during and after the 1911 and 1912 drouth when cattle numbers fell and farms were deserted.

As sheep moved in, there was conflict almost at once with cattlemen who claimed the free range. In South Dakota most conflict was settled peaceably. However Ed Lemmon writes of the killing of a sheepherder in the Fall River country in the early nineties by a Texas cowboy, Ben Harrison, from his outfit. Bitterness is evident, too, in fact that sheepmen were not allowed to use The Strip for trailing to Evarts. In 1909 Chief Forester Pinchot held meetings in Deadwood to decide whether to allow sheep to graze national forest lands of the Black Hills. Determined sheepmen matched angry cattlemen at two all-night meetings, but Pinchot ruled against the sheepmen. One sheepman who leased range on the Standing Rock reservation couldn't understand why his sheep wouldn't stay on the bedground, until a friend told him 15 pounds of pepper had been sprinkled there by stockmen who didn't want sheep on the reservation.

Cattlemen believed sheep would ruin both grass and waterholes. It took the drouth of 1911 - 1912 to convert many of them into sheepmen. After that, many raised both cattle and sheep; some changed back and forth with changing conditions. Sheep provided two income crops: wool in spring and market lambs in fall. Also they did better on skimpy grass and, being herded, could take advantage of isolated patches of grass and the chopped-up range conditions that existed after the first big wave of homesteaders left the country.

For every 1000 - 1200 head of ewes—a band—the sheepman provided a herder, wagon and dog. The herder was the cornerstone of the sheep business, yet he had none of the cowboy's glamour. He was socially at the bottom rung of the ladder. No one has written the story of the sheepherder better than South Dakota's Archer Gilfillan in his classic book *Sheep*. Gilfillan herded sheep west of the Slim Buttes for eighteen years, after dropping his studies for the ministry. Herding sheep was what he called a steady job: 16 to 24 hour days, 7 days a week, 31 days a month. He protests the popular belief that herding is monotonous:

> **Sheep rarely act the same two days in succession. If they run one day they are apt to be quiet the next. They herd differently in a high wind from what they do in a gentle breeze. They travel with a cold wind and against a warm one. They are apt to graze contentedly where feed is plenty and to string out and run where the picking is poor. Herding at one season is so different from herding at another as to almost constitute a different job. No one herding day is exactly like any other day, and there is doubtless much more variety in them than there is in the days spent in office or factory.**

At lambing the sheep bands were brought in close to the lambing pens. Day and night all hands were needed to lamb out, protect the newborn from bad weather, and to mother up the often-cantankerous ewes with their lambs. On the range, the stronger one of twins or triplets was left with the mother. Others were raised as bums, given away, or—if weak—hit in the head.

For shearing, the sheep were again trailed to a central location. In some areas big shearing pens were established and manned by a big crew, such as the pens built by the railroad at Marietta. A good shearer could clip 100 sheep a day with hand shears.

After a week or so of work and socializing at the shearing pens, the herder trailed back to the range. The wagon was located in the vicinity of water, so that sheep could graze off the bedground in the morning, hit water about noon, rest there during the heat of the day, and circle back to the bedground toward dark. Depending on supply of grass, the wagons might not be moved for a month or more.

Sheepherders monuments, also called Stone Johnnies, were built by herders of flat rocks, on a high point where they could watch these sheep. These stood as landmarks, some for more than fifty years. Most were two or three feet high; others were built to a height of six or seven feet.

When it was time to move, the camp tender or the boss came around. Gilfillan describes moving day as the herder's secret sorrow; it could come unexpectedly while he was out with the sheep and unable to defend his possessions. The camp tender piled everything onto the bed, hooked on the team, and set off over rough country to the new location. "At the end of the journey (the herder) may find that the mirror has been again cracked across, or that the kerosene can has been upset on the bed...or that the syrup pail has tipped over and has spread its contents in a thin veneer over all," says Gilfillan.

Sheep were trailed long distances to new grass. One family began their move west one spring in the early 1900's while the older children were still in school. The mother stayed with them in Chamberlain while the father drove the camp wagon, and the younger children followed the grazing sheep. They carried drinking water and picked up every little stick of wood they found for fuel.

"As it became too dark for the sheep to travel, we put up a little tent and dug a small hole in the ground to build a fire with our precious fuel. The sheep quickly learned to bed down around camp," says Winnie Considine, one of the little girls who walked behind the sheep. "I can still see plainly that little beacon ahead, the light that meant supper and rest. But early in the morning we had to be on our way to follow the hungry sheep. 32

Martin Johnson trailed 3000 sheep from Colorado to White Water Creek, taking nearly all summer for the move. Later, during the bad blizzard of May 5, 1905, when rain turned to snow and piled up 17 foot drifts, he lost 3000 head of lambs and 2000 ewes. Many of them went over the Badland Wall; it was a storm during which many cattle, too, were lost over the Wall.

Wool sold for only six to eight cents a pound, and market lambs had to be trailed to Ft. Pierre, ferried across the river, then shipped by rail.

In western South Dakota the herder was never a *shepherd*; the sheephook was never a *crook*; the band or herd of sheep was never a *flock*. Those gentle pastoral terms did not suit the range country where life could be harsh. Local terms reflected

Left, in sheep camp. For a band of 1200 ewes, a herder, dog and wagon were needed.

The herder put his sheep on water about noon, rested them, then circled back toward bedground. This 1891 photo taken near Deadwood.

this harshness, as well as the strong independent spirit of those who lived here.

The Coyote—Natural Enemy

The coyote was the sheepman's natural enemy. A good herder could lose a summer average of one lamb a night to coyotes; a poor herder often lost six or eight lambs each night before he was fired or sent help. Most kills were at night or early morning, but Ole Eggebo of the Lodgepole area recalls he was plagued one summer by a big mangy coyote who struck in the daytime. At noon, as the sheep lay on water, puffing from the heat, the coyote would come in on the run, kill two lambs and disappear in a flash. That night, when the herder and sheep had gone, he would return with other coyotes to eat. Trapping this shrewd killer was impossible, says Eggebo; he would trip the pan of any trap from beneath. Shooting was also impossible: the coyote waited his chance, kept to the opposite side of the sheep from the herder, and killed fast.

Continual vigilance by ranchers and government hunters kept coyote numbers down, but they adapted well to changing conditions.

Outlaw Wolves

The gray wolves, unlike coyotes, could not adapt and were eventually all killed off. But they were a great menace to livestock for many years. They took an enormous toll of horse bands near rough country; some years they killed the entire colt crop. Wolves raised big litters of pups and hunted in family bands of up to 12 or 15. Younger wolves could be trapped, poisoned or shot fairly easily—but an old pair grew more cunning each year.

The most noted outlaw wolf in northwestern South Dakota was Old Three Toes. By 1912, his big three-toed track was plain in dusty sheep corrals where dead lambs were strewn about uneaten. He became known as a killer who seemed to kill for the sport of it. One night he killed many sheep and lambs at three different ranches, but ate only the liver of one lamb. He was killing livestock, including saddle horses and full grown steers, at the rate of $1000 worth a month when caught by a government hunter in 1925. His mate had been killed in 1920, and after that he hunted alone.

Archer Gilfillan tells of the many attempts to trap, shoot or run down Old Three Toes. One man ran him 95 miles during three days in fresh snow, changing horses five times. Sons of a Cave Hill rancher followed him on a ten-mile circle, then he struck out for Short Pine Hills forty miles away. They changed horses once, and by the end of the second day followed disgustedly as the tracks circled back to within a mile of their own ranch. When he was chased by wolf hounds, Old Three Toes tricked them with leaps across high embankments, backtracking, and one time, a thirty-foot jump into water.

Three Toes became notorious throughout the west and as many as 150 men—not counting group hunts—tried to win fame

by killing the outlaw. At last came Clyde F. Briggs, a noted government wolfer who had bagged famous woves in other parts of the United States. Gilfillan describes the 14 sets he made, each with two wolf traps guarded by two coyote sets. When ready, the wolf traps were invisible at ten feet, and baited on a sagebrush with natural wolf urine. The coyote sets were baited with stronger fish scents. Briggs checked his traps daily. The second week he drove over a rise to see Old Three Toes lying quietly, caught tight in two wolf traps. He was muzzled, tied and placed in a car hardly injured. But within a few miles he was dead, a proud old spirit that could not bear captivity.

Another famous wolf was the Blue Blanket Island wolf. He lived on a willow-thicketed and brush-covered wilderness island in the Missouri near the Mobridge area. He and his mate would raise six to eight pups each season, crossing on the ice each fall to hunt when the pups were half grown. When the mate was shot, he lived alone, continuing to do much damage to livestock. The Blue Blanket wolf never returned to a kill, but made fresh ones—so could not be poisoned. A local trapper, Baldy Sours, finally caught him on the island with a snared live rabbit as bait.

Riding the range well after the turn of the century, cowboys often saw five or six big gray wolves on a day's ride. Cattle companies paid $50 bounty on mature wolves on their range; $5 for pups. State bounties were also paid.

Wolves hunting in a pack were skilled at cutting out a mare and colt from a horse band, stampeding the rest before they could form a protective ring. The mare would circle to guard her colt as she tried to reach the other horses. But the wolves would close in, slashing hamstrings just above the hock. Crippled, the mare would struggle to fight them off. But the pack was soon at her throat, quickly killing both mare and colt.

Remington drawing shows wolves getting the worst of it. Dakota wolves were shrewd at cutting out single horses, or mare and colt, for the kill.

12. TERRITORY & STATE

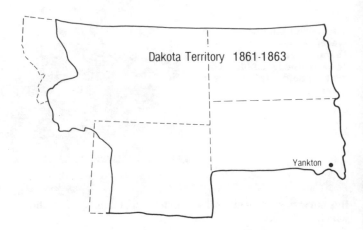

Dakota Territory 1861-1863

Yankton

Dakota Territory in 1861; borders were later changed and in 1889 South Dakota became a state.

Dakota Territory was organized in 1861 to include the lands drained by the upper Missouri—from Minnesota to the Continental Divide. Dr. Wm. Jayne, President Lincoln's personal physician, was appointed first governor. Jayne ventured out for a short time, took census and found 2402 whites living in the territory, about half in the southeastern corner. Yankton was chosen capital.

Yankton was already a wild river town of 300 people. It became commercially important when two railroads arrived in 1873, supplying freight for military posts and Indian agencies. When the Black Hills opened, Yankton became the headquarters for freightlines and stagecoaches heading west. Soon it had a lumber mill, flour mill, packing plant, foundry, population of 3000 and—by 1878—thirty saloons. But it was located in the very corner of a vast territory. Legislators from the Black Hills and northern Dakota objected.

Under vigorous Yankton protest, a nine-man commission considered other towns for the capital. Three of the proposed towns were practically nonexistent, with one building or less, but boasted good locations. Nearly all were located in the southern half, with only three commissioners from northern Dakota. But southern Dakotans split. Bismarck put up a spirited fight, aided by the power of Northern Pacific railroad, and emerged the winner. The first session held there voted to move again, to Pierre, but the governor vetoed the move.

Even earlier southern Dakotans had begun a move for statehood. Now they fought determinedly. They objected to federal control and officials who came from Washington without any knowledge of Dakota, as well as having the capital in Bismarck.

Uncertainty followed. Some legislators wanted statehood without division, looking to Aberdeen as the capital. Some called for two states with a north-south division along the 46th parallel; others wanted an east-west division at the Missouri River. Still others called for division into two territories without statehood. Choosing names caused further dissention. For a time it seemed the northern half would be called *Pembina*, leaving *Dakota* open for the southern half. But in the end, both fought to keep the name Dakota, so the cumbersome *North* and *South* were attached.

Statehood stalled even with the required population. Dakota was largely Republican and a Democratic administration in Washington held off adding two more Republican states. So it was not until 1889, when Republicans came into control of Congress that the four states of South Dakota, North Dakota, Montana and Washington were admitted. The outgoing President Cleveland mixed the papers to disguise the order of signing; however, South Dakota has since been designated the 40th state.

The new state had a ready made constitution. Twice, in 1883 and 1885, constitutional conventions had been held in Sioux Falls to work out details in anticipation of statehood. A big concern had been the two sections of each township reserved for school lands. These were being fast settled by squatters and sold by the federal government at the going rate.

In order to provide longterm financing for education it was decided these lands should not be sold for less than $10 an acre (a high price at the time.) Mineral lands should not be sold for less than appraised value, and all money from these sales should be invested in a permanent school fund with only the interest used.

In writing the constitution, delegates wrestled with two controversial issues: prohibition of liquor, and women's right to vote. Prohibition was finally omitted and brought separately to a vote of the people. It passed in 1889 but was repealed by another vote in 1897. Liquor was again outlawed in 1916, shortly before it was outlawed nationally.

Dakota women were active in the sufferage movement nearly 40 years before they succeeded in getting the vote.

Male delegates at the 1883 Sioux Falls meeting gave the idea slight attention. Deadwood's delegate Moody, later a U.S. Senator, spoke for women saying, "I know of no reason why my wife and daughter are not as able to hold office as I am, though they may not be willing." According to historian Robert Karolevitz, this statement was greeted with bursts of laughter. In 1885 Marietta Bones of Webster, a national officer in the womans sufferage movement, made this plea to convention delegates:

> Let me implore you in behalf of your sister, mother and wife, to place the women of our glorious territory on an equality before the law with yourselves.

But women did not gain the vote in South Dakota until the 19th Amendment was ratified in the state during the last days of 1919.

South Dakota became a mecca for those seeking divorce due to a loophole in the constitution. In 1907 this ended when a new law required a year's residence for divorce.

South Dakota's constitution was very long; much of it was designed to give people power against big corporations. Decisions may be taken directly to the people, and the constitution is easily amended to give people voting power.

Statehood did not end the struggle for relocating the capital. Huron, Aberdeen, Sioux Falls and Mitchell had strong hopes. Pierre and Mitchell waged an expensive fight in 1904 as each town tried to out-entertain the crowds of visitors. But the decisive vote reaffirmed Pierre as capital and proved most people had had enough of the argument.

County seat fights and wasteful county-splitting solutions, however, echoed the earlier struggles for many years.

13. HOMESTEAD AND SETTLEMENT

President Lincoln signed the Homestead Act into law in 1862. It took effect January 1, 1863. This act had a profound influence on the settlement of Dakota Territory and the entire Great Plains.

It was here, in the Great Plains, that most homesteading actually took place—contrary to public opinion which tends to push it farther east. It is interesting that even in college public land classes, two mistaken impressions often prevail about the course of homesteading in the United States. The first mistaken impression is that homesteading began with a bang in states such as Ohio, Michigan and Iowa, moving gradually westward. Second, it is often mistakenly taught that homesteading was pretty much over by 1890.

Statistics show a far different pattern. The Great Plains states dominated homesteading action from the first; the three earliest homesteads were filed in South Dakota and Nebraska. Far from being complete by 1890, homesteading continued strong for another 30 years, not reaching its peak until 1913, when 10,000,000 acres were acquired in a single year.

South Dakota is third highest in homestead numbers. (North Dakota is second; Montana first.) South Dakota's peak homesteading year was 1911.

Mahlon Gore of Vermillion filed the first claim in Dakota Territory and is credited by the Bureau of Land Management—equally with two Nebraskans, William Young and Daniel Freeman—as being officially "first." Instead of partying on that New Years Eve, Mahlon Gore waited in the Vermillion land office. As the clock struck twelve, he filed "immediately." Unfortunately for Gore, his Brule Creek homestead was jumped by one Henry H. Fischer; Gore went north to fight with General Sully in either his 1863 or 1864 campaign.

The first homesteads were proved up five years later. Frank Verzani was the first to prove up in Dakota Territory, at the Vermillion land office January 2, 1868.

Early Settling

Settlement in South Dakota began only a few years before the Homestead Act took effect. In 1860 the population was estimated at 500, most of these in or near the settlements of Vermillion, Bon Homme and Elk Point, and along the James and Vermillion rivers. Then came the 1862 Minnesota Uprising of the Sioux; settlers fled their homes and the next two years saw little new settlement. With the Homestead Act, the Civil War was nearly over. Everyone, it seemed, caught land fever and began moving west.

The first big wave of homesteading into Dakota Territory dried up with the drouth and hard times of 1889 and the early 1890's. Even earlier there had been serious set-backs with the grasshopper plagues of 1874 and 1875, causing South Dakota promoters to scramble in evading the damaging publicity.

With the turn of the century, bountiful rains returned; 1905 was one of the highest rainfall years on record. The grass was growing belly-deep to their horses, said homesteaders who

FINAL HOMESTEAD ENTRIES
1868 - 1961
(includes commuted)

Montana	151,600
North Dakota	118,472
South Dakota	97,197
Dakota Territory	33,951
(Combines North and South Dakota entries to 1889)	
Colorado	107,618
Nebraska	104,260
Oklahoma	99,557
Kansas	89,945
New Mexico	87,312
Minnesota	85,072
Arkansas	74,620
Wyoming	67,315
California	66,738
Oregon	62,926
Idaho	60,221
Washington	58,156
Alabama	41,819
Missouri	34,633
Wisconsin	29,246
Florida	28,096
Mississippi	24,126
Arizona	20,268
Michigan	19,861
Utah	16,798
Iowa	8,851
Nevada	4,370
Alaska	3,277
Ohio	108
Illinois	74
Indiana	30

Bureau of Land Management

Schell notes that of the Dakota Territory filings, the majority were in the southern half every year but 1884.

FINAL HOMESTEAD ENTRIES IN SOUTH DAKOTA

Dakota Territory	Number	Acres
1868	29	4,602
1871	33	5,199
1874	371	54,326
1877	563	88,004
1880	1,147	159,650
1883	1,735	264,843
1886	3,117	489,631
1889	5,814	916,760
South Dakota		
1892	1,588	246,998
1895	896	138,966
1898	928	142,399
1901	2,628	402,590
1904	1,081	161,156
1907	4,180	633,269
1910	6,739	1,035,513
1911	8,584	1,316,234
1913	4,055	621,124
1916	1,477	207,416
1919	1,344	202,959
1922	2,020	436,025
1925	730	195,206
1928	233	59,031
1931	84	20,460

HOMESTEAD LAWS

PRE-EMPTION (1841-1891) — Before homestead. Purchase of 160 acres for $1.25 per acre.

HOMESTEAD (1862) Claim of 160 acres for home; must live there and make improvements 5 years. Liveable house, cultivate 20 acres, other evidence such as well, fences. Residence 7 months each year, no absence of over 6 months allowed.

COMMUTING Homestead claim could be commuted at $1.25 per acre after 6 months residence with improvements and cultivation. Amended to 14 months residence later.

TREE CLAIM (repealed 1891) Plant 40 acres of trees (later 10 acres) care for 8 years; 160 acres; no residence.

STONE AND TIMBER CLAIM 160 acres purchased at $2.50 per acre; land must be valuable for stone and timber on it.

DESERT LANDS Purchase 640 acres of desert lands impossible of cultivation, irrigate 40 acres within 3 years; $1.25 per acre. Amended in 1891 to reduce size to 320 acres.

FOREST HOMESTEAD (1906) 160 acres at $2.50 per acre; 5 year residence; national forest lands classified non-forested (included Black Hills).

ENLARGED HOMESTEAD (1909) 320 acres; must cultivate 80 acres; no commuting; no mineral rights allowed.

RESIDENCE CHANGE (1912) Change from 5 year to 3 year homesteads. Must live on claim 7 months each year, total 21 months.

GRAZING HOMESTEADS (1916) 640 acres; classified grazing only with no possibility of irrigation; 3 years residence; no mineral rights.

DAWES ACT (1887) Opened Indian reservations; encouraged individual Indians to take 160 acre homesteads with "surplus" land sold to U.S. for settlement.

OPENING OF SIOUX LANDS (1889) Homesteaders to pay $1.25 per acre during first 3 years after opening; 75¢ per acre next 2 years; 50¢ an acre next five years. After 10 years unclaimed lands may be homesteaded as free lands, with commutation possible at 50¢ per acre after 14 months residence.

Homesteaders must be age 21 or head of family (only one head of family per household) and a U.S. citizen, or have declared intention to become a citizen before filing. Veterans and veterans widows had special rights and shorter residence time. These laws acquired various amendments and revisions; law piled upon law until there were 3500 land laws.

'A liveable home—among the cotaux,' in 1895.

rushed in to grab lands previously scorned. Much of it had been reservation lands.

In 1889 the great Sioux reservation was cut into six smaller pieces. The so-called surplus lands between were opened—not for free homesteading, because the government had bought it from the Sioux, but at the rate of $1.25 per acre. That rate prevailed for three years, after which it was to drop to 75¢ an acre for two additional years, then to 50¢ an acre. If after 10 years, other lands remained, they could be homesteaded as free lands.

Because of drouths and poor rail service, much of this land was still unclaimed ten years later. So it was freely homesteaded. Commutation (or purchase) was then allowed at 50¢ an acre after 14 months residence.

The creation of national forests had also kept settlers out of the Black Hills. But in 1906, under pressure from western states, certain lands within forests were designated non-forest, agricultural lands and opened to homesteading.

Early homesteaders often managed to get three quarters instead of one. They took a pre-emption and a tree claim, also selecting a homestead claim which they tried to hold while they bought the pre-emption, which required 14 months residence time. In 1891, Congress ended the options of tree claims and pre-emption because of excessive fraud. Then for many years, the homesteader could claim only one quarter.

In 1909 another quarter was added. But to make up for this good deal, 80 acres had to be cultivated, no mineral rights were allowed, and the homestead could not be commuted. In 1916 the 640 acre grazing homestead was created, with similar stipulations and without mineral rights.

Claims Were Too Small

Homesteading worked well enough in the more humid areas of the nation including eastern South Dakota where a family could make a living on one or two quarters of land. But it was soon obvious it could not work in the Great Plains. More land was needed to make a liveable unit. Yet an eastern-based Congress was unable to understand life on the plains, the importance of water and lay of the land. Stockmen were regarded by easterners as wealthy cattle kings to be phased out, instead of the struggling family ranchers that most of them were.

Congress had the report of Major John Wesley Powell stating that the farm unit in the western plains should be at least 2,560 acres. Land should be surveyed by natural boundaries, said Powell, instead of by the rectangular system, so that each unit would have bottomland for hay, natural water on a creek if possible, and higher pasture land.

It was a plan of stunning good sense, but Congress could not bring itself to enact Powell's proposed laws. Says Walter Webb in *The Great Plains*, the Powell plan "fitted too well the needs of the West to get adequate consideration in the East, where the laws for the West were made."

When at last Congress offered the meagre grazing claims of 640 acres, homesteaders were again encouraged to claim land in amounts too small for any practical purpose, investing their savings in useless development. It was shown that this land would graze only 1 cow per 50 acres, for a total of 13 cows per 640 acres. These grazing homesteads, said Will Barnes of the Forest Service, were causing immense damage to the range because people couldn't live on 13 cows and were trying to farm the land. Also they caused a "vast amount of actual suffering," he said, misleading people into a struggle for livelihood on lands that would produce nothing but "Russian thistles and black alkali."

The stipulations attached by Congress did not stop the speculators. But neither did they stop the settlers. They swarmed each new land opening, fought for land rights, won, or lost to others who eventually carried through to final patent. The fraud of homesteading has probably been overemphasized Certainly it existed as crowds of speculators and exploiters of every kind came west to get easy land for resale. But a wide base of honesty also prevailed. Most homesteaders were ordinary people doing their best to comply with inflexible and unreasonable laws.

Homesteading often meant failure and despair. Some quarters were filed on as many as eight or ten times before being proved up. An investigation in Dakota, Kansas and Nebraska in 1888 showed 112 relinquishments of 31 randomly selected quarters.

Yet the rush of settlers could not be stopped. When Indian lands opened, they were there waiting. Five thousand were ready to cross the ice on February 10, 1890 when the signal went off in Chamberlain. In Pierre the same day there was an atmosphere of celebration: flags floated from every building; bands played; cheers were given in the legislature when the signal cannon boomed. All day long teams had been hitched to wagons along the riverbank, awaiting the signal to race across the frozen Missouri to seize the choice quarters.

Two years later on April 15, 1892, the Sisseton Reservation opened. Soldiers strung out in a thin line south to Brown Valley

---

'Well, this is the way it is—'

So you want to know about this land business?

When a man comes here to homestead he picks out a piece of open land, goes to the government land office and describes it. He swears he's taking it for a home and pays $14 filing fees. Within six months he builds a habitable home, digs a well, and remains for 14 months from the time he goes on the land.

Then he gets two neighbors to swear that he has been living on the land and improving it. He pays the land office 50 cents an acre and he has "proved up." As soon as a patent comes from Washington, D.C., the land is his.

Now suppose a fellow named Tarbox takes up a homestead. After six months his feet begin to get cold. Then suppose a fellow named Corey comes looking for land and fancies the piece Tarbox has.

He gets a neighbor, Gaspipe, to take him over to see Tarbox and says, "Tarbox, what'll you take for your relinquishment?"

If Tarbox's feet are awfully cold he may say, "You can have the whole works for $75."

Corey says, "All right. Come on."

Gaspipe takes them to town. Tarbox goes into the land office and says the land he took wasn't what he thought it was and he would like to throw it back so that he will be at liberty to file on another piece. He signs a paper to that effect.

As Tarbox goes out one door, Corey goes in another and he files on his Tarbox relinquishment.

But suppose the day before Corey saw Tarbox, Tarbox had sold 25 bushels of potatoes for $2 a bushel. That warmed his feet. When Corey asks him what he'll take, he says, $1,000.

"That's too darned high," Corey says and returns to town.

Then he meets a Landman, but he doesn't know it. Mr. Landman says, "Looking for land?" When Corey says he has, Mr. Landman asks, "What'd you see?"

Gaspipe speaks up, "Tarbox offered him his relinquishment for $1000 but Corey thinks that's too high."

Then Mr. Landman contests the Tarbox claim. Tarbox goes to court and says he's been living on his place and improving it. Mr. Landman gets Gaspipe to testify that Tarbox offered his claim for $1000 which means that Tarbox is speculating on land instead of keeping it for a home. Tarbox ties what's left of the potato money in his sock and starts back to Kansas.

Now the man who contests has the first right to file on the contested land. But Mr. Landman already has a quarter section and no filing right. All he can do is hold until three months are up. Then it becomes open land again.

In about a week, Johnny Clabbermilk comes along and says to Mr. Landman. "I want land. What can you do for me?"

Mr. Landman says, "Johnny, I can file you on the best claim on the Frozen Man for $75." And Johnny steps into Tarbox's shoes.

If you prove up in fourteen months it will cost you 50 cents an acre or $80. I'm thinking of proving up on the five-year plan. Then I won't have to pay the $80 when I get through.

Bachelor Bess Corey
Homesteading west of Ft. Pierre, 1909

On the '5-year plan' life could be stark for women.

Kadoka, S.D. Apr 5,/07. Just before it moved.
By J.M. Hamilton, Highland, S.D.

If you are seeking a location
In which to start a new creation,
Something devoid of imitation,
Then come and see the great foundation
On which is placed a population,
Made up of men of reputation,
And ladies full of fascination,
On a newly opened reservation,
In Roberts County, South Dakota.

Roberts County History

Town Lot Sale Day in Kadoka April 5, 1907. Businesses were temporarily located as above before the townsite company turned main street around.

TOWN LOT SALE

Yesterday's regular trains were loaded with passengers, and the special of sleepers and dining car which came in about nine o'clock helped to swell the crowd. At about 3 o'clock C. A. Padley opened the sale with a few remarks on the future of the town. He spoke on her chances for county seat and railroad division and promised to intercede with the railroad company in our behalf for a well. After his remarks, the bidding started off at $100 and moved lively from start to finish. Twelve lots on Second Street were reserved to prevent the principal business street from running east and west. First choice was knocked off to G. L. Irwin for $775. After the first six sales disposed of the choice corners, the prices gradually lowered. The first 50 lots all went over base price $110 to $400 and $525.

Proving Up

holding back the sooners. At 12 o'clock noon the cannon on the Minnesota side roared, and the soldiers fired off a volley of rifle shots. An observer states:

> The stampede was on! People in hired rigs, buggies, wagons, carts, foot and horseback set out in a mad rush for free land. On finding a quarter section unclaimed...the homesteader hurriedly threw up a sod marker on each corner of his 160 acres as physical evidence of his claim. Many of the settlers started walking to Watertown that very night to file their land claim, fearing that others with less honest motives than their own might file on the land that was rightly theirs. 33

In 1904 Rosebud Reservation lands were distributed by lottery to avoid such land stampedes. This time avid land-seekers lined up at registration offices in Bonesteel, Chamberlain, Fairfax and Yankton instead of at the reservation edge. Available were 2,412 claims; 106,296 people lined up to register for them at lottery. Again in 1907, over 4,000 applied for the 343 available claims on the Lower Brule Reservation. Again, great crowds converged for the second Rosebud opening in 1907; for the 1909 dispersal of Cheyenne River and Standing Rock reservation lands; for the 1911 Rosebud and Pine Ridge dispersals; and for the final one at Standing Rock in 1915. All this land was acquired by the government in purchase agreements from the tribes.

Promotion Magic

An energetic campaign of land promotion brought thousands of homeseekers into Dakota. Promotion magic was created in the florid style of Col. Pat Donan, an enthusiastic Dakota boomer, and in the official booklet *Dakota* and thousands of leaflets and bulletins distributed by Dakota

Territory. Governors were expected to be promoters. First territorial governor Jayne made this statement:

> As regards soil, climate, beautiful uplands, rich prairies, luxuriant bottoms, productive mountain valleys, mineral wealth, navigable rivers, upon which to float our cereal products and commercial exchange, what section of country within the broad confines of our Republic is fairer, or livelier, or richer, or more inviting as the home of the active, intelligent, and industrious citizen? Before a generation shall have passed, more than a million people will be living in the valley of the Missouri alone.

All joined together to keep the land excitement at fever pitch—speculators, railroads, townsite promoters, even the hard-grubbing settler. The Bison Courier ran this glowing account of area prospects and urged readers to mail it back east to friends:

> Far enough north to reap the benefits of lignite coal, yet not out of the region of sure corn crops or far enough to strike the hills and buttes which characterize the lands adjacent to the Grand River, this region has laid for countless ages only waiting for the advent of the steam horse which should bring the influx of hardy honyockers who should make it blossom and ripen into a rich fruitfulness of waving grain and golden corn fields..

Land Fever

Everyone was in on the boomerism. It was clear that more people would mean more schools, churches, roads, railroad branch lines, economic and cultural wealth, more markets, more supplies. Only the stockman and Indian must have stood aghast as trainloads of people came daily into the most isolated reaches of Dakota.

Real estate agents traveled to foreign countries, lecturing and giving out glowing literature. Colonizing organizations formed in large cities. Railroads advertised cut rates and ran homeseeker specials from Minnesota, Iowa and Illinois. They published a flood of posters, leaflets and guidebooks distributing them through the U.S. and foreign countries, and stationed agents at the port to meet immigrant ships and direct newcomers onto company lines.

Townsite promoters were vigorous land boomers, eager to sell the lots they had platted in what were often non-existent "paper towns" that never materialized. Railroad officials had long understood the profits to be made from townsites and formed their own companies, such as the Milwaukee officers' Northwest Townsite Company. Along railroad lines, the independently platted towns usually faded as these railroad connected companies scooped off the cream of townlot sales as a side benefit to the new track. Existing towns were bypassed; siding and depots were built only at railroad-sanctioned towns. Usually the railroad offered to move businesses from the old to the new town, and the end came quickly.

Town names usually honored the railroaders or their backers. Ed Lemmon was one of the few local people able to influence not only railroad route, but the name of a town. He persuaded Milwaukee officials to build 100 miles north of original plans and to place the town of Lemmon astride the border.

Towns such as Fountain and Medary had to give way to Brookings; Firesteel to Mitchell; Kampeska City to Watertown; Old Madison and Herman to Madison; Edmunds, Freeport and Georgetown to Ipswich. Each new end-of-track town became the jumping off place for hundreds of new settlers.

Up to 18 trains a day brought immigrant cars into Huron. In 1882 it was reported there:

> The railroads much of the time have had two passenger trains a day each way, with from seven to nine coaches full of newcomers, while there have been nine or ten freight trains a day taking their goods, and yet they have not been able to take them fast enough. At a single public house for weeks in succession from 400 to 500 people a day have been fed as they have passed through in search of land and homes. At almost every station goods have been piled up promiscuously in every direction waiting to be moved out to the future home of their owners, and settlements have sprung up like magic. 34

With settlement, counties were organized. Bitter rivalries grew up between towns for county seat. For six years the "Spink County War" raged. County records were forcibly removed from Old Ashton; 300 angry settlers marched upon Redfield which had stolen them; two companies of territorial militia were sent to cool tempers. After years of bitter struggle, "it was a sad day for Lemmon," say pioneers, when office equipment and county records were loaded on wagons and hauled to Bison. All too often the solution to these fights was an agreement to split the counties into areas too small for efficient operation.

Paper railroads flourished as well as paper towns. In land locator offices maps showed a network of proposed branch lines throughout the locality. Aberdeen was called "Hub City of the Dakotas" because a map drawn by the city engineer showed railroads radiating in nine directions like spokes in a wheel. The map circulated widely in the United States and Europe. Many of these branch lines did in fact materialize, with the resulting heavy settlement. (Overbuilding by railroads came to create its own problems.)

Dakota promotion also had detractors. Promoters elsewhere kept alive the memory of disastrous 1874 and 1875 grasshopper plagues and the long drouth that began in 1889. In South Dakota, these detractors charged, "every townsite is a city, every creek a river, every crop a bonanza, every breeze a zephyr and every man a damned liar." 35

Dry Farming Prophet

Western settlement got a big boost from the work of Hardy Webster Campbell, who homesteaded in Brown County in 1879. During the drouth years of the early 1890's Campbell watched and tested his theories. He came to an encouraging conclusion: it was not drouth that had caused crop failure—even in the disastrously dry year of 1894; it was only the failure to use the moisture present through proper farming methods. The answers were in summer fallow, surface packing, seeding grain in widely spaced rows, mulching with dust through frequent cultivation, and deep plowing. (The last two features—widely adopted throughout the Great Plains where huge fields were deeply plowed and left bare of

County splitting was cause for celebration in county seat fights. Picture shows sack race at Murdo's Corn Festival.

vegetation—were directly blamed for the terrible dust storms of the '30's.)

The Northern Pacific railroad was so pleased they hired Campbell to conduct dry farming experiments. By 1895 he was operating five Northern Pacific experiment farms and lecturing widely to farm groups and landseekers. Newspapers had great praise. "Hardy Webster Campbell, the father of dry land farming, has brought a miracle to the plains states," said the Great Falls Tribune. "They will be the last and best garden in the world."

It all coincided neatly with the heavy rainfall years of the early 1900's; seemingly the answers to drouth had been found. There came a resurge of railroad building and the greatest movement of people of all time rushed into the plains to take up land.

Rush of Immigrants

The lure of advertised free lands combined with intolerable conditions in several foreign countries to set off mass migrations to the United States from time to time. Norwegians, Swedes, Dutch, Danes, Welsh and Czechs came early to eastern South Dakota, many from settlements in Minnesota, Iowa and Chicago. A big German-Russian migration began in 1873. This included the Hutterites who settled mainly in the north central part of the state, eventually forming 17 colonies at Bon Homme and along the James River.

Foreign immigration slowed during the nineties; in 1898 only 200,000 entered through the Ellis Island immigration center. Then numbers increased again to one million by 1905. The greatest mass movement in human history came in 1907 when 1,285,349 immigrants entered the United States. Many of these immediately boarded trains for South Dakota and other Great Plains states.

South Dakota immigrants remembered long ship journeys, the crowded quarters and "smell of ship" that lingered on their clothes and possessions for months. Some recalled tragedies such as the sinking of the Titanic.

The hold of the Titanic, like every ship that headed west across the Atlantic in 1912, was filled to capacity with immigrants. Publicity was accorded to the rich and famous, but the Titanic was really an immigrant tragedy. First class passengers were never in much real danger that night; for them there was plenty of space on the lifeboats and time for loading.

It was a different story for third class men. Locked below decks till near the very end, they had little chance for survival.

One who did survive was Ole Abelseth who was returning from Norway to his Perkins County homestead with four friends and relatives, prospective South Dakota settlers. When they were finally allowed on deck, Abelseth waited with his cousin and brother-in-law until the tilting of the ship began spilling people into the water. "I knew there was no chance for us in that ice water," he said. But they clasped each other one more time and jumped; it was the last Abelseth saw of the other two.

Hitting the water, he was seized at once around the neck from behind and dragged under. He struggled free. The water was much colder than he had expected, too cold to stay in for long. All around him in the water swimmers were dropping away with shrill cries. But Ole wore the warm homespun wool underwear his mother had made for him and it gave him the extra endurance he needed that night. The cries grew fewer and fainter as he struck out swimming for a canvas boat he saw dimly ahead. The boat was filled and hands reached to push him away, but Ole crawled aboard. Two others in the boat had dragged themselves from the icy water but both died before morning. With the dawn came a rescue ship. Abelseth died in 1980 at age 94, one of the last of the Titanic survivors, and very likely the final survivor who had actually been in the iceberg filled waters that night.

Immigrants on the boat in 1902.

WE LANDED ON ELLIS ISLAND. At that time, all emigrants must have tickets to their destination and $25 in cash. I had borrowed money for my ticket so was short again. The emigrant train was packed with passengers from all over Europe. The train was slow and had to give way to all other trains. In Chicago we scattered, I was the only one of the group to go on west. 36

AGENTS WORKING in Drammen, Norway, advertised Dakota Territory as Utopia. My father was impressed with the tales of gold and the beauties of the far off land. In April of 1881, I found myself on a combination sail and steamship. Three weeks later we were herded off at Castle Garden. I can still remember the ladies dressed in fine silks and satins who came to watch us disembark. 37

THE SCHRUMN FAMILY arrived in Chicago, hungry, after a 21 day journey which was to have taken only 13 days. They had only bread to eat. They could speak and understand only German and had no addresses of the relatives with whom they planned to live. They roamed the streets of Chicago searching for the Schurtz family, but no one could understand or help them. Mr. Schrumn, in desperation, walked into a school room where a 10-year-old pupil, who understood German and happened to know their relatives, led them to their destination. 38

These immigrants from Russia stopped here in Pukwana in May 1894 on their way to reservation lands across the river.

14. THE SETTLER'S LIFE

THEY CAME—

They came by ox team, by wagon, horseback, on foot, and in immigrant cars. The stories they tell are of crossing flooded rivers, bogging down in wet gumbo, riding "stowaway" in the immigrant cattle car (only one was allowed to ride there caring for livestock). A German father who spent five days on the immigrant train from Iowa to Okaton had the car loaded with one team of horses, harness, wagon, one cow, a crate of chickens, one dog and the yellow cat—and his four sons. After the five cold days on the train, they unloaded and began traveling toward the claim, forgetting the yellow cat. When they discovered she was missing, the boys returned and found her still crouching in a corner of the car.

MY MOTHER MADE BUTTER along the way. We also had a crate of chickens. My mother was always frying potatoes over the campfire in a large skillet. We had cornmeal mush for breakfast. I think sometimes that's all we had besides the dairy products and coffee for Dad. Meat was mostly salt pork, though I can remember we kids played with little wagons made by tying a string through a nail hole in a sardine can, so I suppose we had sardines to lunch on. My mother often remarked on the convenience of a large wooden box of crackers and one equally large of ginger snaps. When the road was bad, they unhitched the hayrack team. Dad or John would drive the covered wagon across and come back for the team with the hayrack. My mother, who knew little of horses or driving, drove the covered wagon, with the hayrack team tied behind. If the road was bad, a steep bank or hill, she stopped the team and waited until one of the men came. Dad always hitched the gentlest team to the covered wagon. 39

WE PUT A 10 X 12 SHACK on the hayrack in sections, then we got a big tent of white canvas also 10 by 12 feet. We put our chickens in crates and loaded all our furniture, household goods, food and clothing. Papa drove four horses on the rack. We three children rode with Grandpa in the spring buggy. Mama rode horse-back and drove about 40 head of cattle and the other horses behind the wagons. Just before we got to Cedar Pass we came to a gate and Grandpa dropped the lines and the team ran away with us. I can see my mother yet speeding up alongside the buggy and catching the team. It was an ordeal to get down Cedar Pass, which wasn't much more than a cow trail then. I can remember my dad taking log chains and rough-locking the hayrack. Then he had to come to the top and drive the buggy down too. 40

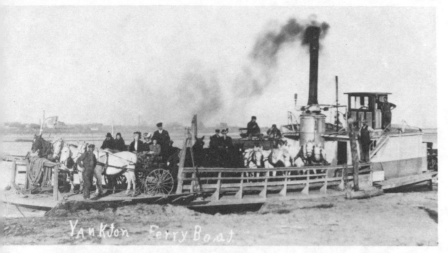

Crossing the Missouri was a worry. Above, the Yankton Ferry loaded with settlers; below, pontoon bridge at Evarts.

WE GOT TO THE MOREAU RIVER on the edge of the Cheyenne Reservation. There was a Catholic mission there and an Indian was the priest. Dad had to get a permit to cross the reservation and the Indian police were all in Evarts and so he asked the priest if he could cross before they came. The priest said the river would be a little lower by four o'clock in the morning and he could have some Indian boys there to help cross the cattle, and he said you could probably get across the reservation before the Indian police came. So we crossed the Moreau River, but it was in flood. We were three days on the reservation and on the third day, just before dark, we saw two posts ahead, no fence or anything, just those two posts, and that was the end of the reservation. Well, here came an Indian on horseback, Dad looked back and he said that could be the police. So Dad rode over to the wagon and he said you drive straight through those two posts and camp and I'll try to get the cattle across. So we did, and Trysinskis followed, so the Indian, he rode out there to Dad and Dad would keep on the other side of the coulee. Dad didn't want to talk to him, afraid he'd ask for a permit. And anyway, they got through the gate all right. 41

Last camp before McIntosh

AT CHAMBERLAIN the train could not cross the river until daylight as the tracks were supported on pontoons so it was dangerous at night. Lodging was hard to find, for many homesteaders were arriving. I remember sleeping on the floor of some house and that my younger brother had a sore throat, so Uncle tied his sock around George's throat. On the way to the homestead the two things I recall are: a woman standing in the doorway of a tar paper house watching us go by, and another house and a lone willow tree on the creek near it. 42

Arriving on Corson County homestead in 1916.

RIDING SLOWLY on top of a wagon load of lumber, my first glimpse of this west river country was on a warm June day in 1905. Never had I seen such vast empty places, no trees, no fences and almost no buildings for mile after mile. Everywhere there were waves of knee-high grass. As the sun became warmer, we girls became thirsty. The men folks stopped the team beside a water hole and dipped up some water, which when we saw it we refused to drink, as did our mother. By the time we reached the next hole we shut our eyes and drank. At our claim shack we found it impossible to put all the things inside and had to leave many right outdoors. Before we really got settled, the rain commenced. The only way we found to keep ourselves dry was to sit on the bed with umbrellas raised over our heads. Through that first monotonous summer, shanties began to dot the prairie but few people lived in them. A woman on the next claim came once, but since she was a soldier's widow she didn't need to stay on her claim to get title to the land. Some would come out the last day of one month and go home the next day—which was the first of next month—so had been there both months. 43

WE HEARD WONDERFUL STORIES about the free land in South Dakota and expected to get rich quick on the golden opportunities in the west. What a disappointment! Nothing here but bare open prairie; no roads, only trails. The second day here a prairie fire swept through and burned all our possessions. But we stayed with neighbors and soon had no thought of ever leaving. 44

IT WAS BLIZZARDING HARD when we got to Sleepy Eye, Minnesota. We were snowbound there for ten days in the passenger train. The immigrant cars with our cows, horses, machinery, and household goods were held up at Winona. We finally arrived in Columbia, Dakota Territory, the end of the railroad. Spent the night at a farmer friends place. There were 17 in our party and Polycarp and 9 in his family. Father had made arrangements to stay with a bachelor who lived in a sod house with a dirt floor. We stayed there six weeks until we got our house built on the claim. Planted 12 acres of wheat that summer, Father cradled it and we children raked and bound it. That winter my father died leaving Mother with six children out on the prairies of Dakota Territory. 45

TRY TO IMAGINE how we felt as we stepped from the coach expecting to land on a platform to find instead just mud, real old gumbo. It was dark, no lights of any kind, then we waded in mud some distance to a place to stay all night. Here again, we got another shock. As we were ushered in we found bunks, one above another, on both sides of a dark passageway. There were three women of us and four small children and my husband who had come in from the claim during the day to meet us. A shock was putting it mildly; however, it was sleep in such a bunk or sit in a chair all night. My husband and I and our two children chose the lower bunk, the other two ladies, my sisters-in-law, and two children took the upper one. All slept. 46

After turn of century, most settlers rode immigrant trains.

We came from every profession and trade,
It did not matter which.
We wanted land
You understand
But not to make a home.
The reason we came
We wanted a claim
Cause we thought it would make us rich.

G. M. Drummond
CALL OF THE PRAIRIE
Ziebach County

THE FARTHER WE CAME the slower the train went. The weather was real warm for that time of year and the train ran out of drinking water because it was so overcrowded. My younger brother Harry got desperate for water and began to cry. Father told him we'd soon be in Murdo and then he could get a drink. It was a real windy day and there was a crowd around the depot, like a celebration. There was a wooden water tank on a flat care shipped in from Presho with warm artesian water. 47

Ox teams moved slowly.

LOCATING

Locating the homestead could be a haphazard decision. New settlers swarmed in to the areas of hottest promotion. Some joined relatives or friends on personal recommendations; immigrants sought settlements where their native tongue was spoken.

First people in an area could be selective and choose land with a spring and rich bottomland. But locators in every area soon had their work down to an efficient system. They hired all available wagons and teams, met the trains filled with landseekers, loaded up everyone—convincing them of the hopelessness of trying to find unclaimed land without a locator, and set off for the nearest block of open land. Each locator worked his own block, filling it up quarter by quarter. He would drive "right down the section line from one survey marker to the next," said one settler, encouraging one man to take the quarter to the north and another the quarter on the south until "the whole country was solid homesteaders." Each person paid from $5 (in earlier years) to $25 or $50, depending on place, distance to travel, and competition. The locator then returned his charges to the land office to file their claims. Many were aboard the next train going east.

People tried to get some evidence of occupation on their claim immediately—especially when the land office was distant as in the earlier years when they were few. A typical marker was the "straddle bug"—three laths or boards nailed together like a tripod. This often straddled the quarter section line to mark two quarters claimed.

Everyone feared claim jumping. Many homesteaders were not actual settlers. They merely put in appearances from time to time to meet minimum requirements. These people were most subject to claim jumping. If they were absent from the claim too long, their rights could be contested.

A homesteader in the northeastern corner of South Dakota once returned to find a shanty on the other end of his quarter. He went to his fur trapper neighbor. The trapper said, "Come back tonight and we'll take care of it." That night they wrapped chains around the shanty, hitched it to a team of horses, and pulled it a mile away.

Other times a claim jumper simply moved into the empty buildings. If he contested and could prove the homesteader had not been there for six months, he had first chance to file on the land.

Relatives and friends tried to 'corner' their claims—locating buildings together at adjacent corners, sharing some facilities.

It seemed a true invasion, this taking possession of the virgin sod, but as I considered, there was a haunting sadness in it, for these shining pine pennons represented the inexorable plow. They prophesied the death of all wild creatures and assured the devastation of the beautiful, the destruction of all the signs and seasons of the sod. Apparently none of my companions shared this feeling, for they all leaped from the wagon and planted their stakes, each upon his chosen quarter-section with whoops of joy, cries which sounded faint and far.

Hamlin Garland
SON OF THE MIDDLE BORDER

OVER THE DOOR was the sign "Cyrus Walts, Surveyor and Locating Agent." This was about all we saw comprising the village of Sioux Falls at that time. We decided to engage Cyrus Walts to show us vacant land. He charged us $5.00 a day for his services. At 10 miles northeast of Sioux Falls we found a government stake near what our guide told us was Slip Up Creek. Looking north from this stake, we could see quite a bit of the creek valley and it looked good to us. Here each of the party selected claims. After filing and making the required land improvements, the party returned home. Late in the fall, it being necessary to be on the land, a second trip was made. We made such improvements as were necessary and returned home for the winter. 48

I CAME OUT in 1908 because my sister was here and wanted me to come. Sis stayed with me the first night, and I felt so far from home and lonely and to help my feelings along, about midnight an old horse roaming around on the prairie came up and pawed on my doorstep. I was scared speechless and Sis said, "Oh, you'll hear a lot of funny noises." I said, "Oh no, I'll not! I'm going back home tomorrow!" But as morning grew near and she talked to me, I became accustomed to all the things that happened. My shack was 12 by 14 feet, had tar paper covering and a rubberoid roof which was not hail proof. How do I know? We had a bad hail storm one night. I had retired, but all of a sudden I felt water dripping on my pillow and elsewhere so I arose. It was coming in through the roof in several places. It was useless to try to sleep. My bedding was wet, so now being so wide awake, I put in several hours writing letters. 49

Sod house near Miller in 1885. Root cellar to left was for cool food storage.

A LIVEABLE HOUSE

The most typical—and in many ways, the best—of the early homes on the open plains and prairies of Dakota were the sod houses. They were cool in summer and warm in winter and stood fast against the wildest wind; but they were also dark, dirty and often infested with mice, bedbugs and other vermin. They usually had a leaky roof. Unprotected, the sod house began deteriorating in 10 to 15 years. But many were improved with plaster, stucco and shingled roofs and used for half a century. (In northwestern South Dakota, several old sod houses are still being lived in.)

Other types of early homes were the dugout (a hole in the hill with a built-out front), log houses, rock houses, and the tar paper shack (which was sometimes missing the tar paper). The tar paper shack became the most common of all for homesteaders who only wanted to staisfy minimum requirements and did not intend to live in it much. In its most crude form, the shack was a small building of twisted planks; black tar paper nailed to the outside helped to keep out the wind and rain. It was baking hot in summer and impossible to heat in winter. Although tar paper shacks were never intended for winter homes, destitute families often did live in them year around. They could be insulated part way up the walls with sod.

THEY BUILT a sod house with a wooden roof and real windows. They made a rickety framework of 2 x 4's and built a roof of planks, extending it over the sides. They they piled blocks of sod along the walls upward to reach the roof, leaving space for windows. This was much better than the dugout. 50

THE TRAIN STOPPED at Groton, the end of the rails. Our home for six weeks was a tent. Each night we made a smudge to smoke out the mosquitoes so we could sleep. During this time my father was building a frame house and digging a well. Mother hauled the dirt out of the well and helped bank the house with sod. Whenever Father went to Aberdeen, he would take his knife and cut clumps of grass as a trail marker to find his way home. 51

Claim shacks were built small and simple—sometimes of green lumber that twisted as it dried.

FIRST HE DUG A HOLE 14 feet square and 3 feet deep. Over this he raised a sod top and relined the whole house with lumber. When he had completed the walls and ceiling, he had only a few boards left, so he covered the floor with straw and rag rugs. One heavy door was the means of entering, and one window high in the wall, was the only light. 52

WE LIVED IN the tar paper shack for 17 years. I remember being on the roof and trying to patch it, and Mother trying to keep the mice out. 53

First school in Watauga township in 1910.

Tarpaper shacks were banked with sod in various styles for winter use.

Stone houses were built with hard labor.

Log houses were favorites in timbered country.

THE CEILING OF THE LEAN-TO kitchen was oilcloth tacked over stringers. As Mary bent over the work table, her head touched the ceiling. It was not uncommon for a mouse to scurry across the top of her head. 54

THEY LIVED IN the covered hayrack several weeks. When the barn was finished, the family moved into it. The floor was of dirt, soon packed hard. The oldest daughter Lucretia became very ill with typhoid fever and was out of her head and kept telling them the horses were coming into the barn, so her brother Ray would pretend he was chasing them out. The house was finished before winter. It had tar paper on the outside and was held together with plenty of nails; the chimney was a stove pipe that went through a cream can. 55

A YOUNG MAN from Iowa sat on his dirt floor paring potatoes. A strong wind came up, tipped over his shack, and left him sitting on the prairie. He left and never came back. 56

Sod strips were thinner in shallow topsoil; were usually laid grass side down.

THE HOUSE WAS an elegant affair as it boasted paper on the outside and beautiful blue building paper on the inside. The chairs were hung on nails on the wall when not in use. The beds were springs that were suspended by wires from the ceiling. 57

Sod house often became the barn for those who stayed. A German-Russian farm.

Woman stands in doorway.

BECAUSE OF MOTHER'S FEAR of snakes, we lived in a tar paper shack instead of a sod house, sodded 2/3 of the way up on the outside. It was furnished with a narrow bunk made of ash poles, a small two-grid camp stove, a tiny homemade table. Mother twisted hay to burn for cooking. Hay was used on the bunk instead of a mattress. With Dad and brother Adolph sleeping on the bunk, it gave the rest of us room to sleep on the floor. In that crowded condition, we nearly suffocated with the door shut. Mosquitoes ate us up if the window was opened. 58

Bachelor decorated his tar paper shack with shiny bottle caps. Right, homesteader family lives in house stripped with tar paper.

143

This family built onto their shanty. Some moved shacks from abandoned claims together to make more rooms.

They improved their homes
when they could

THE LOCKRIDGE GIRLS, Josie and Villa, came out alone to build their homestead shacks. They hired a 16-year-old boy to help them, got a team of mules, loaded their lumber on the wagons and started out. They built their own shacks, with no experience with carpentry; they had no floor, windows or door and were merely tokens that the claim was filed and someone was coming. The girls had a wonderful time, planned to stay the necessary 14 months to prove up, with no thought of making a permanent home. But Josie soon married another homesteader and they increased their holdings as others left. 59

Typical new home for those who could afford it was the 1½ story white frame house with front porch.

A 'real house' with shingled roof and siding (on front, at least.)

Drilling rigs soon made digging wells easier. At right, an Indian family fills water barrels from the Little White River.

Water was Scarce

Homesteads required a liveable home with water available. Dry holes were sometimes dug just so the homesteader could testify that he or she had a well. Near Pierre, a man put this sign by his well:

These improvements might be better
And the water might be wetter.
This hole will answer as a well
Even if water is not found this side of hell.

Early wells were dug with pick and shovel, using a windlass of rope, bucket and crank to haul up the dirt. One person would dig in the well while the other worked the windlass. It could take all summer. A man who came from Germany to central South Dakota in 1883 dug his well alone to a depth of 25 feet. He rigged a special pulley to raise and dump the dirt while he stayed in the well, and could pull himself up and down.

Another couple digging a square well in the same area were curbing it with rock. One of the horses they used to haul rock slipped over the edge and fell down the well. They struggled with him for hours in the tight space. At last they hitched the milk cow with the other horse and succeeded in hauling him out.

Well digging tragedies occurred in deep wells from "fire damp," a shortage of oxygen and increase in fatal gases. A Brule County father and two sons had dug their well to a depth of 30 feet. When the sons again let their father down in the bucket, he fell and lay still. Frightened, they ran to a neighbor for help. The oldest boy was let down, but pulled up quickly when he was nearly overcome. They were finally able to get the father out with an iron hook, but he was dead before he reached the surface.

Another danger was falling down the well. When a child was lost, pioneer mothers ran fearfully to call down the well. Abandoned wells were boarded over, but when boards rotted they were unsafe for livestock.

In some areas water levels were so deep they could not be reached at all by hand digging. West of the Missouri in the south central part of the state, water was below 2500 feet. Later very deep artesian wells of warm water were dug. But in early years the only water sources were rivers, occasional springs and reservoirs.

Dams were built laborously with wheelbarrow and shovel, or with team and scraper, across a side draw. In dry years, these dams held little water. In wet years many were washed out. Settlers sandbagged dams to try to save their water supply in hard rains. Losing the dam was a severe loss as livestock had no other water and had to be moved. Drinking water was hauled from the dams by stoneboat and boiled. As dams began to dry up in late summer, the water had to be strained through a thin white cloth to remove bugs and silt.

The whole process was shocking to many newcomers. Even use of the word "dam". "I considered it a swear word," said one woman from the east. "But every homesteader had to build a dam."

Water witching with "divining rod"—usually a Y-shaped willow—was an art used to locate many wells.

A good well was welcome news to the entire community. They came with water wagons. Most settlers were generous. A Corson County farmer, warned his new well might go dry when so many neighbors came, replied that he just couldn't refuse them. But a Hughes County settler who spilled his last barrel of water one day, went to his neighbor to borrow a pail full and found the well padlocked. The neighbor said firmly that he would not lend any water.

One settler who hauled water from the river by stoneboat said that after the rough trip, "the barrels would be half empty when we got home." People tried to keep several barrels on hand in case of fire.

In towns like Murdo, townsfolk bought their water for 25 to 50 cents per barrel, conserving even the dishwater.

Every shanty had a rain barrel under the eaves to catch the rain off the roof.

This small dam supplied two homesteads. Right, water barrels were hauled on stoneboats, wagons and finally trucks.

Digging coal with shovel and dynamite at Anderson Butte, at left. Above, laying in a winter supply of wood.

Fuel

Buffalo chips and later cow chips were a main fuel of the treeless prairies, as sod houses were the homes. Many a new pioneer was shocked and ashamed of using manure for fuel. Said one, "At first we furtively picked up cow chips, but soon adopted it in the spirit of grim humor," Another said cow chips burned "like paper, but made a very hot fire."

Wood was cut when possible. Push wood was a term used for a long limb of uncut wood which was pushed into the stove as it burned.

South Dakota had little native coal except in the northwestern part of the state where a Corson County pioneer said:

We operated a coal mine on our property also. People came as far as 20 miles to buy coal, hauling it away in wagons or Ford trucks during the fall and the winter. There being very little snow in the area, sleds were seldom necessary. Coal sold for as little as $1 a wagonbox load to 20ᶜ per inch of a standard wagonbox.

Slough grass was twisted and burned in an ordinary cookstove, but it burned quickly unless tightly twisted. Sometimes a washboiler was stuffed with hay and inverted over the open cookstove. This would burn for an hour. Special straw-burning stoves were available as in this Brule County report:

We had two jumbo stoves of sheet iron, round and about two feet across and about five feet high. We would take one to the straw pile and fill it tightly with straw and bring it in and set it up on an iron frame, and put the lid on (like a pail lid). This lid was attached to the stove pipe. There was a small round hole near the top and one near the bottom. We lit it from the top and it would slowly burn all around the outside giving off a nice heat. On nice days it would last nearly all day, but on windy days had to be filled several times. We kept two of these for they had to be filled and the ashes emptied so one was always ready to set up. 60

MANY PEOPLE ask what we burned those days. One year we burned twisted hay. I got to be quite an expert at twisting hay. The amount of twisted hay that it took to do a washing and ironing was staggering. It took one day to get the hay ready. One year we burned corn stalks. They were not very satisfactory as they threw out so little heat and burned so quickly. We also burned cow chips; they made a good fire but left so many ashes. Of all the make-shift fuels I think flax straw is the most satisfactory. We burned it in a straw burner. 61

THE ICE HARVEST was usually a three-day job. Ice was cut at a dam and hauled home on a bobsled and packed in straw or sawdust in a dugout. It was then used in a cooler for our milk and butter and for making ice cream in the summer. Anyone helping with this work felt free to use part of the ice. 62

Boys from Indian Day school cutting ice at Rosebud Agency, 1898.

In the Home

ONE OF THE FAVORITE ROOMS was the kitchen with its big old cooking range, so warm and inviting in the winter. It had a reservoir on one end that would hold a couple of buckets of water for the heat from the stove to warm. There were two warming ovens up over the top where things could be kept warm or skillets could be stored. Of course, there had to be the drawer below the fire pot that held the ashes and had to be emptied all too often, usually leaving a mess. Then there was the oven door on which we would sit to warm up, and it was a good place to dry wet mitts. 63

IN THE ROOT CELLAR were stored vegetables, meat packed in brine and canned in glass jars. It had shelves against one wall of wooden boxes; there were spider webs, sometimes rattlers; dirt chunks fell and we were scared the cracked timbers might fall in. 64

Feeding the laying hens. For hot baths, below, a tea kettle on the stove was needed.

THE SATURDAY NIGHT BATHS were something to remember. We'd put a couple of teakettles of water on the stove to get hot, drag in the washtub that we used to wash clothes in and set it by the cook stove or heater, whichever place was warmest. We'd pour the hot water in and cool it down with cold water until it was just right for the first one. When the next one was to get in we would add more hot water and so on until all were bathed. No clean water for each one as it took too much fuel to heat the water and too much hard work to carry it in and out again. 65

WE CAUGHT AS MUCH rain water in tubs and barrels as we could for laundry use. Mother washed often and always on the washboard, a tiresome task. The wash water was heated on our cook stove. There were no bleaches so the white clothes were boiled in soapy water in the boiler on the stove. It was necessary to cook some starch for each washing. In those days the dresses and skirts were ankle length, many petticoats, with long aprons that were garments of many, many uses. These and other items of clothing required much starch. For the ironing a set of three heavy sad irons were heated on the cook stove, so a hot fire had to be kept till the job was finished. 66

MUCH WILD FRUIT grew along the creeks leading into the river: plums, June berries, chokecherries, buffalo berries. Plenty to can for sauce and pies during the winter. Jams and jellies were made all summer. Mrs. Jensen and I always canned beef together, quarts and quarts, on a wood buring range in boilers. It took two or three days to pressure the big beef, but we always had plenty of good meat. Cottontails were plentiful and very tasty. Prairie chickens and pheasants were very good. 67

A mother had her garden, chickens to care for, many starched petticoats, and always plenty of children.

May 13, 1920: Spring is coming very slowly but by these signs we know it is on the way: The men are shaving again, children are suspiciously silent when wild onions are mentioned, and the women are talking of garden seed and housecleaning. It can't come too soon for most of us. Friend Winter has stayed with us a jolly while. Zeona News.

STEAM BREAKING OUTFIT

REEVES

NEAR MC INTOSH S D

Breaking the virgin sod, ten furrows at a time.

ETERNAL VIGILANCE was the price of a crop from the time it was planted until harvested. When sowing seed in the springtime, millions of blackbirds were on hand to dig it up. We had to be in the field with the shotgun at daylight and stay until dark shooting into the flocks until the seed was sufficiently rooted to withstand their efforts to pull it. Again for a couple of weeks before harvest we had to be on the spot through daylight hours or we had nothing to harvest. 68

haying and harvest

Farmwork

Farm work meant long hours, "from can see to can't see," with the chores done before daylight. Breaking the virgin sod by plowing was the first goal. The breaking plow—with a man walking behind—turned one furrow; 16 or 20 rounds to the end of the quarter and back (half mile each way) was considered a good day's work. Then, just before World War I, big steam tractors came into use, pulling gang plows with up to 10 bottoms, and turning up 20 acres of sod a day.

In the turned sod that first year, pioneers planted corn or potatoes—sometimes chopping the seed in with an ax.

One family plowed a big prairie dog town for the garden and cornfield. There was little grass, but "we had to fight the prairie dogs back, and during the summer we killed 75 rattlesnakes," they said. "It was late when we planted the corn. We thought it would just make fodder, but rains came right and it produced 85 bushels per acre. In the 40 years we lived here, we never again had that kind of crop."

Cooking for threshers in harvest was a big concern for women; they baked many days in preparation. One girl remembers her mother's shock when her father came in at 11 a.m. to tell her the threshers would be there for dinner. "Mother was going to bake bread that day, but there wasn't time. We managed to get a good meal on the table for all those men—15 or more—with fresh squaw bread. And how they ate it!"

Haying: filling the haymow, and stacking in the field, below, with overshot stacker; at left, stacker is moved to field across river.

148

Four-horse team pulls binder through wheat.

Oats bundles are shocked for drying.

Shocking forage.

Neighbors came with teams and hayracks for threshing.

ONE MAN in the community owned a threshing machine and he would travel from one farm to another. The entire neighborhood helped, the men exchanging work. Several farmers would come with their teams and racks to haul the grain to the threshing machine. Others had their wagons with good, tight boxes and they would haul the grain to the granary. Extra men were needed to help pitch bundles and usually an extra one at the granary to help shovel the grain into the bin. Many long hard hours went into the threshing. The women were just as busy preparing good nourishing food to feed the hungry men. 69

ANOTHER BUSY MAN was the "Tankie," with a team on a tank wagon of probably 8 to 10 barrel capacity, with a hand operated pump and long suction hose, pumping water to be converted to steam. Usual source of supply was a creek or slough, often a considerable distance from the threshing. The whistle-code of the engineer would call for water; for grain haulers or sacks; for the bundle haulers to "snap it up;" or to stop the feeding of bundles into the machine, and many more signals. It was not unusual to see a team with grainbox coming at a gallop in response to the proper number of short toots from the engine whistle. 70

Tidball ranch house on Black Horse Creek replaced claim shack in 1918, soon had both running water and windcharger electricity.

Livestock was Vital

Bum lambs on the bottle.

Horses and oxen were both used in field work. Horses were first choice for strength and speed; oxen were less expensive, required less feed other than pasture, were dependable and could be eaten. Men took great pride in a good team. Said one, his team was willing—"Black Prince was so willing to pull the load, and Buckskin Charley so willing to let him".

Most families had a milk cow or two. These had to be herded or kept on a picket before fences were built to keep out of fields and gardens.

The job of herding cows fell to the children. Two girls from Highmore were to knit socks as they herded. But the socks were never the same size: "Bertha held her yarn tightly while Stina held hers loose." Herding could be monotonous. Two boys confessed they hid an egg every day till they had enough eggs to trade for a sack of ginger snaps. They then took the ginger snaps from a hiding place while they herded, dusted off the gnats, and ate a tiny bite at a time, making the ginger snaps last a long time.

Longhorn cattle on the range terrorized the children and even adults. Wild and curious, they'd chase anyone on foot; they'd lure off the milk cows and stampede over the hills.

AFTER WE KIDS WALKED barefoot over cactus patches and an occasional snake, we'd chase the cows into the corral, then wait until the sun went down, so the cows would cool off and the flies wouldn't be so bad. By that time the mosquitoes were out in full force, so we built a smudge and, picking up our milk pails and stools, we went to work. Usually the business of milking was a serious one—we depended on cream checks for part of our living. But there were various diversions, like having a cow kick a pail of milk over, or someone might get a stream of milk on his back if Dad wasn't watching. Afterward the milk had to be separated and fed to the calves. Trouble was, it all had to be done over again the next morning. 71

Hauling pigs to market in wagons.

ANIMAL HEALTH

HORSES: Diarrhea in young foals.
From exposure and lying on damp ground too soon after foaling, from excitement by the mare being turned in with other horses; from the mare's milk being too rich, or too poor; or from sucking while the mother is too heated up from work. Treatment: 1 teaspoon each of whiskey, laudanum, and flour mixed with a little mare's milk; repeat every 4 - 5 hours.

CATTLE: If sick and begin to lose weight examine tail. If hollow or flabby at end of tail bone, split the hollow and fill with salt, wrap with a rag saturated with turpentine.

DOG: Rabies or hydrophobia. In addition to bite of another dog, it is also thought to arise spontaneously in hot weather among some animals. Popular cures are whiskey, strychnine, arsenic, kerosene.

THE PRACTICAL STOCK DOCTOR, 1908
Dr. George Waterman, editor

Rescuing a colt bogged down in the waterhole.

MY BROTHER AND I HIRED OUT to farm for a neighbor, but it turned out to be mostly horse breaking. They were a pretty snakey bunch, but we got along without any runaways. One horse started pitching and kicking and she never stopped until she had lost all her harness except the bridle and halter with which she was still tied to the other horse. Mr. Shives was a good horseman and we got some good "know how" from him. We kept on working broncs and soon had the name of being good horsemen. We broke many horses of our own and for others in later years. 72

Working cattle in pole corral.

Barn has stout braces inside, walls of sod, and roof of poles and branches.

A good team was a pride and joy.

151

A claim cabin school in 1908.

Early schools were dark, with makeshift desks and benches.

School—as soon as possible

As families arrived they struggled to organize schools. Parents often made great sacrifices to get their children educated.

Immediate problems were to find a willing teacher, obtain a building within traveling distance, and to raise the teacher's salary. These problems were sometimes all solved at once: a mother might be persuaded to teach the neighborhood children and her own, in her home without pay. Sometimes she would board children from distant families as well.

First terms were usually short, as little as six weeks. Bachelors often lent their claim shacks for schools—this would count as residence time for them while they went elsewhere to work.

In schools with dirt floors, children were instructed to keep their feet still so they didn't raise a dust. Teachers used the red building paper lining the walls for a blackboard. Furniture was makeshift. One teacher said her desk was made from a parlor organ with the keys taken off and drawers built under the top. In one school, says an early settler, "We sat on boxes, benches and odd chairs around a big rough board table with all the old books we could find piled in the middle. Teacher divided the pupils into three classes, A, B, and C—according to size, I believe."

The first school in South Sioux Falls was a shed-roofed shanty which leaked in the rain so "the scholars huddled together in the northwest corner of the room, the one dry spot." Students there sat at long benches on either side of two long tables held up by two-by-four legs. Games played were Crack-the-Whip, Pull-Away, Anti-Over, and One-Old-Cat. A stout tree branch and homemade ball started a ball game.

The first regular school house in Dakota was said to be at Bon Homme in 1860. It was built of logs, 14 x 15, with a dirt roof and one window. Desks were part of an old wagon box with three-legged stools for seats.

Her first school, says a Jones County pioneer, was an 8 by 10 claim shack with dirt roof. "We had to move the planks to get out the door, therefore we never had recess. The teacher had her bed and other articles in one end of the shack. We all had different books—just those we could find around the home.

As many as four or five would study out of one book. There were no blackboards and we had no paper to write on." When school was held in a home, a tarp or curtain was stretched across one end for family privacy.

In the Bretton district near Pierre in the early '90's, school terms began in November and lasted till March. These would be two terms, with an average of 50 days taught each term; the teacher was paid $30 a month.

Schools often had distinctive names: the Sitting Up school; the Dry Run; Crocus Hill; the Black Shack.

Many children walked or rode long distances to school. One girl who walked three miles said it was often dark when she reached home. The gray wolves would howl along the trail in a bloodchilling sound for her. Two boys walked twelve miles to and from school each day. In winter they used skis and ran a trapline on the way, so if they caught something they'd be late. If the "something" was a skunk, they'd be shunned for the day.

Teachers who rode or drove horses would often pick up students on the way. Horses could be hard for children to control. One Highmore youngster rode a horse named Buster. "He would gallop so fast he wouldn't even slow up for the corner and a couple of times dumped me there—then he'd go back home with my lunch still tied to the saddle. I would walk the other half mile to school."

Two Corson County girls, ages 8 and 10, had a difficult time getting the six miles to school, but a mother determined for them to get an education. They rode horseback along the river. The teacher remembers it often took them until noon to get warm in winter, and she'd let them go early so they wouldn't have so far to go in the dark. One spring the horses had to swim the Grand River in freezing waters. Another time the horses refused to cross, so the girls had to go far around to the bridge. They were so late that their mother took a lantern and went on foot to look for them.

Cold weather and blizzards were constant winter worries for parents. One woman remembers "how cold we got facing that cold northwest wind coming home from school. The horses were cold and anxious to get home to water and grain, and they would run all the way home which only made it that much colder. My feet and legs up to my knees used to feel like stumps when I'd get off my horse at home. How we all suffered from Chilblains."

Children were cautioned to trust a horse's sense of direction. Stories like the following are common:

> One foggy day, after the children started home, darkness set in. The ground was covered with snow, there were very few fences, only poor roads and trails, and the children became lost. About six miles west of Stamford, the buggy dropped into a hole that caused a wheel to break off. The girls rode the horse and the boys held onto his tail and the horse took them home. In the meantime, Mr. Kusick was driving his team and wagon over the prairie holding a lantern in hopes the children would see the lantern light through the fog, but they never saw it. 73

Children were often boarded in homes close to school. Sometimes the mothers moved into town for school term. One family waited until they had five children ready for high school, then sent them all at once into Murdo. High school children often worked for board and room with a town family.

Many teachers were true frontier heroes. Whatever the situation, they were expected to cope: leaky roofs; lack of books; skunks under the schoolhouse; carrying drinking water; rooms full of children of all ages and abilities; keeping the school warm with cow chips; walking miles to school; boarding without privacy in small homes with large families; providing the community with a lively social center.

A Willow Row school teacher in Duel County is remembered as a born teacher, much loved by her students. Says one, "You just had to learn your English when Maria was at the helm. How could you forget her, 'Uffda, how can you be so dumb?' "

Some teachers had little training for their work. If they passed the teacher's exam at the courthouse, they were qualified. At first there was no regular grading system; children were passed according to how many books they completed in reading, arithmetic, geography and history. Sometimes a change of teachers meant pupils were put back to the beginning of their learning.

A Hyde County teacher began teaching in 1901 at the age of 17 on a permit since she was not old enough for a certificate. Her first school was of rough lumber with homemade desks and benches, with 12 pupils, on a salary of $25 paid by warrants worth only $22.50 in cash. The farm where she boarded was 11 miles from school; she drove a horse and cart each morning and evening. At 18 she got her second grade certificate and earned the top available salary of $50 a month, of which she paid $10 for room and board. Another teacher in the same locality earned $45 and paid $20 a month for board and room. Men teachers were customarily paid $5 or more above women teachers.

The teacher often had to discipline unruly students who were bigger, stronger and perhaps older than herself. A certain town was noted for its tough school. In 1907 it had three rooms with about 100 students. Says a former student:

> Hardly any two families had ever gone to school together before, as they came from all over the U.S. and were all nationalities. There were several roughnecks and the others soon got to be that way, as each had to do his own fighting. I often think of Carrie Brackett and the odds she had, how hard she worked to start us right, and how little she accomplished. Several boys who grew up in this country were young cowboys, and handy with a rope. Harry Gage could (and often did) rope a kid across the room and jerk him out of his seat, if the teacher turned her head or left the room. At noon and recess, they'd rope and tie down as many boys as they could and the teacher would have to go out and untie them when school was called. I don't understand why the teachers didn't just cut the ropes instead of untying them, but maybe they were scared of the big boys. 74

Other students trapped skunks under a country schoolhouse. "One day they released a trapped skunk and chased it around the schoolyard. The teacher came out and killed the skunk with a baseball bat and the skunk let loose—smelling up the school for many days."

An early school at Harrold had as many as 68 students for one teacher in 1886, all crowded into one room. Most came from different states, bringing different books (when they had books at all) and having been taught by different standards and divided by different grading systems.

Schools were frequently the scene of practical jokes. Near Chamberlain pioneers remember a girl with long curls who came to school one day with kerosene-soaked hair "to get rid of what they used to call 'livestock.' Franklin Johnson sat behind her and he thought it would be a good joke to touch a lighted match to her hair. This he did and at once her head was in flames, but Franklin jumped up and pulled her head inside his coat and smothered the flames and probably saved her life. But this did not save him from a sound beating from Eustace Ward, the teacher."

Small pleasures were remembered, too. A Jones County teacher tells of her excitement in finding a tree leaf on the way to school. "Now, there was not a tree for miles and miles, I took it on to school and I held it behind me and asked the children to guess what I found. No one could think of a leaf. Well, I put it in a book and pressed it. It was a novelty in that part of the country. I kept it for years until it finally crumbled and was no more a leaf."

In most communities, the school was the social center. The entire community would crowd into the school for school programs, basket socials, church services, debates, spelling bees and dances.

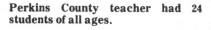

Perkins County teacher had 24 students of all ages.

Violent Weather

Weather changes can come with sudden violence to the usually pleasant Great Plains states. Hailstorms, tornadoes, hard rains with flash flooding, blizzards—as quickly as they come the storms are over. But they sometimes leave a swath of devastation in their wake.

A sudden chill on a hot summer afternoon warns of destructive hail. Large hail threatens not only the crops, but homes and sometimes livestock. A man in southcentral South Dakota remembers an August 1914 hailstorm that came up while he and his brother Donald were bringing home the milk cows. Age 7 and 10, they were riding horseback double, one barefoot and the other without a hat. As the hail pelted them with increased ferocity they jumped off the horse and took shelter under a bank. They took off the saddle and held it over their heads. Meanwhile the horse jerked loose and headed for home, while the water rose high in the ravine. They had to leave their shelter and as the driving rain continued, they drifted with the storm into the darkness. Three hours later they were found by a neighbor's dog, six miles from home. The boys' backs and heads were swollen from the hail and their feet were full of broken cactus spines.

A pioneer woman spent a busy day cleaning her house, finishing by varnishing the floors. Just as she finished the hail began, and created havoc of her day's work. "All the windows on the north side of the house were broken," she said. "Wind and rain coming in the house pasted leaves on the walls. The coal pail was half full of water in the kitchen. Paul was jumping and screaming as the water was coming through the floor to the basement."

In Corson County a 1924 hailstorm caused much damage in the Whitney and Black Horse Creek area. One rancher there found a hail stone "as big as a five-pound lard pail" which hit his Model-T Ford. Bad hail meant the destruction of a year's crops—grain was shelled, corn and grass hammered into the ground, gardens shattered. Yet there are plenty of South Dakotans who report that—even in the face of such destruction—they gathered buckets of hailstones and made ice cream.

Tornadoes occasionally swept the flimsy shacks from the open prairies and broke them to bits. The 1914 tornado which struck near Watertown is recalled by a woman who felt its full force: "All at once we looked and the silo was gone; then the roof of the barn; then the old hog house. You'd close your eyes and something else was gone...We had a hen setting in the barn and, you know, the hen disappeared—and the little chicks hatched out."

Summer thunder and lightning storms brought refreshing rain, but lightning could be a killer of both livestock and people. A Brown County man, whose face had been paralyzed by a gunshot, had a happier experience. He took shelter in the barn doorway from a thunderstorm. Lightning struck close by with an earsplitting crash of thunder and in that moment his paralysis was cured.

Rains have always been welcome in drouth-prone sections of South Dakota. Yet rain, too, has come in violence, causing flash flooding and disaster. One of the heaviest of rains struck Ft. Pierre on the 4th of July 1905. Forty-three homes were wrecked, 17 of them being swept down the raging river. At the Big Bend, below, eight of these homes came against the bank still in fairly good condition. George Harris, who lived there, caught them and tied them up. But he lacked enough rope to hold them secure against the river's force and they all broke away again and plunged on downstream. People salvaged many things from the river in the next days: a good piano; a feather bed, fully made and dry on top; farm wagons and furniture. Thirteen people reportedly died in the flooding there and up the swollen Bad River.

West of the Missouri much of the soil was heavy clay, called gumbo. There a period of hard rain meant good crops, but difficult travel. Freighters would halt and simply wait till things dried out. "We had to pull up and camp when it got wet," one recalls. "The wheels would sink in and ball up so the

Ice jam on the Big White flooded this homestead.

horses couldn't pull the wagons." A woman traveling from Pennsylvania to Sturgis by stagecoach was horrified when the gumbo rolled the wheels full until they locked. Each time this happened the men would climb out and dig off the wheels and push the coach to higher ground.

In the home gumbo was a disaster for the immaculate housekeeper. "The mud was terrible," said one from the southcentral part of the state. "We had no previous experience with that kind of sticky mud, mostly clay, and we tracked in so much of it we were sticking to the floor. We could not remove our shoes on account of the sticky mess, so we scraped off all we could, and after that we learned to leave our shoes out on the porch."

Another said even the animals disliked the gumbo. "The horses would almost run away when the large piece of heavy clay would fly off their feet and hit them. The pet dog would stop to bite off the gumbo from between his toes before he would take more steps and he always seemed very unhappy."

But people in gumbo country rejoiced for the rain. "When it rains the gumbo sticks to us and crops are good; when it's dry, we have faith and stick to the gumbo," they said.

Most learned to take the wet gumbo in stride agreeing that, "wet gumbo is a blessing, It means we've had moisture for our crops, rangeland and water for our livestock, and this is our livelihood."

It was all too clear to South Dakotans—that while violent and sudden storms could cause localized disaster—the most devestating of all weather patterns was neither violent nor sudden. It was the periodic drouth which dragged out endlessly and covered vast regions while settlers watched pitiless skies and prayed for rain.

Blizzards

Sudden blizzards and hard winters caused great hardship to people living in shanties heated with fuels such as cow chips and twisted slough grass.

But in the homes they at least had protection. Those who did not survive were usually caught out in a blizzard's full fury. Often they were children on their way home from school.

Storms could hit suddenly. One mild winter day in 1871 Robert and Sarah Foster, a Minnehaha County brother and sister, ages 15 and 13, went to check their coyote traps. A storm came up and as it worsened their mother, who was home alone with a small child, went many times to the door, calling. Finally the snow drifted so tightly into the doorway she could no longer close the door. She took all the bedding and clothing she could gather and went to bed with her small daughter to keep warm. It was several months before the bodies of Robert and Sarah were found in an abandoned claim shack where they had huddled for shelter.

In 1880, the year of heavy snow, the first October storm lasted three days. A Duel County woman, home with her four small children, went out on the second day to search for the oxen. She found them buried in the straw shelter and shoveled until she could catch their halters in her hands. Afraid to turn them loose in the storm, she led the oxen into the house and sat up with them all night, keeping them on their feet. She worried that if they lay down they would break through the floor and fall into the cellar. On the third day she shoveled again to get the oxen out. When the father returned he could hardly find the house, it was buried so deeply in drifted snow.

By February that year the snow had piled into impassable drifts. Settlers made desperate trips to the river for wood with oxen hitched to wagons that could scarcely be pulled through heavy snow. Food supplies ran low. Some families had only seed grain they had saved or grain intended for stock to eat. This they ground in coffee mills. Others had beans raised on sod the previous summer. Antelope, caught in sheltered river bottoms in deep snow, were an unexpected source of food for some.

What was probably South Dakota's worst blizzard came January 12, 1888. Many settlers and children lost their lives in that storm; much stock was also lost. One Brule County girl, Anna Anderson, stopped on her way to school to warm herself at a neighbor's house, then continued in the storm toward school, only a half mile away. She soon lost direction and walked southeast ahead of the wind. At one point she came so close to safety that she pulled a small dress from a neighbor's clothesline and was still clutching it when found frozen to death the next day. Describing this storm, a pioneer said, "Out of the northwest came a rushing, roaring monster to pour out its fury upon an unsuspecting world, and to blow itself into history as the blizzard of '88."

Another disastrous blizzard swept in May 8, 1905. Dead cattle were found later from the Bad River to the White and many went over the Badlands Wall to their deaths. The blizzard of March 14, 1913 was another terrible killer, and caused people to say, "We need no longer refer to the blizzard of '88 as the worst—it's been replaced by this one." Many towns were shut off completely from the outside world.

In a storm the rule was for teachers to keep all children at school. But not always did this happen. Some who persuaded their teachers to let them go home were lost; parents struggled through the storm to find their children. One young man teacher who had only one boy in school during the 1888 blizzard, decided to take him and go the half mile to the home where he boarded. They got lost, but found a straw pile just before dark, dug a hole and stayed there till morning when the storm abated. The teacher found his way then but lost both feet from frostbite; the boy lost all his toes but one.

In town schools as well as in the country, children waited out blizzards. One pioneer remembers, "It was so bad we couldn't see anything, so we all stayed at school overnight. The teachers cooked some rice for us to eat. We played games and slept on our coats around the register of the two big furnaces." One teacher made a chain and marched her 22 pupils to a nearby home in a blizzard. Others remember square dancing all afternoon, until the last of the school coal was gone. One who recalls a cold hungry night spent at school says, "At daylight a farmer came in with a big kettle of potato soup. I'll never forget that soup!"

Houses and barns were sometimes snowed shut. A man who couldn't get his door open one morning, used a spoon handle to make a small opening. Next he used a large stirring spoon and finally got the door open. After such an experience, some people changed an outward-opening door to swing inward.

A man who shovelled his horses out of the barn said that afterwards he could see their imprint as if they'd been molded there tight against the snow which had blown in wet and settled around them.

In a storm people tied ropes to the door knob and would follow them to barns and outhouses. One teacher going home in a blizzard held his handkerchief before him to tell which way the wind was blowing. He knew that direction would lead him home, and kept going until he stumbled against the back of his house.

Near McIntosh a man went out to do chores in a snowstorm. By the time he finished, the storm turned violent and he lost his way between the shed and shanty. He walked in circles for several hours. His wife grew worried and let the dog out, hoping the dog would find him. As the man continued struggling against the storm, he suddenly saw his dog bouncing ahead of him. He followed and after some time the dog disappeared as suddenly as he had come. The man plunged on and abruptly fell through the snow into a pit, which he finally realized was the entrance to his own shanty.

In the blizzard of 1907, two Seim sisters died. They left their claim shack and were going to their parents' home five miles away. Before they were halfway there, the blizzard began. In less than an hour the two girls were in the midst of a blinding storm, swept by a hard northwest wind. They struggled on; the storm raged through the night and the following day. When it finally broke, rescue parties left the town of Seim to see that everyone in the community was all right. They soon found the Seim girls had left school but hadn't reached home. Articles of their clothing were found along the trail, but there was no trace of the girls. Later, when the weather warmed, the search continued. It was ten days before two of the searchers came upon the girls' frozen bodies.

Digging out after a heavy snow.

The fire in Murdo is now under control. All the business houses on east side of Main street between the elevator and First State Bank are gone; 15 businessess are burned to the ground. The fire started in the office of the Pioneer. The editor had started the fire and returned to his living rooms which were in the same building. In only a few minutes he smelled smoke, rushing to the office door found it filled with smoke. It's probable the stove pipe became somehow disconnected and fire caught either on the ceiling or stationery cabinet. The family rushed out, saving nothing but a coat that hung near the door. Six men pulled the chemical engine downhill and soon had chemcials at work, but the smoke was so dense when the fire was put out at one place it seemed to break out anew at another. The water froze, breaking the hose in several places. It was very disagreeable work, 15° below zero and a cold wind blowing from the north-west. At the First State Bank the buildings were covered with wet blankets kept wet by bucket brigades. Burning pieces of wood were blown onto the bank several times but were extinguished. February 22, 1910.

Fire was a special horror of the settlement years. Home fires, town fires, and prairie fires.

Roof fires from chimney sparks and heating stoves shooting out live cinders were all too common. Tarpaper shacks caught fire easily and burned quickly. A Hyde County farmer refused to let his wife leave sleeping children to work in the field. His sister's children, age two and four, had both burned to death near Highmore one day when his sister was working in the field.

Town fires would wipe out whole blocks of what were typically flimsy wooden buildings set closely together. Deadwood had two destructive fires. Draper lost 18 buildings in three hours during the winter of 1913. The fire began at 2 a.m. in the grocery store and soon roused other people sleeping in stores. Pearl Gallinger remembers her mother saving a silver cracker bowl filled with soup crackers—the only food they had. A blizzard stopped all trains into Draper for two weeks and food became scarce as both groceries and many homes had burned.

Fire breaks did not always protect a home or even a town in high wind. A blazing cow chip jumped a 100-foot fireguard into Ree Heights, starting a fire that wiped out 20 buildings.

Prairie fires were much dreaded and took a toll of crops, buildings, haystacks, livestock and occasionally humans. In earliest settlement days tall cured grass was everywhere. Trains and lightning set many fires in this tall grass which burned for miles in a high wind—until they were stopped by a river in many cases. In harvest season one could always expect prairie fires; many settlers kept barrels of water and gunny sacks in the wagon to fight fire in a hurry.

Everyone soon learned the importance of plowing firebreaks around their homes, their haystacks and fields. They plowed two sets of furrows some 20 or more feet apart, then set fire to the grass between to make a burned-off area too wide for the fire to jump.

A plowed field of summer fallow was a place of safety. As a prairie fire raced toward them, one woman recalls she loaded the wagon with bedding and other provisions and had the grandmother sit in the wagon on the quilts holding the harnessed team, ready to drive to the middle of a plowed field if the fire didn't hold at the firebreak.

A family near Bear Butte "lost everything we had except our stock. When the fire got close to a ranch house there was nothing anyone could do but get in the wagon and drive to a strip of breaking until it passed. George lost 1500 cedar posts that he had spent two years getting out of the breaks. This fire burned all the way to Cheyenne River. After the fire, we lived in my brother's dugout."

A 1910 Corson County fire burned an area 20 miles wide by 35 miles long. Longhorn cattle ran in panic ahead of the fire, stampeding over everything in their path. The worst fire in southcentral South Dakota was said to be in the late fall 1916 when all of eastern Washabaugh and Bennett counties south of the Badlands burned off. That fire burned three days and went far south into Nebraska burning livestock, houses, much rangeland, hay and feed.

After a fire had swept through, the prairies were black as far as the eye could see. In Minneahaha County a fire that burned during nesting season, according to one pioneer, left: "hundreds of prairie chicken's nests, full of eggs, glaring white against the background of blackened prairie—a pitiful sight." Another said she had never realized there were so many rocks until she saw them gleaming white against the black earth.

DURING ONE FIRE Johnnie Gertson was herding cattle when he saw the fire coming. He had no matches to set back fire so ran for an old well nearby. He got there just in time, but unfortunately a lot of Russian thistles which were in the well also caught fire and Johnnie was severely burned about the face and arms. 75

ANNIE SWEENEY WAS ALONE on their farm with the wind blowing 80 miles per hour. The flames leapt through tall buffalo grass and swept through the county to the Missouri river. Annie saw the fire coming and ran to free the stock, but before she had time to escape, fire surrounded the place and she died with the stock. 76

Grasshoppers

From the skies came devestation of another kind: swarms of flying grasshoppers. Early grasshopper plagues which "blackened the skies and shut out the sun" descended on the settlers in 1873 and 1874; other terrible plagues came during the 1930's. Hamlin Garland, in Under the Lion's Paw, describes the despair of settlers:

"Eat! They wiped us out. They chawed everything that was green. They jest set around waitin' f'r us to die t' eat us, too. My God! I ust t' dream of 'em sittin' 'round on the bedpost, six feet long, workin' their jaws. They eet the fork-handles. They got worse 'n' worse till they jest rolled on one another, piled up like snow in winter. Well, it ain't no use."

Rattlesnake hunt near McLaughlin.

ONE YEAR THEY KILLED two rattlesnakes in their claim shack, also a number of them nearby. Emma recalled that two successive nights they heard a rattlesnake and for two days she removed everything in the home searching for it. Finally on the third day she found it coiled in front of the bedroom door. 77

Rattlesnakes

IN THE SPRING OF 1925 Bad River flooded and this drove the rattlers up on higher ground. I taught school in Stanley County that year and I heard that a young girl had been bitten by a rattler. I rode over to see them. The husband told me the story. Their little girl had gone outside to play when the mother heard her scream. The mother ran out, nearly stepped on the snake and it began to rattle. She killed it and picked up the little girl. You can immagine her terror waiting for her husband to come home from a distance of 28 miles. She could carry the child but neighbors were too far away. So she waited, and waited for her husband to arrive. He kept on repeating she was dead—when I got home—she was dead.

Just one week later I fully understood their grief. My wife had gone to Pierre to take a teacher's examination and I was helping Mother extract honey. My father was watching my little girl while she was playing with the dog. They were playing tug-of-war with a stick and she was laughing gayly. Suddenly she screamed and I went to the open door, my father picked her up and I asked him if she was hurt. "No," he said, "she just fell down." Then the dog began to bark and the snake began to rattle. I ran out and killed the snake then asked my father if she was bitten. I then saw the two drops of blood on the back of her hand. I tied a handkerchief above the wound and made incisions with a new razor blade in order to suck the poison out. Then we started for Murdo, seventeen miles away.

When we were half way it was dark and my lights blew out—I felt that this was a bad omen. But we made it safely into town and found the doctor at home. He complimented me on my first aid and then gave her a shot of anti-venom. Then we found she had been bitten on the leg also. "Why," I said, "She's been bitten on the leg also. I've always heard a rattler only strikes once." Later her whole abdomen turned black proving this was a bite, while the bite on the hand did not turn black proving I had gotten most of the poison by sucking the wound.

Now there was nothing to do but wait. We sat around the bed watching her and listening to her loud breathing. One hour passed—two, finally I could take it no longer and went out on the street. The town seemed strange. No sound, it seemed dead. So I went back and watched some more. If she would only cry or say something. We waited when the light of dawn came through the window. Suddenly she sat up and looked around the room. I spoke to her, then she lay down quietly and gave a long sigh. I called the doctor. He looked at her and turned away. I knew then she was dead. Norma Jeanne was dead.

The next morning I went to meet the train. When the train pulled in my wife stepped on the platform—she was radiant. "Why," she said, "It's such a beautiful day, why didn't you bring Norma Jeanne?" 78

Snake trap was used near known dens.

ONE DAY GRETEL, who was three, leaned out the low window sill, cooing and laughing. All at once, Mother saw the dog Jink with open mouth charging directly for her outside the window. Mother grabbed Gretel just as Jink grabbed a rattlesnake and threw it to one side. 79

157

Medical

Early settlers were usually healthy. For their ailments a mustard plaster or dose of kerosene mixed with sugar was administered. Sulphur and molasses purified the blood.

But there were dangerous times: the birth of a baby, pneumonia in winter, dread epidemics. It was not uncommon for new mothers to die of childbed fever—caused by unsanitary conditions such as unclean hands of the doctor or midwife.

Accidents were dealt with quickly. Near Murdo a man who cut a deep gash in his thigh with a mower sickle, was sewn up by his wife Hattie with a three-cornered needle and thread. He was weak with loss of blood, but Hattie gritted her teeth, told him to stretch out straight and sewed the flesh together. Later the doctor told her she had done her job well and possibly saved his life.

Communities were terrorized when fatal infectious diseases swept through. Diptheria, scarlet fever and the Spanish flu were widespread killers. Some epidemics literally struck every home except the most isolated, sometimes killing several family members, especially young children. The young and the elderly were always the most likely to die.

In Sioux Falls about 10% of the population caught typhiod fever in the 1884-1885 epidemic which was traced to a broken water main from the well lying in the bed of the river. One doctor said during the entire winter epidemic there, he only undressed to go to bed four times. In such epidemics doctors had little time to visit country patients—they would send medicine with desperate settlers who had ridden for help.

In 1888 diptheria struck Chamberlain, killing five children of the clothing merchant within a few days.

Another Chamberlain epidemic was of typhoid in 1932-1933, caused by drinking polluted river water. All the towns above ran their sewage into the river, and it was commonly said that the Missouri River purified itself every 20 feet through the silt and sand. This was a year of low water concentrating the pollution. New typoid cases broke out every day and Chamberlain alone had 33 deaths.

The young and the old were most likely to die.

The worst was probably the worldwide Spanish flu epidemic of 1918 which killed over a thousand South Dakotans, with perhaps another 500 or more dying from complications such as pneumonia. Schools closed and public meetings were banned. The White Butte school was closed so much that none of the children were allowed to pass to the next grade. The year didn't count and all had to take their classes over.

Family tragedies were often multiple. In one Hyde County family the mother died when her baby Grace was two weeks old. Neighbors came to help with the burial. Soon after, one of the children died of diptheria and at eight, Grace died of scarlet fever. This time the neighbors stayed away for fear of the disease. The father buried his little girl beside her mother on the prairie.

A family which caught whooping cough kept the newborn baby safe by suspending her in a clothes basket from the ceiling with a pulley. Said the mother, "I would chase the others out in the kitchen while I bathed her, nursed her and changed her. There she slept during the day. She never did get whooping cough."

When his two sons took sick, a father started for the doctor in Gary with a team of horses, but was caught in a bad storm which delayed him two days. He returned to find both his sons dead and his wife so distraught she later had to be institutionalized.

Doctors were scarce and local women often served as midwives, helping in childbirth, sickness and with laying out the dead. Neighbors came in time of sickness and death. Early settlers survived by helping each other and even in deadly epidemics, some neighbor would usually come to help stricken families.

A woman called the "Lodgepole Angel," Mrs. L. T. Larsen, was said to have attended more births than any other midwife in the western Dakotas. She was a trained practical nurse and besides helping at the births of hundreds of babies, spent her days and nights ministering to the sick. Her husband was a locator, so the Larsens also had a stream of newcomers in their home; a dozen or more might spend the night. Nobody was ever turned away. The Larsen hospitality was well known even in a region where hospitality was common. At one time they tried managing a hotel, but had to give it up because Mrs. Larsen was so busy with her nursing. In November 1907, two homesteaders were burned in a bad prairie fire. Mrs. Larsen nursed them in her shack until they could be moved. Then she took them by train to an Aberdeen hospital where they recovered.

Two Minneapolis girls who homesteaded in western South Dakota were also noted for their care of the sick. Jennie Harrington and Robina Littlejohn had adjoining home stead shacks not far from a local saloon. Said Robina, "We were thankful that Jim Owens was there with his saloon and ice house—he supplied the ice we needed so badly for treating typhoid patients when we were drafted into that." The typhoid fever broke out in a railroad building crew and spread to the homesteaders. Both railroaders and neighbors were brought to their shacks for treatment; one neighbor with typhoid stayed six weeks. Another time a woman came there to have her baby and stayed two weeks while the girls cared for mother and baby.

Burials

The first cemetery in Sioux Falls was on the open prairie with only wild flowers and prairie grasses and the song of the meadowlark to honor the graves, said an early settler. Grave markers were of wood with names painted or carved on, at first, or were of rock.

In the Slim Buttes a woman trapper who froze to death in the 1880's while her husband was gone on a ranch job, was buried beneath a rock cairn. Neighbors added rocks from time to time as they rode by through the years.

The graveyard might be in a corner of the homestead. Later, country churches had their own small cemeteries People who lived a greater distance often took the bodies of their loved ones on a long wagon trip to town for burial. In hot weather this was a dread task if the trip was more than a day as it was difficult to keep the body from decomposing. Some people made attempts to preserve the body; others traveled swiftly at night when it was cooler.

In times of epidemic, burials were hasty and few people dared attend. When two brothers died of diptheria near Aberdeen, the family was in quarantine. No one was allowed to go into the home, nor anyone from the house to come out. The father made coffins, sealed them and set them by the road. A neighbor came and picked them up, taking them to the cemetery for burial. In other cases the infected family buried their dead alone while others stayed away.

One cold stormy day in 1911, only four or five people gathered at the cemetery in Van Metre for the funeral of a baby. The teacher saw the bleakness of it from the school window and took her students to the graveside where they sang, "Nearer My God to Thee."

A bit of verse was often written for comfort on the grave marker, such as this from the Highmore cemetery:

> A precious one from us is gone
> A voice we loved is stilled.
> A place is vacant in our house
> Which never can be filled.

In Quarantine

I had been in bed three days with diptheria when my cousin Altene came giggling up the stairs in her father's bathrobe. Close behind came her mother, worried and anxious, and the doctor.

The upstairs was quarantined with only Auntie allowed to come up. After Altene had been in bed one day (it was four for me), we were allowed up. The doctor praised the wonders of Anti-toxin. My Auntie believed him, but Altene and I did not, since it did not lessen our period of quarantine, and my Uncle declared later that Anti-toxin affected us as any intoxicant might.

We spent the next two days sitting at the top of the stairs making known our feelings to the folk below and issuing commands. Finally my cousin Selby, out of kindness for us—or the others, sent us some old books that he had found in the basement, most of them cheap novels. One was a religious book written by a Catholic priest refuting all the statements against Catholicism. We tested the arguments on my aunt till she feared we would turn Catholic, and then the book disappeared. We read and re-read the novels.

But they wouldn't send their good books upstairs to be later burned, and besides they said we were as well as they and could find our own amusements. We tried. Every time we heard the folks eating we would sit on the stairs and sing the last verse of "Tenting Tonight" in so mournful a tone that my uncle threatened to break quarantine and come up. We made parodies on familiar songs:

> Oh blow ye winds over the city,
> And blow ye winds over the town.
> Oh blow ye winds over the city,
> And knock the Health Officer down.

Every time the telephone rang we rushed to the hall to listen. We would hear my aunt or cousins say, "They haven't been sick at all, only in quarantine, and so hilarious." This made us angry as we wanted people to think us very ill. However my mother's first letter contained all that we had hoped for. She was terribly worried. We pinned her letter on the bathroom wall.

We were hard pressed for something to do. We decided to write letters and bake them to kill the germs. We started one to my brother and a friend of his in the Army. Altene would write a paragraph, and then I would write one, but we became so interested writing about each other that we forgot all about the boys until we had used all our stationery. Again we turned to the novels.

Altene cut brown wrapping paper into sheets on which I wrote a novel patterned after the thrilling ones we had been reading. Altene was overjoyed as I made her the fair and lovely heroine. She read it from the head of the stairs that evening while the family were at dinner. But they were not enthusiastic. I had portrayed my uncle as the villian and others as ignorant peasants.

We needed two negative throat cultures to get out of quarantine. The second could be taken at the Health Office. We called Dr. Jones every other day for two weeks to take a throat culture, but always the next day the Health Office would telephone that our cultures were positive. Then would come the saddest hours I have ever experienced. We would go to bed, then stay up all night and mourn.

One day Dr. Jones was too busy to come. We implored Auntie to beg him to let us go down to the Health Office, and he agreed.

There was a mistake somewhere, perhaps because the Health Officer, about whom we had sung so fondly, had resigned. We knew something had happened the minute we told the redhaired girl in the office our names. She said we had broken quarantine, pushed us inside, slammed the door on us and in a few minutes returned with Dr. Kelly, temporary Health Officer, a large man with a large voice.

"Who are your folks?" he roared at Altene.

But Altene could only give her name in a trembling voice. Finally he spied me back of the desk with one foot in the wastebasket. He roared the same questions at me, but I couldn't even think of my name. He made it plain that we had committed the unpardonable sin. He feared that we were planning to leave town and go to my home, so when we were ready to leave he said, "Where are you going now? Are you going to stay here?"

I tried to think of our street. Altene glanced anxiously around the room and replied, "No, downstairs."

My cousin Walt, who had waited outside, put us in the car and we rode home in gloomy silence. We gave up all hope of getting out of quarantine.

We knew we were germ carriers and would have to stay in all our lives. We neither ate, talked, nor heeded telephone calls.

Imagine my surprise when the next morning one of my cousins called to me that my report was negative. I sprang from bed and in three seconds was ready to go downstairs. But Altene was so sorrowful at having me leave that I spent some time in consoling her. I promised to send her magazines, stationery and pictures, and to telephone all her friends that she was seriously ill.

But she was not to be comforted until her sister Clarice called up the stairs that I had better hurry, last night's dishes were waiting.

Marie Barrett
Quarantined in Sioux Falls,
about 1918

Mellette Co Indians
at Home 23

Many Indians had their own homesteads. They preferred teepees and branch-shaded shelters for summer living.

Relations with Indians

Indian scares continued up until the turn of the century, with mostly rumors of Indian outbreaks and false alarms which were all too real for new settlers. Many had never seen an Indian but had heard terrible tales.

In Brown County the summer of 1882, word spread fast that on a certain night the Indians were coming to massacre all the whites. Settlers gathered at one home, waited all night until suddenly they heard a clop, clop of horses' feet. They grabbed their guns and waited, only to find the noise was a gentle rain dripping off the eaves onto the bottom of an upturned wooden washtub.

One scare was started by three men squatting on claims who hoped to hold a fourth claim for a friend and wanted to scare off a newcomer. They staged an Indian raid and the stranger ran into Redfield shouting that everyone was being killed and he alone had escaped. The news spread and a special train was sent from Huron "armed to the teeth."

When word reached settlers in Hughes County that Indians were holding war dances nearby, one family took what they could and hid in a dugout overnight. A scare in the Ft. Pierre area brought crowds of people into town. One family hid in the neighbor's celler and—though the scare amounted to nothing—emerged from the cellar covered with ticks.

During the Ghost Dancing unrest of 1890, word was sent out from Ft. Meade that certain bands had left the reservation; settlers were warned to get together for protection. Men rode day and night to notify settlers north of the Black Hills. In each community people gathered at a defensible home with their possessions, guns and food.

Electa Kerr recalled the defenses: "We went up to Mr. Buck's house in front of a hill. A cellar was made and connected with the kitchen. Men dug a tunnel from the cellar into the side hill and there made a cave supplied with food, water and ammunition for a siege. People up the river had built a fort and those at the log hotel in town took turns standing guards while others enjoyed themselves dancing and playing cards." She said there were many amusing tales of false alarms, such as when a German boy standing guard began to sing in German. Others feared it was an Indian war cry and rushed to their guns, while women and children fled to the cellars.

Another woman remembers turning loose the milk cows with their calves, hitching up the buggy, taking the cat, dog and two little children and setting off for town. "How well I remember that drive. We expected Indians in every gully," she said. "My father's house in Camp Crook was full. The town was full of settlers from miles around." When Indians were discovered riding toward the town, the defenders got ready, but they turned out to be scouts for a military troop.

Newcomers who settled in and near reservations were often startled by the suddenness with which Indian visitors appeared, but soon learned to accept them and get along well as neighbors.

Lunetta Bloomenrader, who had just come to the Highmore community from Iowa, describes her family's first sight of Indians in 1906:

We children were playing in a willow grove about a quarter mile from home when we noticed several open wagons, many horseback riders and lots of dogs coming toward us. We ran to meet them, but to our horror, discovered the riders were Indians, some in full dress, some in buckskins, and the women in shawls and long dresses. We turned tail and ran for home. All of us had seen in the old Cyrs reader the mother who had hidden her children under a huge kettle in the yard so they wouldn't be scalped. A second illustration showed the Indians attacking her with knives. Mother quickly sent us running to the field for our father. He came, running his horses and just as frightened as Mother. By that time the Indians were going by, not even looking our way. They were on their way to the fair in Huron where they spent the entire week camped on the fairgrounds. 80

In visiting, the Indians did not knock, but would come right into the house. Women were understandably alarmed the first time they turned around to find an Indian man sitting at their table, or standing nearby. The visitors would ask for food, according to Sioux custom, or would trade or sell beaded moccasins, berries, and fence posts.

"I was just a few years old," says a Corson County woman, "but was always the target of the 'Oh's and Ah's' as they patted me on the head and exclaimed over my white face. I was plenty scared and managed to hide behind the door a lot." A Hyde County girl had similar fears: "They were always friendly, but I was scared. I was burned brown from the sun by not wearing a sunbonnet, and mother would say that they would mistake me for one of their kin. So I would hide under a feather bed until they left."

A Lodgepole woman, taking her two little girls in the buggy to visit their nearest neighbors five miles away, was horrified to meet 14 spring wagons of Indian people near the top of a hill. She was soon reasuured they were friendly, however, and they explained they had been to the Badlands getting a winter supply of meat.

AN INDIAN FAMILY pitched their tent not far from the Parker house one evening. Two children came to the house with a note asking for milk and eggs. They asked for a note sent back, but Mrs. Parker, a school teacher, did not want to write the note for the Indian handwriting was so much better than hers. Mr. Parker took the things over and was invited into the teepee. The grass had been skinned off in the middle and a small fire was going and everything was neat as a pin. 81

Neighbors needed and trusted each other.

Neighbors

Everybody trusted everyone else. I don't think anyone ever locked their house. The only thing that might have disappeared would be cookies or doughnuts as some of the bachelor homesteaders had a sweet tooth and would stop in. If no one was home they would help themselves and next time around would stop in and tell us what they had done and everyone would have a big laugh. They always brought things from the store that were much more valuable than the cookies. 82

Our mother in the true western spirit, answered many a call for help from sick or sorrowing neighbors in those early days, and many a bachelor's heart was light as he left her door carrying loaves of fresh baked bread or a basket of clean laundry. 83

The code of the land was that if no one was home, a passing traveler could come in and eat—but no dirty dishes. Being a good neighbor meant spending many hours helping others in time of need.

During the drouth of 1910 one neighbor woman had a way of cheering up everyone. She invited us for Sunday dinner saying, "We have a special treat for all." Well, she had the usual pudding, wheat ground in a coffee mill, cooked for hours. We had a light shower a few weeks before and she had gone to the draw that was green with Russian thistles. They were about two inches high, and she had cut them and cooked them for greens. Then she announced they had a fresh cow and we would have cream on our pudding. It was very good and a treat. 84

THE INDIANS WERE FRIENDLY and never disturbed a thing. They never came to the door but stood eight or ten feet from our door and stood like statues. They came in upon invitation and ate meals. They were fond of bread. Sometimes when the squaws ate they would put a piece of bread under their shawls to take home. I always supposed they wanted to take some to their children. The Indian women would trade me beaded moccasins for coffee and sugar. Our children had very few store shoes. The squaws were very fond of white babies and would laugh and play with the children. 85

DAKOTA LAND

Way out west in South Dakota
On my homestead of the plains;
In my shack upon the prairie
Where they say it never rains.

O Dakota Land, Dakota Land
On whose sun-kissed soil I stand

And wonder why it never rains.

THE HONYOCKS FAREWELL

Farewell to my homestead shanty
I have made my final proof,
The cows will hook down the wall
And someone will steal off the roof.

Farewell to my cracker-box cupboard
With gunny sack cloth for a door,
Farewell to my nice little table
That I never shall eat off no more.

Farewell to my buckwheat and sorghum
That none but myself could endure,
Farewell to my sour dough biscuits
They were sure the dyspeptic to cure.

Farewell to my entire homestead,
Farewell to the hills, buttes and sand.
I've covered you up with a mortgage,
Farewell to my quarter of land.

MY GOVERNMENT CLAIM

You'll find me out west on the wide open plain
A starving to death on my government claim.

My clothes are all ragged; my language is rough
I live on fry biscuits, solid and tough.
But happy am I when I crawl into bed
Till a rattlesnake buzzes his tune at my head.

Homesteaders poked fun at their way of life through songs and parodies. These songs had many versions and many verses as they went from singer to singer.

White Butte Ladies Aid met in tar papered house.

Church

As families settled in, they felt the need for churches and cemeteries. First religious groups met in homes, later in schools and local halls. These often began as inter-denominational groups except in nationality settlements where one religious group was strong. Sunday schools and ladies aids were often the first type of organization. Marriages, "real" preaching and baptisms were held whenever a traveling minister came through. Sometimes reservation missionaries came to give services.

The Helping Hand Society was a local non-denominational group which paid visiting ministers two dollars for every service. Since many of the settlers there were Norwegian Lutherans, a Lutheran minister eventually came and most others became Lutheran. Another church was first served by Methodists, then Presbyterians, and finally by a Reformed minister. This caused some confusion for people who were changed back and forth.

A pioneer who was repeatedly switched recalls, "For some time we were Presbyterians, and a preacher came from Belvidere to minister to us. But one Sunday we went over to the school house where these meetings were held and found we had been traded to the Methodists. A preacher from Murdo was to take over."

A certain amount of rivalry existed between churches. According to an Aberdeen story, two revival meetings were set up across the street from each other. One group was singing, "Will there be any stars in my crown?" the other replied, "No, not one; no, not one."

Summer camp meetings were held for several nights each fall along the creek in the Harrington Community. A pioneer recalls, "Families from miles around came in wagons bringing food and camping equipment to remain for a week or more. A big tent was set up with planks on beer kegs, a raised platform with crude pulpit, an altar rail below. Rousing old spiritual songs were sung. It was an opportunity for women to visit with other women, to exchange recipes, patterns, new ideas, discuss child raising problems. Men tested their strength and swapped yarns. Young people had a chance to meet other young people; big boys came on horseback to show off riding skills before giggling girls. Many romances budded and flowered during these camp meetings."

Revival meetings thus became a social time as well as religious. One woman remembers her fashionable sister dressed in a beautiful plum-colored dress. In the midst of the service the plank she sat on broke and she fell into an undignified heap, much to her embarrassment.

In Hyde County a Catholic family lived far from church. One day word came that a priest from Pierre would say Mass at a home some twenty miles away. A daughter recalls, "Father hitched the oxen to the wagon and we made the trip starting very early in the morning. Frankie and I and a host of children were baptized."

Ministers were commonly paid in produce instead of cash. One said he never had ten dollars he considered his own during his whole life in Dakota. For a year he traveled the Aberdeen area in an old buffalo hide coat. Another circuit rider traveled that area in a stoneboat; he stood on a box in the stoneboat and was pulled by one horse.

An early minister north of Sioux Falls organized a Lutheran congregation in a sod house in 1868. One family agreed to give him room and board plus hay and shelter for his horse for $5.50 per month, paid by the congregation. He covered a wide territory, holding services in 17 places.

Ministers occasionally had their own homesteads. One who did was crippled and had to preach sitting down. His wife did most of the work on the claim. Neighbors remember her driving 30 miles to Ipswich to get lumber to build their shanty. She drove an ox team with only a pole hung between the oxen and fastened to a pair of wheels. She rode the pole to Ipswich and brought back the load of lumber.

Towns were Lively

Main street of Faith.

Women followed the custom of calling in the 1880's and 1890's. In Aberdeen and probably in Groton and Frederick this was quite a formal affair. The ladies were always dressed in their best afternoon clothes with hat, gloves, parasol and high button shoes. Usually two ladies went calling together and some were fortunate enough to have a hired man to drive the horse, especially if using a two-seated carriage. Engraved calling cards were left at the home of friends even if that friend was on hand to receive her callers. 86

The towns were full of people in winter. As things on the claims were at a stand-still with nothing to do and no entertainment, it was quite lonely. Many moved into town, a more pleasant place to be with a variety of entertainment. 87

"Resolved that the city of Aberdeen provide some place or places for farmers to hitch their horses when coming to town. This question has now reached a point where something has got to be done in this matter. We must have some place to tie our teams or quit coming to your burg. You must not kick if you farm customers send away for their goods if you do not treat them well. No man can sit in his rig and do business from his wagon seat." Resolution presented to 1911 town board meeting. 88

A bank clerk would carry part of the money home with her for safe keeping. The bank was in a tarpapered shack—not very safe to keep money overnight, so it was split up and taken home by employees until the brick building was built. 89

Along the south wall of the store were men's furnishings, plug hats, garters, arm bands, bow ties, boxes of stiff collars that went with the collarless shirts, shoes. A ladder on wheels ran along the shelves. Along the north wall was women's merchandise: underwear (drawers), kids gloves, jewelry, bolts of material each wrapped in paper to keep the dust off. There were silks, velvets, crepe de chines. serges, linens, calico and sheeting and pillow tubing, also a glass topped counter with fancy buttons, laces and braids, with stools to sit and wait for your order. The grocery was along the west wall. All canned goods came by freight in wooden boxes. On the counter was a coffee mill. Everything was in bulk: cheese, flour, sugar, candy; cookies came in boxes that fit in slotted racks. Eggs and butter were bought from the farmers and kept in the basement. There was a kerosene pump and a vinegar pump to the back. Bananas came on a stalk and hung from a hook in the ceiling. They had crockery, fancy dishes, drawers of different size chimneys, many lamps, tobacco but no cigarettes 90

A roller skating building was put up in Columbia in 1885 with roller skates for rent and seats along side for spectators. Mother and I would frequently go down to watch. The large building was well lighted with kerosene lights. There was always music and some of the skaters became fancy skaters. I never tried roller skating but the place was crowded every evening. 91

Aberdeen in 1911.

Inside the general store—everything from jelly in wooden pails to salt pork, pitchforks and lamps.

Some towns nearly disappeared except for lively general store.

163

These girls trained their heifers to the saddle.

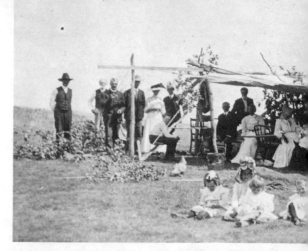

Shelter of canvas and boughs shades this neighborhood gathering.

Baseball game at the Grand River Bridge near Morristown.

A wintertime bobsled party.

Bicycle riding on a Sunday afternoon.

The Happiest Days

SALEM HELD A SPELLING CONTEST benefit in the 1890's, with a fine gold watch donated by businessmen to be awarded the winner. While on her way to the festivities, Miss Kibbe was asked what she thought of her chance to win. She said she thought she had a good chance if she didn't have the word "threshold." She had never spelled it correctly in a public spelling match, but it was the only word she had ever missed. As the contest proceeded, all the spellers were eliminated except Miss Krebs and Miss Kibbe, when the pronouncer turned to Miss Kibbe and gave the word "threshold." She hesitated; her face turned red; then she started to spell "t-h-r-e-s-h." She stopped, became more embarrassed, and in a high pitched voice said, "h-o-l-d," and Miss Krebs won the match—and the gold watch. 92

WOMEN GOT TOGETHER FOR QUILTING BEES and to cut carpet rags for rugs. They had taffy pulls, popcorn and watermelon parties. 93

WE HAD SKATING PARTIES on the Jim River, with huge bonfires. At Verdon we built a good skating rink from the artesian well runoff at the west edge of town. Every evening it was flooded over with water from the we'l and the next morning the surface was like glass. A long bench with high back which could be turned into the wind made a comfortable place with fur coats, robes and bonfire. We could enjoy hot coffee and donuts, skate to harmonica music and sing. 94

ON SUNDAY AFTERNOONS there was a lot of baseball and bronc riding. 95

THE BASEBALL FIELD was somewhere near the Fast Horse cabin as I remember. It seemed like any summer Sunday afternoon, two teams of nine players each would gather to have a game with others sitting on the grass to watch and cheer. 96

BRANDING WAS A TIME WHEN FUN and work combined. The men branded; women fixed a big meal and in the afternoon had a quilting bee or canning session. 97

A MAN WITH A RACE HORSE CAME THROUGH TOWN and the town sports matched his fine looking trotter with a small mare which Taft, a homesteader, used for hauling swill to his hogs. Lots of money was bet on the race. The Taft mare won. The owner of the trotter said he did not mind losing the race but felt disgraced at having his horse beaten by a swill horse. In another horse race there were five entrants for the half-mile dash. Four were conditioned and groomed for the race; the fifth was Blaze Face Doc, a farm horse used on a 4-horse plow team. On the home stretch Doc was bringing up the rear, when the lead horse bolted off the track and the other three followed. Faithful Doc galloped on, the only horse to pass the judges' stand. The announcer shouted, "We hereby declare Blaze Face Doc winner of the first, second and third money, and order him turned out for month in the finest pasture in Brule County." 98

Early day rodeos were in the open.

The homestead days were the happiest days of our lives, said many. Most were young. They came from widely varied backgrounds, with abundant talent. They had little money but much in common; they made their own fun.

Motoring was high adventure with few roads, wooden spoked wheels.

INVITING NEIGHBORS OVER FOR SUNDAY DINNER was common. We kids played many singing games, ran foot races, often played baseball or dominoes. Favorite songs were: Red Wing, The Owl and the Pussy Cat, Merry Widow Waltz, the Preacher and the Bear, I was Seeing Nelly Home, The Sidewalks of New York, I Deam of Jeanie, Bill Bailey Won't you Please Come Home, After the Ball is Over, and A Bicycle Built for Two. Six to twelve of us teenagers would often meet at a neighbor's on a Sunday afternoon, each on a saddle horse or maybe riding double. Then there were the ice skating parties we went to on horseback. We would build big bonfires beside the dam and have hot cocoa and sandwiches before our long, cold ride home. 99

OUR FIRST CHRISTMAS TREE was a branch covered with fringed green wrapping paper, with paper rings and strung popcorn for decorations. 100

WE ALSO PLAYED WHIST, meeting in each other's homes. I remember one we had at our home. We moved out all the big pieces of furniture including the bed and dresser. We could then get three tables of whist going. Children always came too and were bedded down on blankets on the floor to sleep while we all played cards. Friends came horseback, with team and wagon, or in old cars. A good lunch of homemade bread and meat sandwiches with plenty of coffee and cake was always served sometime during the evening. 101

OUR NEIGHBORS WERE VERY FRIENDLY, and we made our own entertainment, such as box socials, shadow and toe socials, picnics, parties and home talent plays. Fourth of July was a big day with a picnic dinner, races of all kinds, bronc riding, and a dance in the evening. 102

THE CHARIVARI WAS FOR NEWLY MARRIED couples. After the neighbors gathered with sticks and pans and other noise-makers, they would be invited into the house and the usual thing was to "pass the hat" for the young couple. The crowd expressed their good wishes, sometimes serving a lunch they had brought along. 103

WHEN JOE LITTLE MARRIED, neighbors gathered. When the newlyweds wouldn't come out after much noisemaking, they threw his 300 pound sow through the window into the house. That brought out the newlyweds! 104

THE PRAIRIE HOME LITERARY, organized in 1906 northwest of Draper, held debates. The affirmative side won this question: Resolved, there is more pleasure in anticipation than in realization. Two men and one woman on each side of that issue. Another debate: Resolved, the bachelor is more benefit to the community than the old maid. No report on how that one turned out. 105

Community get-together often included races, ballgame.

Sunday School picnic in Hegman's Grove near Redfield.

The bachelor life was celebrated in song, story and art—usually with a deep longing for someone to come and share the homestead.

LITTLE OLD SOD SHANTY

I'm looking rather seedy while holding down my claim
And my vittels are not always of the best.
The mice play shyly round me as I nestle down to rest
In my little old sod shanty on the plain.

REFRAIN: O the hinges are of leather and the windows have no glass,
And the roof, it lets the howling blizzard in.
I hear the hungry kiyote as he sneaks up through the grass,
Round my little old sod shanty on the claim.

Yet I rather like the novelty of living in this way
Though my bill of fare is always rather tame,
But I'm happy as a clam, on the land of Uncle Sam
In my little old sod shanty on the claim.

My clothes are plastered o're with dough
And everything is scattered round the room,
But I wouldn't give the freedom that I have out in the West
For the table of an Eastern man's old home.

Still I wish that some kindhearted miss would pity on me take
And extricate me from the mess I'm in.
The angel, how I'd bless her if this her home she'd make
In my little old sod shanty on the claim.

And we would make our fortunes on the prairies of the West
Just as happy as two bedbugs we'd remain.
And we'd forget our trials and our troubles as we rest
In our little old sod shanty on the claim.

THE MEN WOULD THROW IN A QUARTER apiece for the music; the ladies brought cake and sandwiches. Very few boys had buggies; we all had ponies. We would go get the girls—if a girl didn't have a pony, we would take one along if we could get one. I remember one night a friend and I had made a date to take girls to a dance but could scare up only three horses. The girls each rode a horse and we rode double. We went 10 miles, danced all night, and rode home the same way. 106

ONE TIME THERE WAS A MASQUERADE DANCE at Grand Valley to which a few Indians came as well as white. Charlie dressed as an old woman. He followed Felix Fly around and they danced together half the night. 107

Time out at a South Dakota dance in log homestead.

4TH OF JULY was held in a large grove of trees near the creek. The neighbors for miles around came with well filled food baskets and the men built a dance pavilion. I remember vividly one 4th it clouded up and we had a cloudburst about the time the dance started. The people all ran for cover and our house had standing room only. Many had to stay all night. No one tried to sleep, so the hours were passed singing and story telling. At the break of dawn people got their teams or cars and tried to make it home. The tall grass in the picnic area was covered with black grease from the cars—the grease ended up on our skirts as we walked through the grass. 108

MY FATHER AND A NEARBY HOMESTEADER built a bowery dance platform near our claim shack. Music was furnished by the "Little Bohemian Band" of Belvidere. People came from near and far, cowboys, homesteaders and ranchers, to enjoy the biweekly dances. In the afternoon someone took a hayrack and gathered up the people for the dance, as many did not have their own horses. 109

I REMEMBER ONE NIGHT at our house, we had laid a new linoleum, thinking a dance would help stretch it so it would lay better, but a fast square dance was in progress someone slipped on one corner and off it went. The dancing would start at eight and many times the sun was coming up as we got home, so rather than go to bed for a short time we would change clothes, gather up the milk pails and head for the barn. After the milking was done, calves fed, separator washed and breakfast over we either went to bed until a pesky fly tickled our nose, or just did whatever the day required. 110

ONE EVENING A. T. WILSON got a covered wagon and invited several families to go to the Hobeck ranch to a dance. We were never allowed to dance, but our parents relented and let us youngsters go. They were dancing in a very small room and Ethel and I were so surprised to see cowboys dancing with overalls on and wearing spurs on their boots. Stella and I knew nothing about dancing, so Mr. Lyman took us up to the ranch home and one, two, threed us around the dining table till we were ready to go back to the hall and dance. 111

WE HAD WONDERFUL HAYRIDES to dances ten or twenty miles away. The sleighs were filled with hay or straw, plenty of thick quilts and hot rocks or sad irons wrapped in paper and old socks, and no one was ever cold even in near zero and lower temperatures. 112

EVEN IN OUR SMALL HOUSE, which was 14 by 20, it was common to move out the beds and dance. I remember once when the beds were taken outside to make room for dancing. A hard rain came and with people walking in the wet gumbo from the fence, where they tied their horses, the floor became matted with gumbo. Of course they danced until morning. When they left it took a shovel to dig off the hard packed gumbo before bringing in the beds which were completely soaked from the rain. 113

Always someone to strum a guitar or make music with violin, accordian or harmonica.

167

Early auto might need tow uphill with horse and rope.

15. WAR YEARS

Steam tractors and other machinery began replacing horses before World War I. Ford trucks and cars soon answered the desperate needs of South Dakotans for long distance travel. A generation of young men were tinkering with engines. Recalls one:

> Along about 1914 or 1915 the Badlands were invaded by Model T's, Chevies, Maxwells and Stars. Most of us got one. They usually started by turning the engine over with a crank. If this failed we jacked up the rear wheel, dropped in the clutch and cranked some more. There were no roads, just trails and sometimes very rough in places where wagon wheels had cut them up when wet. It was bad to hang up on a 'high center'; you couldn't get off. Everyone carried a spade for this emergency. Tires were poor and blowouts common. There were no spare tires. You had to take it off and patch it and pump it up with a hand pump. If the patch held you could go on, if not you could go on the rim. That was motoring! [114]

War meant more machinery, with higher production needed. The 1910-1911 drouth had already thinned out the settlers, so farms were larger.

Those who survived the drouth had watched, with a measure of despair and envy, as long caravans of covered wagons headed east. Most wagons had a barrel of water on the side, a cow, chickens, maybe some pigs—with women and children walking behind. One pioneer says that as a boy he watched this steady stream going east through that long hot summer. His family was desperate too, but his father said he was "too hard up to finance a trip back to Iowa, so we had to stay," and his mother wondered where the next sack of flour was coming from. One wagon he saw carried the terse message: "40 miles to water, 50 miles to wood; I'm leaving South Dakota, I'm leaving it for good." A Draper pioneer recalls 1911 as a year when the grass didn't turn green until after August first. They had planted corn in spring and it didn't come up till after an August rain.

Farm prices rose swiftly with war. Wheat shot up from 90¢ to nearly $2.00 by 1917 and $2.40 in 1919; it was at a low of 69¢ in 1912. Corn went from 50¢ to $1.20. Hay doubled in price to $10 a ton. Beef cattle rose from $21.50 per head in 1910 to $53.90 in 1919. Wool went to 91¢ a pound. Farm lands skyrocketed; in Beadle County, for instance, prices went from $4.60 an acre in 1900, to $42.45, to $93.75. Demand was heavy and South Dakota farmers responded to the call to increase production. They bought machinery and land. They plowed up marginal land and overstocked pastures. They went deeply into debt—and had to repay later under desperately changed conditions.

More than 32,000 South Dakota men served in World War I; 210 were killed in action. At home family and friends bought war bonds, raised money for Red Cross, knit, sewed hospital garments, made surgical dressings.

Every community raised money for Red Cross and Liberty Bonds. Kadoka boasted the best benefit sale in the state in May 1918 by taking in $6,182 as in this partial account:

> Fred Sears got the high priced puppy at $16. The tumbleweed given by our little Boy Scouts was sold and resold by Auctioneer Leedom until it brought in around $150. Jim Judge was the fortunate purchaser of the yell given in honor of the Jackson County soldier boys who have gone to war. It cost Jim twenty bucks but he says it was worth seven hundred...The rifle sent in by Julius Hurley, who week before last left for war and who at the present time is dangerously sick with pneumonia at Jefferson Barracks, was sold and resold for $265. The gun was finally sold to B. L. McNally who will return it to the parents of Julius. [115]

Emotions ran high. Wartime hysteria caused a spirit of intolerance nationwide. In South Dakota, as elsewhere, witch hunts were on for the supposedly unpatriotic. Anyone heard making comments against the draft, the war, the Red Cross efforts, or elected officials could be charged with treason. Strong action was taken against the IWW—Industrial Workers of the World—headquartered in Aberdeen, which was trying to organize a socialistic labor union of farm workers. Known as the "Wobblies" and "I Won't Work," they disrupted harvests by such acts as throwing pitchforks into threshing machines. Many Nonpartisan League organizers were also run out of the state.

Speaking German on the telephone or in public was forbidden. German language churches were required to change to English overnight, though neither members nor ministers understood it. After much protest a brief summary of the English sermon was permitted in German at the close of each service. German names were changed: Rhine Creek became Marne and German-fried potatoes disappeared from menus. German language newspapers in Aberdeen and Sioux Falls were forced to stop publication. Their editors were sent to federal prison. Local zealots burned German textbooks, dumped German heirlooms and books into the Missouri, smeared yellow paint on property, and publicly mocked their victims.

Hutterites were easy targets for intolerance. A branch of the Mennonites, they lived communally, dressed distinctively, spoke German and had made little effort to learn English. They refused to salute the flag or wear a uniform. They had a long European history of religious persecution (burned at the stake by Catholics; beheaded or drowned by the Protestants). Many had come to South Dakota from Russia in 1873 and 1874 and formed three colonies. By World War I these had increased to 17 colonies with a population of about 2000.

Those who were drafted had many unfortunate experiences. Many of the 47 Hutterite men called into service were married and had as many as four children. They were instructed to refuse to wear the uniform or to do any work which helped the war effort, and as a result were harrassed, ridiculed and beaten. Four from the Rockport colony near Alexandria were forced to run around the compound at the point of a bayonet in a Missouri camp. Later they were sent to prison in Alcatraz, then to Leavenworth where they slept without blankets and were fed on bread and water. Punishment included being chained to bars so they had to stand on tiptoe. When they became seriously ill, two were sent home. But two brothers, John and Michael Hofer, died there. When the wife of one came to claim the body, she found him in the coffin dressed in the uniform he had refused to wear in life.

At home, Hutterite colonies faced increasing persecution. Some still refused to make donations to the Red Cross or buy Liberty Bonds. Near Yankton a local committee levied a quota of $10,000 in Liberty Bonds for the Jamesville colony. The colony refused and was raided one night by a local group which drove off a herd of steers and 1000 sheep. They invested in Liberty Bonds for the colony with the $16,000 the livestock brought at auction. Hutterites protested that the cattle and sheep were worth $40,000, and charged that some of the raiders got their own cuts from the clouded transaction.

Lawsuits seeking to dissolve the Hutterite corporations further discouraged them, and they began moving to Canada until all were gone except the Bon Homme colony. (Some returned and others multiplied until in 1972 there were 30 colonies in South Dakota with a total population of nearly 3000, holding 135,000 acres of land.)

World War I also brought a worldwide epidemic of Spanish flu which killed huge numbers of people. More than a thousand died in South Dakota during 1918 and 1919; 65,839 cases were reported. John Reiger of Corson County came home on furlough to attend the funeral of his mother and sister who had both died of the flu. During the funeral the mourners heard an amazing sound: the freedom bell rang announcing the end of the war. Reiger said the minister turned to prayers of thanksgiving, and he had never heard a minister praise God as on that day.

16. HARD TIMES

Farm prices dropped after the war. Wheat went down to 87¢ by 1921; corn was 26¢; cattle averaged $29.20 a head.

The roaring twenties brought prohibition, from 1920 to 1933, in an era of homemade brew sold in quart canning jars. South Dakota had its share of bootleg whiskey and moonshine available in "blind pigs," or hidden back rooms from which a bartender could identify any newcomers through a hole in the door.

In 1927 Gutzon Borglum began his work on the Rushmore memorial which took the rest of his life, until his death at 74 in 1941. The same year President Calvin Coolidge established the summer White House in the Black Hills (at the Game Lodge in Custer State Park). He came on horseback, in cowboy boots and western hat, to dedicate the memorial and promote the use of federal funds, which were soon forthcoming.

Early in the 1920's there were brief price rallies, but from 1925 to 1940 South Dakota farmers and ranchers saw very few years when both prices and crops were good enough to give them a liveable income. Banks had loaned out too much money and began to fail. Nine closed in 1922; 36 in 1923. During the '20's, 70 percent of South Dakota banks failed, one of the highest rates in the nation. Depositers lost an estimated $39,000,000.

Dakotans were in desperate circumstances, particularly in the west, long before the stock market crash on Black Friday in October of 1929. Hundreds of families had left their land; hundreds more were deeply in debt. The 1930's brought a drouth like never before, and relentlessly low markets.

Farm land fell in value. In Turner County, land which sold for $227 an acre in 1920, had dropped to $42 by 1940. In the same years land in Hutchinson County dropped from $151 to $28; in Sully County, from $38 to $5.

One farmer summed up the early drouth years in this way: "1930 was pretty dry; 1931 was DRY; 1932 was a wet year but the prices for produce were very low; 1933 was very dry and in 1934 nothing grew but the leaves on the cottonwood trees." The grass didn't turn green in 1934—but the worst was yet to come.

In 1936 three state records were shattered: hottest, driest, coldest. A long cold spell that began Christmas day dropped temperatures to 58 below zero at McIntosh, February 17, 1936. Temperatures reached 120 degrees on July 3 at Gann Valley. Ludlow recorded a total of 2.89 inches of moisture that year,

One settler tried to save ten spruce trees from grasshoppers with screens—but lost them all.

Even rangeland began to blow, with little grass to hold the soil.

Many loaded up their belongings and headed west.

and many other points in western South Dakota had only five or six inches. Despair and uncertainty were widespread:

> There was no rain, over 100 degree temperatures every day, and hot nights, too. The grass disappeared, the wind blew hard every day, the sand moved and covered fences, machinery or whatever was there. Sometimes the air was so full of dust we had to put wet towels over our faces to breathe. The grasshoppers came like clouds and ate every bit of grass and even clothes on the wash line. If they would get in the house, they'd eat holes in curtains. You could look toward the sun and the sky was just thick with flying hoppers. [116]

Dust storms from the big plow-up darkened the skies. The first big one hit November 1933 after fall plowing. The Minnehaha County history calls it the "Black Blizzard of 1933" and says the wind shifted to the north, blowing 40-60 miles and hour, dropping temperatures at the rate of six degrees every half hour. "When it was spent, there was a heavy deposit of dirt and grit sifting through every crevice through which the wind could pass."

It was only the first of many black blizzards. People fixed gauze masks on baby faces, tied damp handkerchiefs over their own, and cautioned children to lie down in a low place if caught out in a duststorm. A Jones County farmer said, "We were milking 14 cows in the barn, but the milk would be so full of dirt we just dumped it in the hog troughs. We would take a two-quart jar and hold it up close, then put the lid on quickly so we had milk to use. Cattle and horses could walk right over fences. We would have to have our car lights on even in daylight in order to drive to town for groceries."

Another said, "Creek beds were dry. The prairie was covered with mammoth cracks from lack of moisture, until you gave up hope that anything would ever grow again."

Migrating hordes of grasshoppers descended "so thick you couldn't see the sides of the buildings." Fenceposts were twice

Making hay from Russian thistles.

their normal size with grasshoppers, and highways were slushy and slick.

One pioneer remembers a flight which killed a big cotton-wood tree by the house. "As soon as they hit the ground they headed for the tree and started up it and began to eat the leaves. The next morning they had eaten every leaf, and there were a lot of hoppers left eating the young branches. It didn't take very long and they killed the tree." [117]

Another tried in desperation to save two tomato plants just setting on green tomatoes. She spread dish towels over the plants, tucking the edges down and covering them tightly with soil so no hole showed. Later she returned to the garden to find the grasshoppers had eaten every bit of the dishtowels. The tomato plants were gone and the roots eaten right into the ground. One woman talks of their fight against grasshoppers: "One day we would have a nice field of corn that was all tassled out and the next day the hoppers would have it all eaten up. When we washed clothes, we would want a windy day or the hoppers would have the clothes dirty. The men would get up early in the morning and put out poison, but it seemed for every grasshopper killed, a hundred relatives came for the funeral." [118]

People tried hard to stay off welfare. But by 1934, conditions were so bad that 39 percent of South Dakotans were on relief—the highest in the nation. Local committees set up stringent rules for those on relief. According to a Hyde County history such families could not own a radio or have a telephone. "If they lived in town they were not to use a car; if they came in from the rural area they were allowed one trip per week. Women on relief could not have beauty parlor work done. Also prohibited was any use or purchase of liquor, attendance at dances, picture shows or anything that required payment of an admission."

A woman there remembers going to town to ask if she could charge a sack of potatoes until the WPA check came. She was told, "No credit," went home in tears and cooked more beans. But in 1938 she and her husband were able to get a $1600 loan, buy four horses, ten milk cows, and rent a farm. The cows kept them in groceries and necessities until they raised a little crop and got on their feet again.

A Wanblee farmer said, "We were on relief as most of the people in the county were. I helped build a bridge for WPA, cut firewood for schools on another project, and had charge of a crew to finish the auditorium at Wanblee. Prices dropped to a drastic low—butterfat 3¢ a pound, eggs—2¢-3¢ a dozen, hogs from 2¢ to 3¢ a pound. I had some shoats weighing 75 pounds which I took to Kadoka to sell to Nels Nielsen. He remarked that he was buying them by the dozen and would pay me $9 a dozen—75¢ a head! Now and then I would take a can of cream to Wanblee and get just enough from it to pay for gasoline to get the Model A pickup back home and have some in the tank for emergencies." Conditions among Indian people on the reservation were especially acute; most were at a bare survival level.

In 1933 President Roosevelt took office and launched a flood of relief measures as promised. But many were ill conceived and poorly managed.

For example the livestock purchase program of 1934 was supposed to give meat to the needy, financial aid to the stockman, and raise the price of beef. It made few friends in Dakota: stockmen were paid only a fraction of what their stock were worth, and they had to watch the killing and wanton destruction of meat from many of their sheep, hogs and cattle. Top price paid on cows was $20 a head; calves went for $4 or less. Market price was even less and those who shipped privately often found the check did not pay the railroad bill.

'I just sat down and cried—nine years we've tried.'

APPROACHING DUST STORM IN MIDDLE WEST.   CONARD

A dust storm billows in; 'black blizzards' blotted out the sun.

With no grass and no possibility of hay that summer, ranchers had little choice.

Many of the livestock sold to the government were killed and buried on the spot to save shipping expenses. Officially these condemned animals were in very poor condition, but ranchers found a quota of each herd was condemned. People were forbidden to eat any of the meat.

In all 915,039 cattle, or about 42 percent of all South Dakota cattle were purchased by the government at an average price of $10 each. Of these 10 percent, or 87,000 were condemned, killed and buried. Hogs were purchased and killed in 1933; 150,000 sheep purchased in 1934 and 1935.

A woman from southcentral South Dakota remembers helping her father trail their cattle to town. "Daddy cried and said, 'This sure hurts.' It hurt me too as we took Daisy, our Holstein cow. A couple of miles west of us a large cistern had been left idle, so the cattle were hauled to this cistern in trucks. They were then knocked in the head and thrown into this cistern. I was horrified at this sight as a young girl, and I still shudder when I think of it. The cattle were so thin and gaunt. It seemed too cruel, but there was no feed for them." Another wept when a favorite black cow was condemned and killed, but once condemned there was no recourse.

Some of the cattle were branded ERA, for Emergency Relief Administration, and were sent to Indian reservations as milk cows and to start beef herds. But Indians were even more desperate than whites. ERA, many said, meant "Eat Right Away"—and they did.

Those who kept a few cattle fed thistles, with cottonwood leaves and weeds stacked along with the thistles. A Corson County rancher who held back 2,700 sheep, finally had to ship them all to Chicago in 1935. When he got the papers there was no check, only a bill for the difference of $125 he owed the railroad. He almost lost his mind over this cruel twist.

Many who could not pay taxes or redeem mortgages lost their land. By 1938 four northwestern counties had over a million acres on delinquent tax rolls.

The hopeless conditions had a disturbing effect on the human spirit. People grew depressed, some lost their minds, others grew silent, bitter or violent.

The Farm Holiday movement grew out of this anger and despair. In most cases the Holiday association worked peaceably, trying to halt foreclosures and raise prices. But as tempers tightened, they stood ready with threats of violence. Foreclosure sales were halted through intimidation such as the "Penny sales." A forced farm auction turned into a penny sale when Farm Holiday members and loyal neighbors in-

filtrated the crowd to bid a few pennies against each other—intimidating other buyers with baleful stares and threats as needed. A tractor might be sold for 23¢, the milk cow for 15¢, the kitchen table for a penny—all to be returned to the owner debt-free, while the mortgage holder had to take his payment. Usually the auctioneer or the sheriff stopped the sale before long.

Farm Holiday also called strikes—a "holiday" from selling—and set up picket lines and blockades to keep livestock, grain and milk from getting to market in an effort to force prices up. Thirteen roads into Sioux Falls were blockaded the fall of 1932 to stop cattle shipments. In another incident a Sioux City blockade resulted in the killing of a dairy farmer at Jefferson.

As people left the country, towns began to fold up. Post offices were dropped, depots moved away, schools and shipping stockyards torn down. In gumbo country those who stayed were reminded of the old saying, "If you stick to the gumbo (or to South Dakota) when it's dry, the gumbo will stick to you when it's wet"—and held out. Delinquent tax land was purchased for two and three dollars an acre under the Federal Land Utilization program, divided into community pastures and leased to ranchers bordering the land. Much was reseeded with resistant grasses. Nearly a million acres was acquired under this plan, with two-thirds of it going into "government pastures" for 660 ranchers, the other third becoming game refuges and recreation sites.

Buried machinery in the farmyard of Gregory county commisssioner in 1936.

Federal New Deal programs poured money into the state. They included WPA, ERA, CCC, PWA, FSA, AAA, RA—alphabet soup, some called them. Many public buildings, roads and dams were built under the WPA, PWA and CCC work programs, as well as forest improvements in the Black Hills. CCC was a popular youth program which employed 23,049 young men in 19 South Dakota camps. They were paid $30 a month of which $25 was sent home to their families.

In 1936 Bertyne Birkland wrote to the *Dakota Farmer* saying she was moving and had a dozen coats, children's overshoes, and other clothing to give away. Readers could write her, giving sizes needed. Within two weeks she had over 700 requests in letters such as these: "I'm sure I can use all the clothes you mention in Dakota Farmer. We threshed only 3½ bushels wheat and 21 bu. oats. We have 10 children...we are not shiftless, rather very saving"; "If the coats and clothing does not fit I will make it over. I sure would be glad to get some. If you would give me your future address I would like to repay you"; "We have no crop for last 10 years—cattle dying—hope we can get some WPA work." From Deuel County a mother of seven wrote on a torn piece of ledger paper, "I can use anything you have to spare as I make over." "I'm to become a mother for the tenth time," wrote a Perkins County mother. "Anything in baby clothes. We were hit by drought." A few weeks later a western South Dakota woman wrote her gratitude to Birkland, who had collected clothes for most of the requests:

> You can't imagine how tickled we were when our neighbor brought the box out from town. I had to wash at night when all were in bed so the clothes would be clean for next day. I just sat down and cried, nine years we've tried. The girls took a bath, put on the clean underwear.. The little boy put his helmet under his pillow. The red dress fits fine, tight in bust but set belt in each side and fits fine...I put curtains in front room and fixed the other ones for kitchen with ruffles. Are they ever nice.
> (Dakota Farmer Sept. 1970)

Thus with fortitude, humility and raw endurance, people survived the hard times of the 20's and 30's—into the next decade which was to bring again the disturbing combination of war and prosperity. For all the hardship and suffering of the depression, life continued, even smoothly in some quarters. Young people fell in love, married; babies were born, reared, and educated. People coped, with amazing resiliancy and stamina. War loomed, but after war came a new era.

With fortitude and humor, people survived the hard times on countless homesteads like this one near Rapid City.

17. WORLD WAR II AND LATER EVENTS

Again during wartime, agriculture production reached a peak. Townspeople, teachers and students took time off to help labor-short farmers with harvest. The war hysteria of the first world war was not so evident, but rather it was with determination and commitment that men went away to serve and their wives and sweethearts went to work in war plants. Victory Bond drives, Red Cross fund drives, and other war efforts were carried on by networks of volunteers, raising a third of a billion dollars in bonds and two and a quarter million for the Red Cross.

Some 64,560 South Dakotans went into military service; 1560 were killed in action; 484 died of other causes. The Rapid City Air Base, later renamed Ellsworth Air Base, was built, as well as other training camps in the state.

With war over, South Dakota swept into modern times with a rush. Building projects neglected for years because of economic depression, then labor and material shortages, went ahead. Rural electrification reached out to the most isolated farms and ranches. The interstate highway system was soon underway; new bridges were built across the Missouri to allow crossing at eleven points.

The Missouri River dams were major building projects. Under the Pick-Sloan plan, construction began on the Ft. Randall dam in 1946. Oahe was begun in 1948, Gavins Point in 1952, Big Bend in 1960. Each took five to sixteen years to complete. Oahe, largest rolled-earth dam in the world, is 242 feet high and backs water up for 250 miles. An alternate plan for 21 locks and dams between Sioux City and Ft. Peck, which would have provided much needed transportation for farm products to world markets, was scrapped due to costs and the determination that upper Missouri needs were for irrigation and domestic water. Lower Missouri interests were for flood control from above and navigation—they held out for a nine-foot channel and only small dams with locks in their region which would flood a minimum of cropland. The Dakota dams were built primarily for irrigation use, electric power and flood control downstream.

Disaster struck the Black Hills and towns of Rapid City, Keystone, Rockerville and Black Hawk the night of June 8 and early morning hours of June 9 in 1972 when sudden heavy rains filled the narrow canyons with walls of rushing water. Houses, trailer homes, bridges, chunks of highway and cars were swept away and smashed into other buildings and obstructions. Propane tanks became lethal weapons as they shot downstream tearing screaming people from tree branches and floating supports. When it was over 232 persons were confirmed dead by the Rapid City police department, with five missing. Over a hundred million dollars in property was destroyed and a massive cleanup needed. New zoning laws were put into effect to control building in the flood plain, especially along Rapid Creek.

Dissatisfaction and dissent among Indian people brought on the confrontation at Wounded Knee, which started the night of February 27, 1973, and lasted 71 days. About 250 people took control of the town of Wounded Knee, holding it against the tribal police and tribal government of Pine Ridge. Federal FBI agents and marshalls sealed off the area and attempted negotiations. Sporadic gunfire from both sides wounded nine and killed two before the occupation came to an end in May. Russell Means, a leader in the AIM-oriented occupation, challenged tribal leadership in the 1974 elections, but was not able to unseat the tribal president.

REFERENCE NOTES

1. T. C. McLuhan, *Touch The Earth* (Pocket Books, 1971), p.36.
2. Ibid., pg.39.
3. Ibid., p.42.
4. Sarah Emilia Olden, *The People of Tipi Sapa* (Morehouse Publ., Milwaukee, 1918).
5. *S. D. Hist. Collections Vol. 7* Truteau's Journal, (S.D. Hist. Society, Pierre).
6. J. Leonard Jennewein and Jane Boorman, *Dakota Panorama* (Brevet Press, Sioux Falls, 1961), p.47.
7. *SDHistCol 25*, p.197.
8. Ibid., p.111.
9. Ibid., p.148.
10. John R. Milton, *The Literature of South Dakota* (Dakota Press, Vermillion, 1976), p.34.
11. Henry A. Boller, *Missouri River Fur Trader* (Hist. Society of N.D., Bismarck, 1966).
12. Robert F. Karolevitz, *Challenge: The South Dakota Story* (Brevet Press, Sioux Falls, 1975), p.139.
13. William E. Lass, *A History of Steamboating on the Upper Missouri* (U. of Nebr., 1962), p.31.
14. Dee Brown, *Bury My Heart at Wounded Knee* Holt, Rinehart & Winston, 1970), p.141.
15. *SDHistCol 29*, p.408.
16. Ibid., p.347.
17. Ibid., p.498.
18. Brown
19. James McLaughlin, *My Friend the Indian* (Houghton Mifflin, 1910), p.174.
20. *SDHistCol 29*, p.188.
21. Karolevitz, p.123.
22. SDHistCol 36.
23. McLuhan, p. 134.
24. McLaughlin.
25. Vine Deloria, Jr., *Of Utmost Good Faith* (Simon & Schuster), p. 162.
26. *SDHistCol 29*, pg. 52.
27. Ibid., p.25.
28. McLuhan, p.103.
29. Herbert Krause and Gary D. Olson, eds., *Custer's Prelude to Glory* (Brevet Press, Sioux Falls, 1974), p.131.
30. Bob Lee, ed., *Gold-Gals-Guns-Guts* (S. D. Bicentennial Com. 1976), p.92.
31. Ibid., p.51.
32. Ruth Iverson, Marj Strait, Margie Peters, eds. *Proving Up: Jones County History* (Book & Thimble Club, Murdo, 1969), p.179.
33. *Roberts County History* (Dakota Territory Centinnial, 1961).
34. Herbert S. Schell, *History of South Dakota* (U. of Nebr., Lincoln, 1961), p. 166.
35. *SDHistCol 23.*
36. *Proving Up: Jones County*
37. *Early History of Brown County* (Territorial Pioneers, Western Printing, Aberdeen, 1965).
38. *Deuel County Historical Collections.*
39. Marie Barrett, reminiscences.
40. *Jackson-Washabaugh Counties: 1915-1965,* (Jackson-Washabaugh Historical Society, 1965).
41. William Barrett, reminiscences.
42. *Proving Up: Jones County*
43. Ibid.
44. Ibid.
45. *Brown County*
46. *Jackson-Washabaugh.*
47. *Jones County*
48. Charles A. Smith, *Minnehaha County History* (Educator Supply Co. Mitchell, 1949).
49. *Jones County*
50. *Hughes County History* (Office of County Superintendent of Schools, 1934).
51. *Brown County*
52. *Hughes County*
53. *Proving Up: Jones County*
54. *Hyde Heritage* (Hyde County Hist. Society, State Publishers, Pierre, 1977).
55. *Jones County.*
56. Ibid.
57. Ibid.
58. Ibid.
59. *Brown County*, p. 145.
60. *SDHistCol 23.*
61. Ibid.
62. *Jones County*
63. Ibid.
64. Ibid.
65. *Hyde Heritage.*
66. *Jackson-Washabaugh.*
67. Rose Tidball, *Taming the Plains* (Tidball, 1976).
68. *Deuel County Historical Collections.*
69. *Jones County*
70. *Roberts County.*
71. *Jones County.*
72. Ibid.
73. *Jackson-Washabaugh*
74. *Jones County.*
75. *SDHistCol 23.*
76. *Hughes County.*
77. *Jackson-Washabaugh*
78. *Jones County*
79. *SDHistCol 23.*
80. *Hyde Heritage.*
81. *Jones County.*
82. *Jones County.*
83. Ibid.
84. Ibid.
85. *Homestead Years* (Bison Courier, Bison).
86. *Brown County.*
87. *Jones County*
88. *Brown County*
89. *Jones County.*
90. *Deuel County*
91. *Brown County*
92. *SDHistCol 25.*
93. *Jones County*
94. *Brown County*
95. *Jackson-Washabaugh.*
96. *Tidball.*
97. *Jones County.*
98. *SDHistCol 23*
99. *Jones County*
100. *Brown County.*
101. *Tidball.*
102. Ibid.
103. *Deuel County.*
104. *Brown County.*
105. *Jones County*
106. Ibid.
107. *Tidball.*
108. *Jackson-Washabaugh.*
109. Ibid.
110. *Hyde Heritage.*
111. *Jones County.*
112. *Ibid.*
113. *Mato Paha; Land of the Pioneers; Northwest Meade County.*
114. *Jackson-Washabaugh.*
115. Ibid.
116. *Tidball.*
117. *Jones County.*
118. Ibid.

ACKNOWLEDGMENTS

I want to acknowledge the help of many people in the research and preparation of this book. Thanks to the many state officials who gave willing help with information and photo search, especially the people in Game, Fish and Parks, in Tourism, and in the Historical Society. My thanks to the editors of local and county books who have gathered a wealth of authentic pioneer stories, and those who shared their experiences in these books; I feel the stories are a vital South Dakota heritage deserving wide readership. I thank all others who have shared their poetry, their writings and their experiences here. I also acknowledge a debt to my South Dakota mother and grandparents and to homestead stories told around the supper table as I was growing up.

The photos have come from many sources and I'm grateful to all who shared their family photos here; special thanks to Ed and Beulah Aske who lent so many excellent historical photos. Among modern day photographers, my personal thanks go to Richard Oge, Dave Johnson, Wilford Miller, Chuck Post, and Ron Spomer. I'm grateful also to the many others whose photography is used here. In the book's physical makeup I sincerely thank Gaye, Cheryl and Ralph at the Adams County Record for their willingness, their patience and care in typesetting. Also to the North Plains Press of Aberdeen for their printing skill and integrity.

In writing this book my goal has been to search out the personal and meaningful from the great abundance of material available. I have attempted a fresh look at history from the human viewpoint of those who live and lived here. Because of space limitations, much that I valued had to be omitted, but I sincerely hope this book succeeds in weaving some strong fibers into the rich fabric of South Dakota's heritage. F.M.B.

PICTURE CREDITS

Cover photo - S. D. Tourism
Aberdeen Chamber of Commerce - 26d
Aske, Hazel - 125; 127c; 128b; 134; 135; 138c;
  142a; 144a; 145b,c,d; 147b; 149c; 150b,c;
  151b,c,d; 152a,b; 156; 158; 160a; 163b; 164a,b;
  165a,c; 166;
Barrett, Margaret - 81b, 147a,c; 148b; 153; 162;
  163c; 164d.
Berg, F. - 2a; 11a,b,d; 14b,c,d; 15c; 17b; 20a,b,c;
  21b; 23b; 24a,b; 29a,b; 32b,d; 35a,e; 36b,d; 37f;
  41b; 53b,d; 55a; 56a,b; 61e; 64c; 65a,b,c; 66b;
  68a,b; 70b; 71b; 72c; 74a; 75c; 78; collages 25,
  50, 63, 174, 175.
Bison High School - 36c; 60c; 61d; 63a; collage 25.
Cheyenne-Eagle Butte High School - 57; 60b;
  61b; collages 25, 50, 63.
Foster, Lenore - 139a; 163d.
Foster, Ruth - 148a.
Harpers Weekly - 96; 129b.
Haugen, Dorothy - 133, 143c.
Homestake Mining Co. - 76a,b,c.
Johnson, Dave - 27c; 30b
Lib. of Congress - 141a; 171a.
Mammoth Site - 48a.
McFarland, Pearl - 147d; 151a; 155; 169b; 170b.
Miller, Wilford - 5b; 26a.
N. D. Game & Fish - 5c; 40a.
N. D. Hist. Soc. - 85b; 89; 90; 95; 105.
N. D. Travel - 6c; 8a; 10; 40b; 72a; 92b.
Northern State College - 3; 37a; 49a; 62b; 64f.
Oge, Richard - 35d; 49b; 52a,c; 53a; 54a,b; 58c;
  59.
Olson, Gertrude - 142c; 143a,b,e; 151e; 161; 163a;
  167a.
Platte Enterprise - 37c; 61a; collages 25, 50.
St. Francis Mission - 100.
S. D. Extension Service - 69a,c; 70a,c; 72b; 75b;
  149b,d.
S. D. Game, Fish & Parks - 1; 2b; 4a,c; 8d; 9b;
  12b; 13c; 16a; 18b; 19d; 23a,c; 26b,c; 27a,b,c;
  30a,b; 31a,b; 32c; 33; 34-all; 38a,b,c; 39a,d;
  40c,d,e,f; 41a,c,d,e,f; 42a,b,c,d; 43b,c; 51; 58a;
  71a; 157a,b; collages 50.
S. D. High Liner - 6a,b; 67; 72d; 74b; 75a; 80.
S. D. Hist. Soc. - 32a; 81a; 86a,b; 87; 88; 91; 98;
  99a; 101; 102a,b,c,d,e; 103; 106; 108; 109; 110;
  111a,b; 113a,c; 114a,b,c; 115; 116a,b; 117a,b,c;
  119; 121; 123; 124; 126; 127a,b; 129a; 137;
  138a,d; 140; 146c; 160b; 164c; 168; 170a; 171b;
  172.
S.D.S.U. - 62c,e,f; 64b; collage 50.

S.D. Tourism - 4b; 5a,d; 7; 8b,c,e; 9a; 11c;
  12a,c,d,e; 13a,b; 14a; 15a,b,d,e; 16b,c,d,e; 17a;
  18a,c,d; 19a,b,c,e; 20d; 21a; 22a,b,c,d; 35b,c;
  36a; 37b,d,e; 39b,c; 48b; 52b; 53c,e; 55b; 58b;
  63b; 64a,d,e; 66a; 71c; 73; 77; 79a,b,c,d,e; 85a;
  92a; 99b; 113b; 120; 122; 139b; 142d; collages
  25, 50, 63.
Spink County Hist. Museum - 132; 141b; 144b;
  149a; 165d.
Spomer, Ron - 4c.
Strait, Marj - 128a; 143d; 148c,d; 154; 165b.

Tidball, Rose - 138b; 142b; 144c; 145a; 146a,b;
  150a; 164e; 167b.
USDA - 69b; 136; 169a.
USD - 62a,d; collages 25, 50.
USD Archaeology Lab. - 82; 83; 84.
Van Wyk, Caroline - 43a.
Walsh, Dennis - 65d; 66c.
Warner High School - 36e; 53f; 60a; 61c; collages
  25, 50, 63, 173.

Letters designate photos in clock-wise order, beginning with upper left corner of page.

Color Separations by courtesy of South Dakota Department of Game, Fish & Parks, South Dakota Department of Tourism, and Aberdeen Chamber of Commerce.

Louisa Mosier lived with her mother, twin sister Ella and brother Walt, here in Madison home of seven gables. She was an "old maid school marm" of 33 when she married cattle-and-horse rancher Tom Barrett in 1899. They had four children in six years, ranching at Wagner, then set off on a 400-mile covered wagon trip north-west to claim a homestead on the Grand River. Louisa drove a four-horse team on the wagon, with a loaded hayrack and extra team hitched behind, a baby in her arms and three lively little ones (Author Berg's mother, Marie, and uncles, Will and Chet) scrambling over the piled bedding. Off to the side of the wagon, Tom pushed a herd of 35 cattle and rode ahead to scout out camping places and waterholes. At the mouth of Lodgepole Creek they built their homestead shack.

photo by Bob Runner

Francie M. Berg writes on the heritage of the northern Great Plains. Born on a Missouri River homestead, raised on a Montana ranch, she lives in North Dakota within a few miles of her grand-parents' South Dakota homestead. Her earlier book *NORTH DAKOTA: Land of Changing Seasons* is the first volume of the *Old West Region Series* which will span five states. *SOUTH DAKOTA: Land of Shining Gold* is second in this series.

Berg also writes on self-help subjects. Her book *HOW TO BE SLIMMER, TRIMMER & HAPPIER: An Action Plan for Young People,* published in 1980 has been acclaimed by doctors, dietitians and youth professionals.

Francie and her husband Bertram, a Hettinger veterinarian, are active in 4-H work, including international programs. They have been IFYE delegates to Switzerland and England, and were leaders for a 4-H Labo exchange in Japan. They have four children.

Ms. Berg holds a masters degree in family social science and anthropology from the University of Minnesota and a B.S. in home economics education and extension from Montana State University. She has taught home economics and worked as an extension home economist; now works full time in writing and publishing.

BIBLIOGRAPHY

Agenbroad, Larry. *Mammoth Site of Hot Springs.* Caxton Printers, 1977.

Amiotte, Arthur, ed. *Photographs and Poems by Sioux Children.* Indian Arts Board, U. S. Dept. Interior, 1971.

Anderson, Robert; Brown, Joanna; Lerner, Jonny; Shafer, Barbara Lou, eds. *Voices from Wounded Knee.* Akwesasne Notes, 1973.

Badhorse, Beverley. *Press Coverage of Native American Affairs.* Thesis, Laramie, Wyo., 1979.

Blasingame, Ike. *Dakota Cowboy: My Life in the Old Days.* Putnam, U. of Nebr. Press, 1958.

Boller, Henry A. *Missouri River Fur Trader: Letters & Journal.* Mattison, Ray, ed. State Hist. Society of N. D., Bismarck, 1966.

Bradfield, Byron. *White River Pete Sez.* Lame Johnny Press, 1978.

Brown, Dee. *Bury My Heart at Wounded Knee.* Holt, Rinehart & Winston, 1970.

Bye, John O. *Back Trailing in the Heart of the Short Grass Country.* Alexander Print. co. Everett, Wash.

Call of the Prairie. Ziebach County Golden Jubilee, Dupree, 1960.

Carstensen, Vernon, ed. *The Public Lands: Studies in the History of the Public Domain.* U. of Wisc. Madison, 1962.

Casey, Robert. *The Black Hills and Their Incredible Characters.* Bobbs-Merrill, 1949.

Clark, Badger. *Grass Grown Trails.* Gorham Press, 1917.

Deloria, Ella. *Dakota Texts.* American Ethnological Society, U. of South Dakota, 1932.

Deloria, Vine, Jr. *Custer Died for Your Sins: An Indian Manifesto.* MacMillan, 1969, *God is Red.* Dell 1975. *Of Utmost Good Faith.* Simon & Schuster. *We talk, You listen.* Dell, 1972.

Dick, Everett. *The Sod-House Frontier 1854-1890.* U. of Nebr. Lincoln, 1937.

Doll, Don and Alinder, Jim, eds. *Crying for a Vision: Rosebud Sioux Trilogy.* Morgan & Morgan, 1976.

Early History of Brown County. Territorial Pioneers, Western Printing, Aberdeen, 1965.

Fielder, Mildred. *A Guide to Black Hills Ghost Mines.* North Plains Press, Aberdeen, 1972.

Garland, Hamilin. *Main Travelled Roads.* Harper, 1893. *A Son of the Middle Border.* Grossett & Dunlap with Macmillan, 1914. *Prairie Song and Western Story.* Norwood Press, 1928.

Gates, Paul W. *History of Public Land Law Development.* U.S. Gov. Printing, 1968. *Free Homesteads for All Americans: The Homestead Act of 1862.* Civil War Centennial Commission, Washington, D.C., 1962

Gilfillan, Archer B. *Sheep: Life on the South Dakota Range.* U. of Minnesota Press, 1928. *A Goat's Eye View of the Black Hills.* Dean & Dean, Rapid City 1953.

Glut, Donald F. *The Dinosaur Dictionary.* Citadel Press, 1972.

Hayes, T. E. *Memories: South Dakota's Depression Years.* Oxcart Press, Grand Forks.

Homesteads. Interior Department, Bureau of Land Management, 1962.

Homestead Years. Bison Courier, Bison.

Hughes County History. Office of County Superintendent of Schools, 1934.

Hyde Heritage. Hyde County Historical Society, State Publishers, Pierre, 1977.

Ise, John. *Sod & Stubble.* U. of Nebr. Lincoln, 1936.

Iversen, Ruth; Strait, Marj; Peters, Margie, eds. *Proving Up: Jones County History.* Book & Thimble Club, Murdo, 1969.

Jackson-Washabaugh Counties: 1915-1965. Jackson-Washabaugh Historical Society, 1965.

Jennewein, J. Leonard and Boorman, Jane. *Dakota Panorama.* Dakota Territory Centennial Commission, Brevet Press, Sioux Falls, 1961.

Karolevitz, Rovert F. *Challenge: The South Dakota Story.* Brevet Press, Sioux Falls, 1975.

Kraenzel, Carl. *The Great Plains in Transition.* U. of Oklahoma, 1955.

Krause, Herbert, and Olson, Gary D. eds. *Custer's Prelude to Glory: A Newspaper Accounting of Custer's 1874 Expedition to the Black Hills.*

Brevet Press, Sioux Falls, 1974.

Lame Deer, John Fire, and Erdoes, Richard. *Lame Deer: Seeker of Visions.* Simon & Schuster, 1972.

Lass, William E. *A History of Steamboating on the Upper Missouri.* U. of Nebr. Lincoln, 1962.

Lee, Bob, ed. *Gold-Gals-Guns-Guts.* With S. D. Bicentennial Commission 1976.

Lemmon, ED. *Boss Cowman: The Recollections of Ed Lemmon, 1857-1946.* Yost, Nellie S., ed. U. of Nebr. Lincoln, 1969.

Mama Said there'd be days like this, but she never said there'd be years of it: An Anthology of Poetry by the Inmates of the S. D. State Penitentiary. South Dakota Arts Council, Sioux Falls.

Mato Paha: Land of the Pioneers. Northwest Meade County, 1969.

McGowen, Tom. *Album of Prehistoric Animals.* Rand McNally, 1974.

McLaughlin, James. *My Friend the Indian.* Houghton Mifflin, 1910.

McLuhan, T. C., ed. *Touch the Earth.* Pocket Books, N. Y., 1971.

Milton, John R., ed. *The Literature of South Dakota.* Dakota Press, Vermillion, 1976.

Moberg, Vilhelm. *The Emigrants.* Simon & Schuster, 1951.

Mobridge: The Bridge City, It's First 50 Years 1906-1956.

O'Harra, Cleophas. *The White River Badlands.* S. D. School of Mines, Rapid City, 1920.

Olden, Sarah Emilia. *The People of Tipi Sapa.* Morehouse Publ., Milwaukee, 1918.

Pommersheim, Frank, and Remerowski, Anita. *Reservation Street Law: A Handbook of Individual Rights and Responsibilities.* Sinte Gleska College Press, Rosebud, S. D., 1979.

Rapid City Flood. Boone Publ., 1972.

Ritter, Dr. *The People's Home Library: Dr. Ritter's Home Medical Book.* 1910.

Robbins, Roy M. *Our Landed Heritage: The Public Domain 1776-1936.* U of Nebr. Lincoln, 1962.

Roberts County History. Dakota Territory Centennial, 1961.

Rolvaag, O. E. *Giants in the Earth.* Harper & Row, 1927.

Schell, Herbert S. *History of South Dakota.* U. of Nebr., Lincoln, 1961.

Shannon, Fred A. *The Farmer's Last Frontier.* N. Y. 1945.

Simpson, George Gaylord. *Horses.* The Natural History Library, Doubleday, 1961.

Smith, Charles A. *Minnehaha County History.* Educator Supply Co., Mitchell, S.D. 1949.

South Dakota Historical Collections: Volumes 1-37. S. D. State Historical Society, Pierre, 1902-1974.

Taft, Philip B., Jr. *Behind Prison Walls Indians Reclaim Their Heritage,* and *Indian Offender Programs: And then There Was One.* Corrections Magazine, June 1981.

Thwaites, Rueben, ed. *Original Journals of the Lewis & Clark Expedition.* 8 volumes, Arno, 1904.

Tidball, Rose. *Taming the Plains.* Tidball, 1976.

Waterman, George. *The Practical Stock Doctor.* 1908.

Webb, Walter Prescott. *The Great Plains.* Grosset & Dunlap, N. Y., 1931.

Typesetting by Adams County Record

Printed by North Plains Press

INDEX